Studies of Unionism in Government

The Unions and the Cities

HARRY H. WELLINGTON *and* RALPH K. WINTER, JR.

The Unions and the Cities

THE BROOKINGS INSTITUTION, WASHINGTON, D.C.

1775 Massachusetts Avenue, N.W., Washington, D.C. 20036

ISBN 0-8157-9294-8
Library of Congress Catalog Card Number 79-179327

9 8 7 6 5 4 3 2 1

THE BROOKINGS INSTITUTION is an independent organization devoted to nonpartisan research, education, and publication in economics, government, foreign policy, and the social sciences generally. Its principal purposes are to aid in the development of sound public policies and to promote public understanding of issues of national importance.

The Institution was founded on December 8, 1927, to merge the activities of the Institute for Government Research, founded in 1916, the Institute of Economics, founded in 1922, and the Robert Brookings Graduate School of Economics and Government, founded in 1924.

The general administration of the Institution is the responsibility of a Board of Trustees charged with maintaining the independence of the staff and fostering the most favorable conditions for creative research and education. The immediate direction of the policies, program, and staff of the Institution is vested in the President, assisted by an advisory committee of the officers and staff.

In publishing a study, the Institution presents it as a competent treatment of a subject worthy of public consideration. The interpretations and conclusions in such publications are those of the author or authors and do not necessarily reflect the views of the other staff members, officers, or trustees of the Brookings Institution.

Foreword

The rapid growth of militant unionism in public employment over the past half decade presents a difficult challenge to local governments: how to respond fairly to the demands of public employee unions without compromising the legitimate interests of taxpayers and recipients of public services. Because the unions have power to withhold essential public services, urban governments cannot ignore their claims on municipal budgets—or their involvement in local government affairs ranging from the design of school curricula to the provision of health services. Indeed, since few other groups can so profoundly affect the life of a community, union pressures may overwhelm the needs of others and thereby distort the political process.

The problem is of mounting importance to persons concerned with labor law, industrial relations, the provision of public services, and the shaping of urban government. As these specialists devise new policies to accommodate rapidly changing circumstances, their choices among alternative approaches to the problem need to be based on a broad knowledge of collective bargaining in the public sector. To assist them in making informed decisions, the Brookings Institution, with the encouragement of the National Civil Service League and financial support from the Ford Foundation, began in 1967 a program of research on unionism in government at the state and local levels. This book—portions of which have appeared in somewhat different form in Volumes 78 and 79 of the *Yale Law Journal*—is the first of a series of volumes to grow out of that program. The authors address the political, economic, and legal problems confronting American cities and other units of local government as a result of the growing importation of collective bargaining into the public sector.

Harry H. Wellington and Ralph K. Winter, Jr., are professors of law at Yale University. During the preparation of this volume, they were members of the associated staff of the Brookings Institution. They wish to acknowledge their good fortune in having access to the research of others who have generously shared the fruits of their labors with them. In particular, they want to thank two of their colleagues on the Brookings project, Arnold R. Weber, Associate Director of the Office of Management and Budget, and John F. Burton, associate professor of industrial relations and public policy in the Graduate School of Business, University of Chicago. They permitted Wellington and Winter to use their extensive files containing the results of many months of interviews of government and union officials conducted by a team of graduate students working under their supervision. Although the authors rely on these interviews for many factual propositions, they have not cited particular ones in order to spare the officials involved, and the students who interviewed them, possible embarrassment. Nor have they attempted to keep track of local developments since the time of the interviews. As a result, practices cited by the authors for illustrative purposes may be referred to in the present tense although circumstances have changed in the interim.

They also wish to thank the scores of state and local officials with whom they corresponded, and who furnished them a vast quantity of information about local practices.

They would like to thank as well Professor Ward S. Bowman, Jr., of the Yale Law School and Professor Albert J. Reiss, Jr., of Yale's Department of Sociology, who read the manuscript and contributed helpful suggestions. They are grateful, too, for the useful comments of the Brookings reading committee consisting of Professors Harold M. Levinson, Bernard D. Meltzer, Albert Rees, and David L. Shapiro.

They also acknowledge their debt to students at the Yale Law School who participated in their research seminar on collective bargaining in the public sector. The students' diligence in research and rigor in analysis provided the authors with large amounts of empirical data organized in a fashion that exposed all of the problems in this difficult area, as well as many ways of coping with them. They were Thomas D. Allison, Jr., Jay E. Bovilsky, Stephen S. Dunham, Judith A. Futch, Paul D. Gerwirtz, Thomas P. Humphrey II, Daniel M. Lewis, Francis C. Lynch, Jr., William J. O'Brien III, Michael T. Schaffield, and Michael H. Walsh. Particular thanks go to Thomas W. Brunner and Joseph H. Wender, who not only participated in the seminar but also did a great deal of extra work on the subject.

The authors received valuable research assistance from Richard D. Diamond, Harriet Taylor, and Paul Davies. Their special gratitude goes to J. Michael Eisner, who was their research assistant throughout this enterprise. His contribution was substantial indeed.

Finally, their thanks go to Elizabeth B. Manley, Eileen Quinn, Stephanie Remiszewski, and others who typed the manuscript; to Gene Coakley, S. Charles Smith, and other members of the staff of the Yale Law School library; to Ruth Kaufman, who edited the manuscript; to Evelyn P. Fisher and Genevieve Wimsatt, who checked the entire manuscript for accuracy; and to Joan C. Culver, who prepared the index.

The views expressed in this book are, of course, those of the authors and should not be attributed to the trustees, officers, or staff members of the Ford Foundation or the Brookings Institution.

KERMIT GORDON
President

July 1971
Washington, D.C.

Contents

PART TWO: *Organization and the Establishment of Collective Bargaining*

PART THREE: *Bargaining in the Public Sector*

PART FOUR: *The Strike and Its Alternatives*

"If the city has $2 billion a year for the bums on welfare, how come they have no dough for us?"—a New York City fireman quoted in the New York Times, *December 27, 1970.*

Introduction

The state of municipal government is one of the dominant political issues of our time, dominant to the point of being central to what, in the rhetoric of the day, is known as the "urban crisis." The causes of this "crisis" are hardly self-evident although the symptoms are all too obvious. Under the pressure of the strident demands from conflicting groups, municipal budgets are inadequate to meet the political claims made upon them. New money must be found if these claims are to be satisfied but whether or how the states or the nation should extend financial help to the cities is a constant source of intense debate. Some want the cities to be self-supporting, others prefer revenue sharing schemes, while yet others advocate earmarked funds or a federal takeover of some local programs.

The quality and nature of services provided by cities is also a source of controversy. The extent to which the conduct of the police should be subject to independent review, the nature of the curriculum offered by public schools, the disciplining of students in those schools, and the functions to be performed by welfare workers are just examples of existing controversies. The very structure of government under which municipal services are to be delivered is challenged by demands that control over them be decentralized and assumed by various "communities" within the municipality. Finally, all of these problems are exacerbated by the existence of racial and ethnic tensions.

These issues are all part of the "urban crisis" and have a number of common aspects. One such common aspect is the central role played by public employee unionism. Budgetary issues and the manner in which other political entities are to help the cities financially must be resolved with an eye to the monetary demands such unions make. Regulation of the delivery of municipal services often strikes at the heart of the conditions under which public employees must work and these employees are often professionals who have their own ideas as to what kinds of services are best for the cities. A restructuring of government clearly affects collective bargaining and may well meet union resistance. Furthermore, public employee unions may have racial or ethnic characteristics different from those predominant in the areas of the community they serve. Labor disputes may thus aggravate existing tensions in the cities. Finally, strikes further complicate many of these problems.

One important aspect of the urban crisis, therefore, is the role of public employee unionism, a role that will be importantly shaped by the direction law takes in regulating collective bargaining in public employment. This century has seen what might be called, figuratively at least, a revolution in labor policy. Federal and state laws encouraging the development and practice of collective bargaining represent a sharp departure from earlier laissez-faire and antiunion policies. Until the decade of the 1960s, however, this legislation largely excluded public employment from its coverage. One reason for this exclusion doubtless was the failure of the labor movement to use its political muscle on behalf of public employees. Another was a persistent belief that public employment is not the same as private employment; a belief, therefore, that, whatever the merits of contemporary labor policy in the private sector, the public sector called for a different approach.

This book examines that position. It is about the applicability of collective bargaining to the public sector. And collective bargaining in public employment is now taking hold in one form or another, both through practice and law, in much of the nation. Indeed, increasingly, the belief that there is a difference between the sectors is being abandoned. Increasingly the claim is heard that the considerations determining what collective bargaining policy should be are virtually identical in private and public employment, and that a law that's good for one is good for the other. This book questions that claim. It speaks, to put it another way, to the assertion that government is "just another industry."

Accepting the challenge of this claim compels us to take the private sector as we find it. We will assume—although many on both the political right and left challenge the assumption—that collective bargaining in the private sector is a valid policy. If this assumption is not made, no extension of collective bargaining to public employment can be justified.

The scheme of the book is simple. Part I sets out the theory upon which our skepticism about a total transplant of collective bargaining to public employment is based, sketches in, from a mass of data, the background in which contemporary regulation is taking place, and discusses the role law ought to play at various levels of government.

Drawing upon the extensive experience that municipalities have had with collective bargaining in the past few years, the rest of the book elaborates in detail the kind of regulations law ought to erect on this theoretical foundation. Part II deals with rights of organization and the establishment of bargaining. Part III discusses contract formation and administration, including problems of structuring the public employer to bargain effectively and the scope of permissible bargaining. And Part IV addresses the resolution of impasses and the strike question.

PART ONE

The Framework for Regulating Collective Bargaining in Public Employment

CHAPTER ONE

The Limits of Collective Bargaining in Public Employment

Writing in the March 1969 issue of the *Michigan Law Review*, Mr. Theodore Kheel, the distinguished mediator and arbitrator, placed the weight of his considerable authority behind what is fast becoming the conventional wisdom. In the public sector, as in the private, Mr. Kheel argues, "the most effective technique to produce acceptable terms to resolve disputes is voluntary agreement of the parties, and the best system we have for producing agreements between groups is collective bargaining—even though it involves conflict and the possibility of a work disruption."[1] Clearly for Kheel, as for others, the insistence upon a full extension of collective bargaining—including strikes—to public employment stems from a deep commitment to that way of ordering labor-management affairs in private employment. While such a commitment may not be necessary, a minimal acceptance of collective bargaining is a condition precedent to the Kheel view. Those skeptical of the value of collective bargaining in private employment will hardly press its extension. But even if one accepts collective bargaining in the private sector (as we have said in the

1. "Strikes and Public Employment," 67 *Michigan Law Review* 931, 942 (1969).

Introduction we shall for the purposes of this book), the claims that support it there do not, in any self-evident way, make the case for its full transplant. The public sector is *not* the private, and its labor problems *are* different, very different indeed.

The Claims for Collective Bargaining in the Private Sector

Four claims are made for private-sector collective bargaining. First, it is said to be a way to achieve industrial peace. The point was put as early as 1902 by the federal Industrial Commission:

> The chief advantage which comes from the practice of periodically determining the conditions of labor by collective bargaining directly between employers and employees is that thereby each side obtains a better understanding of the actual state of the industry, of the conditions which confront the other side, and of the motives which influence it. Most strikes and lockouts would not occur if each party understood exactly the position of the other.[2]

Second, collective bargaining is a way of achieving industrial democracy, that is, participation by workers in their own governance. It is the industrial counterpart of the contemporary demand for community participation.[3]

Third, unions that bargain collectively with employers represent workers in the political arena as well. And political representation through interest groups is one of the most important types of political representation that the individual can have. Government at all levels acts in large part in response to the demands made upon it by the groups to which its citizens belong.[4]

Fourth, and most important, as a result of a belief in the unequal bargaining power of employers and employees, collective bargaining is claimed to be a needed substitute for individual bar-

2. *Final Report of the Industrial Commission* (Government Printing Office, 1902), p. 844.

3. See, for example, testimony of Louis D. Brandeis before the Commission on Industrial Relations, Jan. 23, 1915, in *Industrial Relations,* Final Report and Testimony Submitted to Congress by the Commission on Industrial Relations, S. Doc. 415, 64 Cong. 1 sess. (1916), 8, 7657–81.

4. See generally H. Wellington, *Labor and the Legal Process* (Yale University Press, 1968), pp. 215–38.

gaining.[5] Monopsony—a buyer's monopoly,[6] in this case a buyer of labor—is alleged to exist in many situations and to create unfair contracts of labor as a result of individual bargaining. While this, in turn, may not mean that workers as a class and over time get significantly less than they should—because monopsony is surely not a general condition but is alleged to exist only in a number of particular circumstances[7]—it may mean that the terms and conditions of employment for an individual or group of workers at a given period of time and in given circumstances may be unfair. What tends to insure fairness in the aggregate and over the long run is the discipline of the market.[8] But monopsony, if it exists, can work substantial injustice to individuals. Governmental support of collective bargaining represents the nation's response to a belief that such injustice occurs. Fairness between employee and employer in wages, hours, and terms and conditions of employ-

5. See, for example, *Final Report of the Industrial Commission,* p. 800:

> It is quite generally recognized that the growth of great aggregations of capital under the control of single groups of men, which is so prominent a feature of the economic development of recent years, necessitates a corresponding aggregation of workingmen into unions, which may be able also to act as units. It is readily perceived that the position of the single workman, face to face with one of our great modern combinations, such as the United States Steel Corporation, is a position of very great weakness. The workman has one thing to sell—his labor. He has perhaps devoted years to the acquirement of a skill which gives his labor power a relatively high value, so long as he is able to put it to use in combination with certain materials and machinery. A single legal person has, to a very great extent, the control of such machinery, and in particular of such materials. Under such conditions there is little competition for the workman's labor. Control of the means of production gives power to dictate to the workingman upon what terms he shall make use of them.

6. The use of the term monopsony is not intended to suggest a labor market with a single employer. Rather, we mean any market condition in which the terms and conditions of employment are generally below those that would exist under perfect competition.

7. There is by no means agreement that monopsony is a significant factor. For a theoretical discussion, see F. Machlup, *The Political Economy of Monopoly: Business, Labor and Government Policies* (Johns Hopkins Press, 1952), pp. 333–79; for an empirical study, see R. Bunting, *Employer Concentration in Local Labor Markets* (University of North Carolina Press, 1962).

8. See L. Reynolds, *Labor Economics and Labor Relations* (3d ed. Prentice-Hall, 1961), pp. 18–19. To the extent that monopsonistic conditions exist at any particular time one would expect them to be transitory. For even if we assume a high degree of labor immobility, a low wage level in a labor market will attract outside employers. Over time, therefore, the benefits of monopsony seem to carry with them the seeds of its destruction. But the time may seem very long in the life of any individual worker.

ment is thought more likely to be ensured where private ordering takes the collective form.[9]

There are, however, generally recognized social costs resulting from this resort to collectivism.[10] In the private sector these costs are primarily economic, and the question is, given the benefits of collective bargaining as an institution, what is the nature of the economic costs? Economists who have turned their attention to this question are legion, and disagreement among them monumental.[11] The principal concerns are of two intertwined sorts. One is summarized by Professor Albert Rees of Princeton:

> If the union is viewed solely in terms of its effect on the economy, it must in my opinion be considered an obstacle to the optimum performance of our economic system. It alters the wage structure in a way that impedes the growth of employment in sectors of the economy where productivity and income are naturally high and that leaves too much labor in low-income sectors of the economy like southern agriculture and the least skilled service trades. It benefits most those workers who would in any case be relatively well off, and while some of this gain may be at the expense of the owners of capital, most of it must be at the expense of consumers and the lower-paid workers. Unions interfere blatantly with the use of the most productive techniques in some industries, and this effect is probably not offset by the stimulus to higher productivity furnished by some other unions.[12]

9. See *Labor Management Relations Act,* § 1, 29 U.S.C. § 151 (1964).

10. The monopsony justification views collective bargaining as a system of countervailing power—that is, the collective power of the workers countervails the bargaining power of employers. See J. Galbraith, *American Capitalism: The Concept of Countervailing Power* (Houghton Mifflin, 1952), pp. 121 ff. Even if the entire line of argument up to this point is accepted, collective bargaining nevertheless seems a crude device for meeting the monopsony problem, since there is no particular reason to think that collective bargaining will be instituted where there is monopsony (or that it is more likely to be instituted there). In some circumstances collective bargaining may even raise wages above a "competitive" level. On the other hand, the collective bargaining approach is no cruder than the law's general response to perceived unfairness in the application of the freedom of contract doctrine. See Wellington, *Labor and the Legal Process,* pp. 26–38.

11. Compare, e.g., H. Simons, "Some Reflections on Syndicalism," *Journal of Political Economy* 1–25 (1944), with R. Lester, "Reflections on the Labor Monopoly Issue," 55 *Journal of Political Economy* 513 (1947).

12. A. Rees, *The Economics of Trade Unions* (University of Chicago Press, 1962), pp. 194–95. Also see H. Johnson and P. Mieszkowski, *The Effects of Unionization on the Distribution of Income: A General Equilibrium Approach,* 84 *Quarterly Journal of Economics* 539 (1970).

The other concern is stated in the 1967 Report of the Council of Economic Advisers:

> Vigorous competition is essential to price stability in a high employment economy. But competitive forces do not and cannot operate with equal strength in every sector of the economy. In industries where the number of competitors is limited, business firms have a substantial measure of discretion in setting prices. In many sectors of the labor market, unions and managements together have a substantial measure of discretion in setting wages. The responsible exercise of discretionary power over wages and prices can help to maintain general price stability. Its irresponsible use can make full employment and price stability incompatible.[13]

And the claim is that this "discretionary power" too often is exercised "irresponsibly."[14]

Disagreement among economists extends to the quantity as well as to the fact of economic malfunctioning that properly is attributable to collective bargaining.[15] But there is no disagreement that at some point the market disciplines or delimits union power. As we shall see in more detail below, union power is frequently constrained by the fact that consumers react to a relative increase in the price of a product by purchasing less of it. As a result any significant real financial benefit, beyond that justified by an increase in productivity, that accrues to workers through collective bargaining may well cause significant unemployment among union members. Because of this employment-benefit relationship, the economic costs imposed by collective bargaining as it presently exists in the private sector seem inherently limited.[16]

13. *Economic Report of the President Together With the Annual Report of the Council of Economic Advisers,* January 1967, p. 119.

14. *Ibid.,* pp. 119–34. See generally J. Sheahan, *The Wage-Price Guideposts* (Brookings Institution, 1967).

15. See H. Lewis, *Unionism and Relative Wages in the United States: An Empirical Inquiry* (University of Chicago Press, 1963), and earlier studies discussed therein.

16. See generally J. Dunlop, *Wage Determination Under Trade Unions* (Macmillan, 1944), pp. 28–44; M. Friedman, "Some Comments on the Significance of Labor Unions for Economic Policy," in D. Wright (ed.), *The Impact of the Union,* p. 204 (Harcourt, 1951); Rees, *The Economics of the Trade Unions,* pp. 50–60.

In A. Ross, *Trade Union Wage Policy* (University of California, 1948), the argument is made that the employment effect of a wage bargain in not taken into account by either employers or unions (pp. 76–93). One reason given in support of this conclusion is the difficulty of knowing what effect a particular wage bargain

The Claims for Collective Bargaining in the Public Sector

In the area of public employment the claims upon public policy made by the need for industrial peace, industrial democracy, and effective political representation point toward collective bargaining. This is to say that three of the four arguments that support bargaining in the private sector—to some extent, at least—press for similar arrangements in the public sector.

Government is a growth industry, particularly state and municipal government. While federal employment between 1963 and 1970 increased from 2.5 million to 2.9 million, state and local employment rose from 7.2 to 10.1 million,[17] and the increase continues apace. With size comes bureaucracy, and with bureaucracy comes the sense of isolation of the individual worker. His manhood, like that of his industrial counterpart, seems threatened. Lengthening chains of command necessarily depersonalize the employment relationship and contribute to a sense of powerlessness on the part of the worker. If he is to share in the governance of his employment relationship as he does in the private sector, it must be through the device of representation, which means unioniza-

will have on employment. But the forecasting difficulty inheres in any pricing decision, whether it is raising the price of automobiles or of labor, and it certainly does not render the effect of an increase on the volume purchased an irrelevant consideration. Uncertainty as to the impact of a wage decision on employment does not allow union leaders to be indifferent to the fact that there is an impact. If it did, they would all demand rates of $100 per hour.

Ross's second argument is that there is only a loose connection between wage rates and the volume of employment. It is not clear what he means by this assertion. It may be a rephrasing of the uncertainty argument. Presumably he is not asserting that the demand curve for labor is absolutely vertical; although proof of that phenomenon would entitle him to the professional immortality promised by Professor Stigler (see G. Stigler, *The Theory of Price* [3rd ed., Macmillan, 1966] p. 24), the unsupported assertion hardly merits serious consideration. But if the curve is not vertical, then there is a "close connection" since the volume of employment is by hypothesis affected at every point on a declining curve. Probably he means simply that the curve is relatively inelastic, but that conclusion is neither self-evident, supported by his text, nor a proposition generally accepted on the basis of established studies.

17. U.S. Bureau of the Census, *Public Employment in 1970* (1971), Table 1, and Bureau of the Census, *State Distribution of Public Employment in 1963* (1964), Table 1.

tion.[18] Accordingly, just as the increase in the size of economic units in private industry fostered unionism, so the enlarging of governmental bureaucracy has encouraged public employees to look to collective action for a sense of control over their employment destiny. The number of government employees, moreover, makes it plain that those employees are members of an interest group that can organize for political representation as well as for job participation.[19]

The pressures thus generated by size and bureaucracy lead inescapably to disruption—to labor unrest—unless these pressures are recognized and unless existing decision-making procedures are accommodated to them. Peace in government employment too, the argument runs, can best be established by making union recognition and collective bargaining accepted public policy.[20]

Much less clearly analogous to the private model, however, is the unequal bargaining power argument. In the private sector that argument really has two aspects. The first, just adumbrated, is affirmative in nature. Monopsony is believed sometimes to result in unfair individual contracts of employment. The unfairness may be reflected in wages, which are less than they would be if the market were more nearly perfect, or in working arrangements that may lodge arbitrary power in a foreman, that is, power to hire, fire, promote, assign, or discipline without respect to substantive or procedural rules. A persistent assertion, generating much heat, relates to the arbitrary exercise of managerial power in individual cases. This assertion goes far to explain the insistence of unions on the establishment in the labor contract of rules, with an accompanying adjudicatory procedure, to govern industrial life.[21]

Judgments about the fairness of the financial terms of the public employee's individual contract of employment are even harder to make than for private sector workers. The case for the existence of private employer monopsony, disputed as it is, asserts only

18. See *Final Report of the Industrial Commission,* p. 805; C. Summers, "American Legislation for Union Democracy," 25 *Mod. L. Rev.* 273, 275 (1962).

19. For the "early" history, see S. Spero, *Government as Employer* (Remsen, 1948).

20. See, for example, *Governor's Committee on Public Employee Relations, Final Report* (State of New York, 1966), pp. 9–14.

21. See N. Chamberlain, *The Union Challenge to Management Control* (Harper, 1948), p. 94.

that some private sector employers in some circumstances have too much bargaining power. In the public sector, the case to be proved is that the governmental employer ever has such power. But even if this case could be proved, market norms are at best attenuated guides to questions of fairness. In employment as in all other areas, governmental decisions are properly political decisions, and economic considerations are but one criterion among many. Questions of fairness do not centrally relate to how much imperfection one sees in the market, but more to how much imperfection one sees in the political process. "Low" pay for teachers may be merely a decision—right or wrong, resulting from the pressure of special interests or from a desire to promote the general welfare—to exchange a reduction in the quality or quantity of teachers for higher welfare payments, a domed stadium, and so on. And the ability to make informed judgments about such political decisions is limited because of the understandable but unfortunate fact that the science of politics has failed to supply either as elegant or as reliable a theoretical model as has its sister discipline.

Nevertheless, employment benefits in the public sector may have improved relatively more slowly than in the private sector during the last three decades. An economy with a persistent inflationary bias probably works to the disadvantage of those who must rely on legislation for wage adujstments.[22] Moreover, while public employment was once attractive for the greater job security and retirement benefits it provided, quite similar protection is now available in many areas of the private sector.[23] On the other hand, to the extent that civil service, or merit, systems exist in public employment and these laws are obeyed, the arbitrary exercise of managerial power is substantially reduced. Where it is reduced, a labor policy that relies on individual employment contracts must seem less unacceptable.

The second, or negative, aspect of the unequal bargaining power argument relates to the social costs of collective bargaining. As has been seen, the social costs of collective bargaining in the private sector are principally economic and seem inherently lim-

22. This is surely one reason that might explain the widely assumed fact that public employees have fallen behind their private sector counterparts. See J. Stieber, "Collective Bargaining in the Public Sector," in L. Ulman (ed.), *Challenges to Collective Bargaining* (Prentice-Hall, 1967), pp. 65, 69.

23. See G. Taylor, "Public Employment: Strikes or Procedures?" 20 *Industrial and Labor Relations Review* 617, 623–25 (1967).

ited by market forces. In the public sector, however, the costs seem economic only in a very narrow sense and are on the whole political. It further seems that, to the extent union power is delimited by market or other forces in the public sector, these constraints do not come into play nearly as quickly as in the private. An understanding of why this is so requires further comparison between collective bargaining in the two sectors.

The Private Sector Model

Although the private sector is, of course, extraordinarily diverse, the paradigm is an industry that produces a product that is not particularly essential to those who buy it and for which dissimilar products can be substituted. Within the market or markets for this product, most—but not all—of the producers must bargain with a union representing their employees, and this union is generally the same throughout the industry. A price rise of this product relative to others will result in a decrease in the number of units of the product sold. This in turn will result in a cutback in employment. And an increase in price would be dictated by an increase in labor cost relative to output, at least in most situations.[24] Thus, the union is faced with some sort of rough trade-off between, on the one hand, larger benefits for some employees and unemployment for others, and on the other hand, smaller benefits and more employment. Because unions are political organizations, with a legal duty to represent all employees fairly,[25] and with a treasury that comes from per capita dues, there is pressure on the union to avoid the road that leads to unemployment.[26]

This picture of the restraints that the market imposes on collective bargaining settlements undergoes change as the variables change. On the one hand, to the extent that there are nonunion firms within a product market, the impact of union pressure will be diminished by the ability of consumers to purchase identical

24. The cost increase may, of course, take some time to work through and appear as a price increase. See Rees, *The Economics of Trade Unions,* pp. 107–09. In some oligopolistic situations the firm may be able to raise prices after a wage increase without suffering a significant decrease in sales.

25. *Steele* v. *Louisville & Nashville Railroad Co.,* 323 U.S. 192 (1944).

26. The pressure is sometimes resisted. Indeed, the United Mine Workers has chosen more benefits for less employment. See generally M. Baratz, *The Union and the Coal Industry* (Yale University Press, 1955).

products from nonunion and, presumably, less expensive sources. On the other hand, to the extent that union organization of competitors within the product market is complete, there will be no such restraint and the principal barriers to union bargaining goals will be the ability of a number of consumers to react to a price change by turning to dissimilar but nevertheless substitutable products.

Two additional variables must be noted. First, where the demand for an industry's product is rather insensitive to price—that is, relatively inelastic—and where all the firms in a product market are organized, the union need fear less the employment-benefit trade-off, for the employer is less concerned about raising prices in response to increased costs. By hypothesis, a price rise affects unit sales of such an employer only minimally. Second, in an expanding industry, wage settlements that exceed increases in productivity may not reduce union employment. They will reduce expansion, hence the employment effect will be experienced only by workers who do not belong to the union. This means that in the short run the politics of the employment-benefit trade-off do not restrain the union in its bargaining demands.

In both of these cases, however, there are at least two restraints on the union. One is the employer's increased incentive to substitute machines for labor, a factor present in the paradigm and all other cases as well. The other restraint stems from the fact that large sections of the nation are unorganized and highly resistant to unionization.[27] Accordingly, capital will seek nonunion labor, and in this way the market will discipline the organized sector.

The employer, in the paradigm and in all variations of it, is motivated primarily by the necessity to maximize profits (and this is so no matter how political a corporation may seem to be). He therefore is not inclined (absent an increase in demand for his product) to raise prices and thereby suffer a loss in profits, and he is organized to transmit and represent the market pressures described above. Generally he will resist, and resist hard, union demands that exceed increases in productivity, for if he accepts such demands he may be forced to raise prices. Should he be

27. See H. Cohany, "Trends and Changes in Union Membership," 89 *Monthly Lab. Rev.* 510–13 (1966); I. Bernstein, "The Growth of American Unions, 1945–1960," 2 *Labor History* 131–57 (1961).

unsuccessful in his resistance too often, and should it or the bargain cost him too much, he can be expected to put his money and energy elsewhere.[28]

What all this means is that the social costs imposed by collective bargaining are economic costs; that usually they are limited by powerful market restraints; and that these restraints are visible to anyone who is able to see the forest for the trees.[29]

The Public Sector Model: Monetary Issues

The paradigm in the public sector is a municipality with an elected city council and an elected mayor who bargains (through others) with unions representing the employees of the city. He bargains also, of course, with other permanent and ad hoc interest groups making claims upon government (business groups, save-the-park committees, neighborhood groups, and so forth). Indeed, the decisions that are made may be thought of roughly as a result of interactions and accommodations among these interest groups, as influenced by perceptions about the attitudes of the electorate and by the goals and programs of the mayor and his city council.[30]

Decisions that cost the city money are generally paid for from taxes and, less often, by borrowing. Not only are there many types of taxes but also there are several layers of government that may make tax revenue available to the city; federal and state as well as local funds may be employed for some purposes. Formal allocation of money for particular uses is made through the city's budget, which may have within it considerable room for adjust-

28. And the law would protect him in this. Indeed, it would protect him if he were moved by an antiunion animus as well as by valid economic considerations. See *Textile Workers Union of America* v. *Darlington Manufacturing Co.*, 380 U.S. 263 (1965).

Of course, where fixed costs are large relative to variable costs, it may be difficult for an employer to extricate himself.

29. This does not mean that collective bargaining in the private sector is free of social costs. It means only that the costs are necessarily limited by the discipline of the market.

30. See generally R. Dahl, *Who Governs? Democracy and Power in an American City* (Yale University Press, 1961). On interest group theory generally, see D. Truman, *The Government Process: Political Interests and Public Opinion* (3d printing; Alfred A. Knopf, 1955).

ments.[31] Thus, a union will bargain hard for as large a share of the budget as it thinks it possibly can obtain, and even try to force a tax increase if it deems that possible.

In the public sector, too, the market operates. In the long run, the supply of labor is a function of the price paid for labor by the public employer relative to what workers earn elsewhere.[32] This is some assurance that public employees in the aggregate—with or without collective bargaining—are not paid too little. The case for employer monopsony, moreover, may be much weaker in the public sector than it is in the private. First, to the extent that most public employees work in urban areas, as they probably do, there may often be a number of substitutable and competing private and public employers in the labor market. When that is the case, there can be little monopsony power.[33] Second, even if public employers occasionally have monopsony power, governmental policy is determined only in part by economic criteria, and there is no assurance, as there is in the private sector where the profit motive prevails, that the power will be exploited.

As noted, market-imposed unemployment is an important restraint on unions in the private sector. In the public sector, the trade-off between benefits and employment seems much less important. Government does not generally sell a product the demand for which is closely related to price. There usually are not close substitutes for the products and services provided by government and the demand for them is relatively inelastic. Such market conditions are favorable to unions in the private sector because they permit the acquisition of benefits without the penalty of unemployment, subject to the restraint of nonunion competitors, actual or potential. But no such restraint limits the demands of public employee unions. Because much government activity is,

31. See, for example, W. Sayre and H. Kaufman, *Governing New York City: Politics in the Metropolis* (Russell Sage, 1960), pp. 366–72.

32. See M. Moskow, *Teachers and Unions* (University of Pennsylvania, Wharton School of Finance and Commerce, Industrial Research Unit, 1966), pp. 79–86.

33. This is based on the reasonable but not unchallengeable assumption that the number of significant employers in a labor market is related to the existence of monopsony. See R. Bunting, *Employer Concentration in Local Labor Markets,* pp. 3–14. The greater the number of such employers in a labor market, the greater the departure from the classic case of the monopsony of a single employer. The number of employers would clearly seem to affect their ability to make and enforce a collusive wage agreement.

and must be, a monopoly, product competition, nonunion or otherwise, does not exert a downward pressure on prices and wages. Nor will the existence of a pool of labor ready to work for a wage below union scale attract new capital and create a new, and competitively less expensive, governmental enterprise.

The fear of unemployment, however, can serve as something of a restraining force in two situations. First, if the cost of labor increases, the city may reduce the quality of the service it furnishes by reducing employment. For example, if teachers' salaries are increased, it may decrease the number of teachers and increase class size. However, the ability of city government to accomplish such a change is limited not only by union pressure but also by the pressure of other affected interested groups in the community.[34] Political considerations, therefore, may cause either no reduction in employment or services, or a reduction in an area other than that in which the union members work. Both the political power exerted by the beneficiaries of the services, who are also voters, and the power of the public employee union as a labor organization then combine to create great pressure on political leaders either to seek new funds or to reduce municipal services of another kind. Second, if labor costs increase, the city, like a private employer, may seek to replace labor with machines. The absence of a profit motive, and a political concern for unemployment, however, may be deterrents in addition to the deterrent of union resistance. The public employer that decides it must limit employment because of unit labor costs will likely find that the politically easiest decision is to restrict new hirings rather than to lay off current employees.

Where pensions are concerned, moreover, major concessions may be politically tempting since there is no immediate impact on the taxpayer or the city budget. Whereas actuarial soundness would be insisted on by a profit-seeking entity like a firm, it may be a secondary concern to politicians whose conduct is determined by relatively short-run considerations. The impact of failing to adhere to actuarial principles will frequently fall upon a different mayor and a different city council. In those circumstances, conces-

34. Organized parent groups, for example. Compare the unsuccessful attempt of the New York City Board of Education to reduce the employment of substitute teachers in the public schools in March 1971. *New York Times*, March 11, 1971, p. 1.

sions that condemn a city to future impoverishment may not seem intolerable.

Even if a close relationship between increased economic benefits and unemployment does not exist as a significant deterrent to unions in the public sector, might not the argument be made that in some sense the taxpayer is the public sector's functional equivalent of the consumer? If taxes become too high the taxpayer can move to another community. While it is generally much easier for a consumer to substitute products than for a taxpayer to substitute communities, is it not fair to say that, at the point at which a tax increase will cause so many taxpayers to move that it will produce less total revenue, the market disciplines or restrains union and public employer in the same way and for the same reasons that the market disciplines parties in the private sector? Moreover, does not the analogy to the private sector suggest that it is legitimate in an economic sense for unions to push government to the point of substitutability?

Several factors suggest that the answer to this latter question is at best indeterminate, and that the question of legitimacy must be judged not by economic but by political criteria.

In the first place, there is no theoretical reason—economic or political—to suppose that it is desirable for a governmental entity to liquidate its taxing power, to tax up to the point where another tax increase will produce less revenue because of the number of people it drives to different communities. In the private area, profit maximization is a complex concept, but its approximation generally is both a legal requirement and socially useful as a means of allocating resources.[35] The liquidation of taxing power seems neither imperative nor useful.

Second, consider the complexity of the tax structure and the way in which different kinds of taxes (property, sales, income) fall differently upon a given population. Consider, moreover, that the taxing authority of a particular governmental entity may be limited (a municipality may not have the power to impose an income tax). What is necessarily involved, then, is principally the redistribution of income by government rather than resource alloca-

35. See generally R. Dorfman, *Prices and Markets* (Prentice-Hall, 1967).

tion,[36] and questions of income redistribution surely are essentially political questions.[37]

For his part, the mayor in our paradigm will be disciplined not by a desire to maximize profits but by a desire—in some cases at least—to do a good job (to implement his programs), and in virtually all cases by a wish either to be reelected or to move to a better elective office. What he gives to the union must be taken from some other interest group or from taxpayers. His is the job of coordinating these competing claims while remaining politically viable. And that coordination will be governed by the relative power of the competing interest groups. Coordination, moreover, is not limited to issues involving the level of taxes and the way in which tax moneys are spent. Nonfinancial issues also require coordination, and here too the outcome turns upon the relative power of interest groups. And relative power is affected importantly by the scope of collective bargaining.

The Public Sector Model: Nonmonetary Issues

In the private sector, unions have pushed to expand the scope of bargaining in response to the desires of their members for a variety of new benefits (pension rights, supplementary unemployment payments, merit increases). These benefits generally impose a monetary cost on the employer. And because employers are restrained by the market, an expanded bargaining agenda means that, if a union negotiates an agreement over more subjects, it generally trades off more of less for less of more.

From the consumer's point of view this in turn means that the price of the product he purchases is not significantly related to the

36. In the private sector what is involved is principally resource allocation rather than income redistribution. Income redistribution occurs to the extent that unions are able to increase wages at the expense of profits, but the extent to which this actually happens would seem to be limited. It also occurs if unions, by limiting employment in the union sector through maintenance of wages above a competitive level, increase the supply of labor in the nonunion sector and thereby depress wages there.

37. In the private sector the political question was answered when the National Labor Relations Act was passed: the benefits of collective bargaining (with the strike) outweigh the social costs.

scope of bargaining. And since unions rarely bargain about the nature of the product produced,[38] the consumer can be relatively indifferent as to how many or how few subjects are covered in any collective agreement.[39] Nor need the consumer be concerned about union demands that would not impose a financial cost on the employer, for example, the design of a grievance procedure. While such demands are not subject to the same kind of trade-off as are financial demands, they are unlikely, if granted, to have any impact on the consumer. Their effect is on the quality of life of the parties to the agreement.

In the public sector the cluster of problems that surround the scope of bargaining are much more troublesome than they are in the private sector. The problems have several dimensions.

First, the trade-off between subjects of bargaining in the public sector is less of a protection to the consumer (public) than it is in the private. Where political leaders view the costs of union demands as essentially budgetary, a trade-off can occur. Thus, a demand for higher teacher salaries and a demand for reduced class size may be treated as part of one package. But where a demand, although it has a budgetary effect, is viewed as involving essentially political costs, trade-offs are more difficult. Our paradigmatic mayor, for example, may be under great pressure to make a large monetary settlement with a teachers' union whether or not it is joined to demands for special training programs for disadvantaged children. Interest groups tend to exert pressure against union demands only when they are directly affected. Otherwise, they are apt to join that large constituency (the general public) that wants

38. The fact that American unions and management are generally economically oriented is a source of great freedom to us all. If either the unions or management decided to make decisions about the nature of services provided or products manufactured on the basis of their own ideological convictions, we would all, as consumers, be less free. Although unions may misallocate resources, consumers are still generally able to satisfy strong desires for particular products by paying more for them and sacrificing less valued items. This is because unions and management generally make no attempt to adjust to anything but economic considerations. Were it otherwise, and the unions—or management—insisted that no products of a certain kind be manufactured, consumers would have much less choice.

39. The major qualification to these generalizations is that sometimes unions can generate more support from the membership for certain demands than for others (more for the size of the work crew, less for wage increases). Just how extensive this phenomenon is, and how it balances out over time, is difficult to say; however, it would not seem to be of great importance in the overall picture.

to avoid labor trouble. Trade-offs can occur only when several demands are resisted by roughly the same groups. Thus, pure budgetary demands can be traded off when they are opposed by taxpayers. But when the identity of the resisting group changes with each demand, political leaders may find it expedient to strike a balance on each issue individually, rather than as part of a total package, by measuring the political power of each interest group involved against the political power of the constituency pressing for labor peace. To put it another way, as important as financial factors are to a mayor, political factors may be even more important. The market allows the businessman no such discretionary choice.

Where a union demand—such as increasing the disciplinary power of teachers—does not have budgetary consequences, some trade-offs may occur. Granting the demand will impose a political cost on the mayor because it may anger another interest group. But because the resisting group may change with each issue, each issue is apt to be treated individually and not as a part of a total package. And this may not protect the public. Differing from the private sector, nonmonetary demands of public sector unions do have effects that go beyond the parties to the agreement. All of us have a stake in how school children are disciplined. Expansion of the subjects of bargaining in the public sector, therefore, may increase the total quantum of union power in the political process.

Second, public employees do not generally produce a product. They perform a service. The way in which a service is performed may become a subject of bargaining. As a result, the nature of that service may be changed. Some of these services—police protection, teaching, health care—involve questions that are politically, socially, or ideologically sensitive. In part this is because government is involved and alternatives to governmentally provided services are relatively dear. In part, government is involved because of society's perception about the nature of the service and society's need for it. This suggests that decisions affecting the nature of a governmentally provided service are much more likely to be challenged and are more urgent than generally is the case with services that are offered privately.

Third, some of the services government provides are performed by professionals—teachers, social workers, and so forth—who are keenly interested in the underlying philosophy that informs their work. To them, theirs is not merely a job to be done for a salary. They may be educators or other "change agents" of society. And this may mean that these employees are concerned with more than incrementally altering a governmental service or its method of delivery. They may be advocates of bold departures that will radically transform the service itself.

The issue is not a threshold one of whether professional public employees should participate in decisions about the nature of the services they provide. Any properly run governmental agency should be interested in, and heavily reliant upon, the judgment of its professional staff. The issue rather is the method of that participation.

Conclusions about this issue as well as the larger issue of a full transplant of collective bargaining to the public sector may be facilitated by addressing some aspects of the governmental decision-making process—particularly at the municipal level—and the impact of collective bargaining on that process.

Public Employee Unions and the Political Process

Although the market does not discipline the union in the public sector to the extent that it does in the private, the municipal employment paradigm, nevertheless, would seem to be consistent with what Robert A. Dahl has called the " 'normal' American political process," which is "one in which there is a high probability that an active and legitimate group in the population can make itself heard effectively at some crucial stage in the process of decision," for the union may be seen as little more than an "active and legitimate group in the population."[40] With elections in the background to perform, as Mr. Dahl notes, "the critical role . . . in maximizing political equality and popular sovereignty,"[41] all seems well, at least theoretically, with collective bargaining and public employment.

But there is trouble even in the house of theory if collective

40. R. Dahl, *A Preface to Democratic Theory* (University of Chicago Press, 1956), p. 145.

41. *Ibid.*, pp. 124–25.

bargaining in the public sector means what it does in the private. The trouble is that if unions are able to withhold labor—to strike—as well as to employ the usual methods of political pressure, they may possess a disproportionate share of effective power in the process of decision. Collective bargaining would then be so effective a pressure as to skew the results of the " 'normal' American political process."

One should straightway make plain that the strike issue is not simply the importance of public services as contrasted with services or products produced in the private sector. This is only part of the issue, and in the past the partial truth has beclouded analysis.[42] The services performed by a private transit authority are neither less nor more important to the public than those that would be performed if the transit authority were owned by a municipality. A railroad or a dock strike may be more damaging to a community than "job action" by police. This is not to say that governmental services are not important. They are, both because the demand for them is inelastic and because their disruption may seriously injure a city's economy and occasionally impair the physical welfare of its citizens. Nevertheless, the importance of governmental services is only a necessary part of, rather than a complete answer to, the question: Why be more concerned about strikes in public employment than in private?

The answer to the question is simply that, because strikes in public employment disrupt important services, a large part of a mayor's political constituency will, in many cases, press for a quick end to the strike with little concern for the cost of settlement. This is particularly so where the cost of settlement is borne by a different and larger political constituency, the citizens of the state or nation. Since interest groups other than public employees, with conflicting claims on municipal government, do not, as a general proposition, have anything approaching the effectiveness of the strike—or at least cannot maintain that relative degree of power over the long run—they may be put at a significant competitive disadvantage in the political process.

The private sector strike is designed to exert economic pressure on the employer by depriving him of revenues. The public em-

42. See, for example, Spero, *Government as Employer,* pp. 1–15.

ployee strike is fundamentally different: its sole purpose is to exert political pressure on municipal officials. They are deprived, not of revenues but of the political support of those who are inconvenienced by a disruption of municipal services. But precisely because the private strike is an economic weapon, it is disciplined by the market and the benefit/unemployment trade-off that imposes. And because the public employee strike is a political weapon, it is subject only to the restraints imposed by the political process and they are on the whole less limiting and less disciplinary than those of the market. If this is the case, it must be said that the political process will be radically altered by wholesale importation of the strike weapon. And because of the deceptive simplicity of the analogy to collective bargaining in the private sector, the alteration may take place without anyone realizing what has happened.

Nor is it an answer that, in some municipalities, interest groups other than unions now have a disproportionate share of political power. This is inescapably true, and we do not condone that situation. Indeed, we would be among the first to advocate reform. However, reform cannot be accomplished by giving another interest group disproportionate power, for the losers would be the weakest groups in the community. In most municipalities, the weakest groups are composed of citizens who many believe are most in need of more power.

Therefore, while the purpose and effect of strikes by public employees may seem in the beginning designed merely to establish collective bargaining or to "catch up" with wages and fringe benefits in the private sector, in the long run strikes may become too effective a means for redistributing income; so effective, indeed, that one might see them as an institutionalized means of obtaining and maintaining a subsidy for union members.[43]

As is often the case when one generalizes, this picture may be considered overdrawn. In order to refine analysis, it will be helpful to distinguish between strikes that occur over monetary issues and strikes involving nonmonetary issues. The generalized picture sketched above is mainly concerned with the former. Because there is usually no substitute for governmental services, the citizen-consumer faced with a strike of teachers, or garbage men, or

43. Strikes in some areas of the private sector may have this effect, too. See below, p. 32.

social workers is likely to be seriously inconvenienced. This in turn places enormous pressure on the mayor, who is apt to find it difficult to look to the long-run balance sheet of the municipality. Most citizens are directly affected by a strike of sanitation workers. Few, however, can decipher a municipal budget or trace the relationship between today's labor settlement and next year's increase in the mill rate. Thus, in the typical case the impact of a settlement is less visible—or can more often be concealed—than the impact of a disruption of services. Moreover, the cost of settlement may fall upon a constituency much larger—the whole state or nation—than that represented by the mayor. And revenue sharing schemes that involve unrestricted funds may further lessen public resistance to generous settlements. It follows that the mayor usually will look to the electorate that is clamoring for a settlement, and in these circumstances the union's fear of a long strike, a major check on its power in the private sector, is not a consideration.[44] In the face of all of these factors other interest groups with priorities different from the union's are apt to be much less successful in their pursuit of scarce tax dollars than is the union with power to withhold services.[45]

With respect to strikes over some nonmonetary issues—decentralization of the governance of schools might be an example—the intensity of concern on the part of well-organized interest groups opposed to the union's position would support the mayor in his resistance to union demands. But even here, if the union rank and file back their leadership, pressures for settlement from the gen-

44. Contrast the situation in the private sector: ". . . management cannot normally win the short strike. Management can only win the long strike. Also management frequently tends, in fact, to win the long strike. As a strike lengthens, it commonly bears more heavily on the union and the employees than on management. Strike relief is no substitute for a job. Even regular strike benefits, which few unions can afford, and which usually exhaust the union treasury quite rapidly (with some exceptions), are no substitute for a job." E. Livernash, "The Relation of Power to the Structure and Process of Collective Bargaining," 6 *Journal of Law & Economics* 10, 15 (October 1963).

45. A vivid example was provided by an experience in New Jersey. After a twelve-hour strike by Newark firefighters on July 11, 1969, state urban aid funds, originally authorized for helping the poor, were diverted to salary increases for firemen and police. See *New York Times,* Aug. 7, 1969, p. 25. Moreover, government decision makers other than the mayor (for example, the governor) may have interests different from those of the mayor, interests that manifest themselves in pressures for settlement.

eral public, which may be largely indifferent as to the underlying issue, might in time become irresistible.[46]

The strike and its threat, moreover, exacerbate the problems associated with the scope of bargaining in public employment. This seems clear if one attends in slightly more detail to techniques of municipal decision making.

Few students of our cities would object to Herbert Kaufman's observation that:

> Decisions of the municipal government emanate from no single source, but from many centers; conflicts and clashes are referred to no single authority, but are settled at many levels and at many points in the system: no single group can guarantee the success of any proposal it supports, the defeat of every idea it objects to. Not even the central governmental organs of the city—the Mayor, the Board of Estimate, the Council—individually or in combination, even approach mastery in this sense.
>
> Each separate decision center consists of a cluster of interested contestants, with a "core group" in the middle, invested by the rules with the formal authority to legitimize decisions (that is to promulgate them in binding form) and a constellation of related "satellite groups" seeking to influence the authoritative issuances of the core group.[47]

Nor would many disagree with Nelson W. Polsby when, in discussing community decision making that is concerned with an alternative to a "current state of affairs," he argues that the alternative "must be politically palatable and relatively easy to accomplish; otherwise great amounts of influence have to be brought to bear with great skill and efficiency in order to secure its adoption."[48]

It seems probable that such potential subjects of bargaining as school decentralization and a civilian police review board are, where they do not exist, alternatives to the "current state of affairs," which are not "politically palatable and relatively easy to accomplish." If a teachers' union or a police union were to bargain with the municipal employer over these questions, and were able to use the strike to insist that the proposals not be adopted, how much "skill and efficiency" on the part of the proposals' advocates would be necessary to effect a change? And, to put the

46. Consider also the effect of such strikes on the fabric of society. See, for example, M. Mayer, *The Teachers Strike: New York, 1968* (Harper and Row, 1969).

47. "Metropolitan Leadership," quoted in N. Polsby, *Community Power and Political Theory* (Yale University Press, 1963), pp. 127–28.

48. Polsby, in *ibid.*, p. 135.

shoe on the other foot, if a teachers' union were to insist through collective bargaining (with the strike or its threat) upon major changes in school curriculum, would not that union have to be considerably less skillful and efficient in the normal political process than other advocates of community change? The point is that with respect to some subjects, collective bargaining may be too powerful a lever on municipal decision making, too effective a technique for changing or preventing the change of one small but important part of the "current state of affairs."

Unfortunately, in this area the problem is not merely the strike threat and the strike. In a system where impasse procedures involving third parties are established in order to reduce work stoppages—and this is common in those states that have passed public employment bargaining statutes—third party intervention must be partly responsive to union demands. If the scope of bargaining is open-ended, the neutral party, to be effective, will have to work out accommodations that inevitably advance some of the union's claims some of the time. And the neutral, with his eyes fixed on achieving a settlement, can hardly be concerned with balancing all the items on the community agenda or reflecting the interests of all relevant groups.

The Theory Summarized

Collective bargaining in public employment, then, seems distinguishable from that in the private sector. To begin with, it imposes on society more than a potential misallocation of resources through restrictions on economic output, the principal cost imposed by private sector unions. Collective bargaining by public employees and the political process cannot be separated. The costs of such bargaining, therefore, cannot be fully measured without taking into account the impact on the allocation of political power in the typical municipality. If one assumes, as here, that municipal political processes should be structured to ensure "a high probability that an active and legitimate group in the population can make itself heard effectively at some crucial stage in the process of decision,"[49] then the issue is how powerful unions will be in the

49. Dahl, *Preface to Democratic Theory*, p. 145.

typical municipal political process if a full transplant of collective bargaining is carried out.

The conclusion is that such a transplant would, in many cases, institutionalize the power of public employee unions in a way that would leave competing groups in the political process at a permanent and substantial disadvantage. There are three reasons for this, and each is related to the type of services typically performed by public employees.

First, some of these services are such that any prolonged disruption would entail an actual danger to health and safety.

Second, the demand for numerous governmental services is relatively inelastic, that is, relatively insensitive to changes in price. Indeed, the lack of close substitutes is typical of many governmental endeavors.[50] And, since at least the time of Marshall's *Principles of Economics,* the elasticity of demand for the final service or product has been considered a major determinant of union power.[51] Because the demand for labor is derived from the demand for the product, inelasticity on the product side tends to reduce the employment-benefit trade-off unions face. This is as much the case in the private as in the public sector. But in the private sector, product inelasticity is not typical. Moreover, there is the further restraint on union power created by the real possibility of nonunion entrants into the product market. In the public sector, inelasticity of demand seems more the rule than the exception, and nonunion rivals are not generally a serious problem.

Consider education. A strike by teachers may never create an immediate danger to public health and welfare. Nevertheless, because the demand for education is relatively inelastic, teachers rarely need fear unemployment as a result of union-induced wage increases, and the threat of an important nonunion rival (competitive private schools) is not to be taken seriously so long as potential consumers of private education must pay taxes to support the public school system.

The final reason for fearing a full transplant is the extent to

50. Sometimes this is so because of the nature of the endeavor—national defense, for example—and sometimes because the existence of the governmental operation necessarily inhibits entry by private entities, as in the case of elementry education.

51. A. Marshall, *Principles of Economics* (8th ed.; Macmillan, 1920), pp. 383–86.

which the disruption of a government service inconveniences municipal voters. A teachers' strike may not endanger public health or welfare. It may, however, seriously inconvenience parents and other citizens who, as voters, have the power to punish one of the parties—and always the same party, the political leadership—to the dispute. How can anyone any longer doubt the vulnerability of a municipal employer to this sort of pressure? Was it simply a matter of indifference to Mayor Lindsay in September 1969 whether another teachers' strike occurred on the eve of a municipal election? Did the size and the speed of the settlement with the United Federation of Teachers (UFT) suggest nothing about one first-rate politician's estimate of his vulnerability? And are the chickens now coming home to roost because of extravagant concessions on pensions for employees of New York City the result only of mistaken actuarial calculations? Or do they reflect the irrelevance of long-run considerations to politicians vulnerable to the strike and compelled to think in terms of short-run political impact?

Those who disagree on this latter point rely principally on their conviction that anticipation of increased taxes as the result of a large labor settlement will countervail the felt inconvenience of a strike, and that municipalities are not, therefore, overly vulnerable to strikes by public employees. The argument made here, however—that governmental budgets in large cities are so complex that generally the effect of any particular labor settlement on the typical municipal budget is a matter of very low visibility—seems adequately convincing. Concern over possible taxes will not, as a general proposition, significantly deter voters who are inconvenienced by a strike from compelling political leaders to settle quickly. Moreover, municipalities are often subsidized by other political entities—the nation or state—and the cost of a strike settlement may not be borne by those demanding an end to the strike.

All this may seem to suggest that it is the strike weapon—whether the issue be monetary or nonmonetary—that cannot be transplanted to the public sector. This is an oversimplification, however. It is the combination of the strike and the typical municipal political process, including the usual methods for raising revenue. One solution, of course, might well be a ban on strikes, if it could be made effective. But that is not the sole alternative, for there may be ways in which municipal political structures can be changed so as to make cities less vulnerable to strikes and to reduce the potential power of public employee unions to tolerable levels. (The relative merits of these alternatives are weighed in Part IV.)

All this may also seem to suggest a sharper distinction between the public and private sectors than actually exists. The discussion here has dealt with models, one for private collective bargaining, the other for public. Each model is located at the core of its sector. But the difference in the impact of collective bargaining in the two sectors should be seen as a continuum. Thus, for example, it may be that market restraints do not sufficiently discipline strike settlements in some regulated industries or in industries that rely mainly on government contracts. Indeed, collective bargaining in such industries has been under steady and insistent attack.

In the public sector, it may be that in any given municipality—but particularly a small one—at any given time, taxpayer resistance or the determination of municipal government, or both, will substantially offset union power even under existing political structures. These plainly are exceptions, however. They do not invalidate the public-private distinction as an analytical tool, for that distinction rests on the very real differences that exist in the vast bulk of situations, situations exemplified by these models. On the other hand, in part because of a recognition that there are exceptions that in particular cases make the models invalid, we shall argue that the law regulating municipal bargaining must be flexible and tailored to the real needs of a particular municipality. The flexibility issue will be addressed directly, and in some detail, after consideration of the contemporary setting in which public bargaining is now developing.

CHAPTER TWO

The Contemporary Setting

The legal status of unionism among employees of federal, state, and municipal government has long been one of the loose ends of labor policy. A loose end, that is, in the sense that there is no national legislation, and, until recently, state and municipal policies were largely unformulated except for occasional statutes and sporadic pronouncements by judges exercising the power of common law courts. A legal vacuum, however, does not inevitably entail harmful consequences. So long as the interest of public employees in unionism was mixed and the public labor sector was relatively quiescent, the ambiguities in legal status were tolerable. But in an age in which attitudes and conditions undergo swift and unforeseeable changes, what are loose ends in the law one day quickly become vexatious and intractable problems the next.

So it is with the issue of public employee unionism. From 1960 to 1970 employment in state and local government jumped from roughly 6 to 10 million while the number of federal employees rose from 2.4 to 2.9 million. This jump has made government employment a significant determinant of labor market conditions (see Figure 1). At the same time, all units of state, county, and municipal government—police and fire departments, schools, welfare systems, sanitation bureaus, and so forth—are facing persistent and vocal demands for the provision of steadier and better services and for greater control over these services by affected citizen groups within the community.

FIGURE 1. *Federal and State and Local Employment and Payrolls, 1959–70*[a]

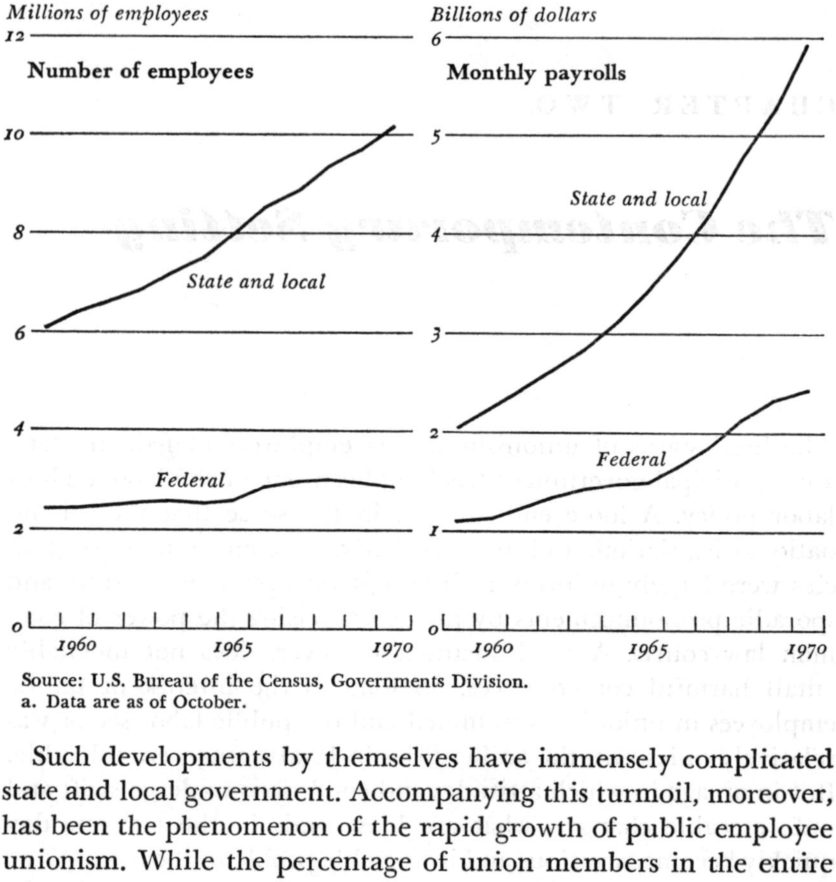

Source: U.S. Bureau of the Census, Governments Division.
a. Data are as of October.

Such developments by themselves have immensely complicated state and local government. Accompanying this turmoil, moreover, has been the phenomenon of the rapid growth of public employee unionism. While the percentage of union members in the entire labor force has been declining, or remaining stable, many public employee unions have doubled, and more than doubled, their membership. In a twelve-year span from 1956 to 1968, the percentage of all union members (those in both the private and public sector) who were employed by government jumped from 5 percent to almost 11 percent.[1] Indeed, the public sector is the only one in which the union movement has done significantly more than hold its own in recent years. This increase in membership has been accompanied by a perceptible rise in militancy, fre-

1. Advisory Commission on Intergovernmental Relations, *Labor-Management Policies for State and Local Government* (1969), pp. 1, 5; U.S. Bureau of the Census, *Statistical Abstract of the United States, 1970* (1970), p. 239.

quently manifesting itself in a determination to achieve union goals regardless of the law.

The result has been conflict: between public employee unions and political leaders and between unions and those groups seeking enhanced control over governmental decisions affecting them. Some disputes have been settled, but only under the threat of a disruption of governmental services. Others—more than a few—have been settled only after an illegal strike that creates the atmosphere of a crisis if not the fact itself. And those disputes involving highly charged political issues, such as a police civilian review board or school decentralization plan, or touching society's most sensitive nerves by pitting a union of one race against a citizenry of another, have frequently left an ugly residue of racial and ethnic tension. The effect of such labor disputes on the social and political fabric of New York City—and of the events of Memphis on the nation—surely demonstrates their deadly potential. Thus, the questions left unanswered by law—whether and to what extent collective bargaining is the appropriate labor policy for the public sector—now demand answers.

It is the aim of this book to suggest some answers to those questions. The answers will build upon the theoretical difficulties of transplanting full collective bargaining to public employment, as developed in Chapter 1, and upon a general framework to be outlined in Chapter 3. Before proceeding to that framework, however, the contemporary setting, de jure and de facto, in which the law is developing will be sketched in order briefly to describe where collective bargaining by public employees is now and how it got there, and to lay out the basic contours of the social landscape in which the legal structures must be erected. For the details of those structures must take into account a large number of considerations—legal and nonlegal—arising from what has gone before and from what is happening now.

The Developing Legal Structure

THE INITIAL RESPONSE AND ITS CRITICS

A unique aspect of American life is that courts confront most problems of social change—and are thus the source of the first formal governmental response—before legislatures. The initial ju-

dicial response to collective bargaining by public employees was generally hostile. Although the court rulings were by no means uniform, many decisions limited the power of employees to organize unions and restrained governmental authorities from recognizing unions of their employees or entering into collective agreements with them. Other rulings permitted organization; some allowed the execution of collective agreements but limited the matters on which unions and governmental employers might agree. Arbitration clauses or union shop provisions, for instance, were occasionally prohibited. All decisions forbade strikes.

The rationales supplied in support of judicial hostility varied, but the most significant were based on the concept of the sovereignty of the public employer, and its offspring, the doctrine of the illegal delegation of power.[2] Good lawyers, however, are good critics, and these two lawyer-made constructs have for some years been sharply attacked by union lawyers and academic commentators. Their criticism, strengthened by the changing nature of government employment and the ever visible example of collective bargaining in the private sector, has led to a liberalized common law, as well as a growing body of enacted law, and has reduced to a whisper the counsel of restraint voiced by these constructs.[3]

Consider sovereignty, that concept so elusive as an analytical tool, yet so fundamental to all notions of government. A law dictionary advises that it is the "supreme, absolute, and uncontrollable power by which any independent state is governed. . . ."[4]

2. For the flavor of the rhetoric, see *Railway Mail Association* v. *Murphy*, 180 Misc. 868, 875, 44 N.Y.S. 2d 601, 607, rev'd on other grounds *sub nom. Railway Mail Association* v. *Corsi*, 267 App. Div. 470, aff'd, 293 N.Y. 315, 56 N.E.2d 721 aff'd, 326 U.S. 88 (1945):

> To tolerate or recognize any combination of civil service employees of the government as a labor organization or union is not only incompatible with the spirit of democracy, but inconsistent with every principle upon which our government is founded. Nothing is more dangerous to public welfare than to admit that hired servants of the State can dictate to the government the hours, the wages and conditions under which they will carry on essential services vital to the welfare, safety and security of the citizen. To admit as true that government employees have power to halt or check the functions of government unless their demands are satisfied, is to transfer to them all legislative, executive and judicial power. Nothing would be more ridiculous. 180 Misc. N.Y. at 875.

3. The most important of the "liberal" common law decisions is the Connecticut case of *Norwalk Teachers Association* v. *Board of Education of City of Norwalk*, 138 Conn. 269, 83 A.2d 482 (1951).

4. H. Black, *Black's Law Dictionary* (4th ed., West, 1968), p. 1568.

Since collective bargaining in the private sector is believed by many to be a system of countervailing power—a means, that is, by which the power of employees is increased to offset that of employers—one might easily see its establishment in the public sector as an infringement on governmental power and the sovereignty of the state itself. Viewing the "supreme, absolute, and uncontrollable" sovereign in its role as an employer, therefore, Franklin Roosevelt understandably said, "A strike of public employees manifests nothing less than an intent on their part to obstruct the operations of government until their demands are satisfied. Such action looking toward the paralysis of government by those who have sworn to support it is unthinkable and intolerable."[5]

But to the lawyer-critics, sovereignty seems a weak reed when the private analogy is pressed. It was 1836 when a judge observed that if collective bargaining in the private sector were "tolerated, the constitutional control over our affairs would pass away from the people at large, and become vested in the hands of conspirators. We should have a new system of government, and our rights [would] be placed at the disposal of a voluntary and self-constituted association."[6] Such sovereignty-related assertions are no longer thought to have applicability to the private sector, for private collective bargaining has served as the nation's labor policy for more than a generation—not without criticism, but surely without any sign of the apocalypse. And so, conclude the critics, the notion of sovereignty as a bar to collective bargaining is not a concept peculiar to the public employer, but is merely an anti-union makeweight left from an earlier day when the law was hostile to all collective bargaining.

Sovereignty must also seem to the critics too elusive and too remote a concept to be of practical significance in the fashioning of labor policy. The issue is not, they say, whether government's power is "supreme," but how government as an employer ought to exercise that power. And the concept of sovereignty, while it lo-

5. Letter from Franklin D. Roosevelt to L. C. Stewart, president, National Federation of Federal Employees, Aug. 16, 1937, cited in I. Vogel, "What About the Rights of the Public Employee?" 1 *Labor Law Journal* 604, 612 (May 1950).

6. *The Case of the Twenty Journeymen Tailors, People* v. *Faulkner*, N.Y. (1836), *New York Courier and Enquirer*, May 31, 1836, reproduced in J. Commons and E. Gilmore, *A Documentary History of American Industrial Society* (Cleveland: Arthur H. Clark Co., 1910), Vol. 4, p. 322.

cates the source of ultimate authority, does not seem to speak to that issue.

The doctrine of the illegal delegation of power, however, does address itself to that question, for it is a constitutional doctrine that sometimes forbids government from sharing its powers with others.[7]

The doctrine of illegal delegation commands that certain discretionary decisions be made solely on the basis of the judgment of a designated official. And because a great deal of shared control is implicit in any scheme of collective bargaining, the delegation doctrine has been employed in the past to prevent all bargaining between government and its employees. Even today it serves as a basis for establishing limits on the scope of collective bargaining in public employment. Often subjects of vital interest to employees are subjects that cannot be resolved through the collective bargaining process, because they are by law nondelegable.[8] In some jurisdictions, however, the delegation doctrine places in doubt the binding force of bargains struck;[9] and in others is employed as an excuse for not bargaining even though such bargaining is legally permissible.[10]

Again, however, the lawyer-critics press the analogy of the private sector and again find the limiting doctrine an inadequate basis for a distinction. Private employers from the beginning of American labor history have insisted upon management prerogatives. Certain decisions, their rhetoric claims, must be made by management alone and cannot be subject to shared control.[11]

7. See *Mugford* v. *Mayor and City Council of Baltimore,* reprinted in C. Rhyne, *Labor Unions and Municipal Employee Law* (National Institute of Municipal Law Officers, 1946), pp. 161–64, aff'd, 185 Md. 266, 44 A.2d 745 (1946).

8. See, for example, Executive Order 10988, "Employee-Management Cooperation in the Federal Service," 27 *Fed. Reg.* 551 (Jan. 19, 1962). Cf. *In re Farmingdale Classroom Teachers,* 68 *Labor Relations Reference Manual* 2761 (N.Y. Sup. Ct. 1968).

9. See *Amalgamated Transit Union, Local Division 1338* v. *Dallas Public Transit Board,* 430 S.W.2d 107 (Texas Ct. Civ. App., 1968), cert. denied, 396 U.S. 838 (1969).

10. Compare *Regents* v. *Packing House Workers,* 68 *LRRM* 2677 (Iowa Dist. Ct., 1968), with *Fort Smith* v. *Arkansas State Council No. 38, AFSCME, AFL-CIO,* 245 Ark. 409, 433 S.W.2d 153 (1968).

11. Consider the following statement of Charles E. Wilson made in 1948 when he was president of General Motors:

> If we consider the ultimate result of this tendency to stretch collective bargaining to comprehend any subject that a union leader may desire to bargain

While the decisions at issue have changed over the years—from wage rates to subcontracting, from hours of work to automation —the assertion of management prerogatives has been the private sector's analogue to the illegal delegation of power;[12] management is charged with the lawful responsibility for making management decisions; the decision in question is a management decision, it cannot be shared, for to share would be to give control to those without legal responsibility.[13]

In the private sector the establishment of collective bargaining is itself a rejection of these arguments. Based on a belief that bargaining is likely to be unfair when the individual employee is ranged against the employer, and that "industrial democracy" is necessary to rescue the employee from the psychological emasculation of modern industry, collective bargaining inevitably entails shared control of "wages, hours, and other terms and conditions of employment."[14] And there is nothing in any realistic description of the management function to require that the quoted language be given anything other than an expansive reading.[15] Given the conservative ideology of the American labor movement, we need not fear that the unions will intrude on matters that in fact are "solely of interest to management." They are hardly likely to

---

on, we come out with the union leaders really running the economy of the country; but with no legal or public responsibility and with no private employment except as they may permit.

Under these conditions, the freedom of management to function properly without interference in making its everyday decisions will be gradually restricted. The union leaders—particularly where they have industry-wide power—will have the deciding vote in all managerial decisions, or at least, will exercise a veto power that will stop progress.

. . . .

Only by defining and restricting collective bargaining to its proper sphere can we hope to save what we have come to know as our American system and keep it from evolving into an alien form, imported from East of the Rhine. . . . N. Chamberlain, *The Labor Sector* (McGraw-Hill, 1965), p. 342.

12. See, for example, *Inland Steel Co.* v. *NLRB,* 170 F.2d 247 (7th Cir. 1948), cert. denied, 336 U.S. 960 (1948); *Fibreboard Paper Products Corp.* v. *NLRB,* 379 U.S. 203 (1964).

13. The earliest American labor cases sometimes contained rhetoric of this sort. Compare *State* v. *Glidden,* 55 Conn. 46, 72, 8 A.890, 894 (1887), with *The Philadelphia Cordwainers Case, Commonwealth* v. *Pullis* (1806), Commons and Gilmore, *A Documentary History,* Vol. 3 (1910), pp. 59, 229.

14. Labor-Management Relations Act of 1947, § 8(d), 29 U.S.C. § 158(d) (1964).

15. See generally H. Wellington, *Labor and the Legal Process* (Yale University Press, 1968), pp. 63–90.

expend their limited power in disputes over issues having no impact on the worker. Nor are there lines to be drawn on grounds of economic efficiency. Since the efficiency of an employer is reflected in the cost of his product, whether that cost is imposed through high wages or a restriction on the introduction of machinery is a matter of indifference to society. Thus, in our system of private collective bargaining, economic power and the parties' desires are the only rational determinants of what matters should be subjects of bargaining.[16]

Therefore, ask the lawyer-critics, is not the doctrine of illegal delegation to be treated in the public sector in the same way as the management prerogatives question is in the private?[17] And are not the reasons for collective bargaining in the public sector the same as those in the private?

As Chapter 1 insists, the answers to these questions are considerably different from those offered by our lawyer-critics. There is a concept of sovereignty entitled to count as a reason for being skeptical about the legalizing of strikes by public employees without corresponding protective changes in the typical urban political process. For what sovereignty should mean here is not the location of ultimate authority—on that the critics are dead right—but the right of government, through its laws, to insure the survival of the " 'normal' American political process." As hard as it is for some of the critics to accept, strikes by public employees may, as a long-run proposition, skew that process by concentrating too much power in one parochial interest group. Unless the vulnerability of the typical municipal political process to strikes is reduced, therefore, that threat is appropriately met by a prohibition of strikes.

Moreover, the public stake in some issues makes it appropriate for government either not to have to bargain with its employees on these issues at all or to follow bargaining procedures radically

16. See A. Cox and J. Dunlop, "Regulation of Collective Bargaining by The National Labor Relations Board," 63 *Harvard Law Review* 389 (January 1950); Committee for Economic Development, *The Public Interest in National Labor Policy* (New York: CED, 1961), p. 82.

17. In the private area, many subjects have been held not to be mandatory subjects of bargaining. As to nonmandatory subjects, neither employer nor union has a duty to bargain. Indeed, to press bargaining about such a subject is itself an unfair labor practice. See *NLRB* v. *Wooster Division of Borg-Warner Corp.*, 356 U.S. 342 (1958).

different from those of the private sector. It is in this respect that the judicial doctrine of illegal delegation of power should have relevance. For the traditional procedures of bargaining, when employed to resolve issues that are not only terms and conditions of employment but also controversial political issues, may drastically reduce the influence other groups will have on the decision-making process and thereby work an undesirable change in the distribution of political power in a community.

THE STATE OF THE LAW

Nevertheless, the critics of sovereignty and delegation are carrying the day, in part because the differences between the public and private sectors have not been articulated clearly and are not sufficiently appreciated. As important is the fact that the judicial elaboration of sovereignty and illegal delegation was shrouded in abstractions and resulted in expansive and unevenhanded limitations on public employees. If one accepts the claims for collective bargaining in the private sector as legitimate, the danger to the political process posed by public employee unions does not call for a complete prohibition on collective bargaining. Because the courts too often reached that result under the doctrine of sovereignty, that doctrine no longer counts with many of the critics who view it as a construct that rejects the claims for collective bargaining generally. It seems, however, that this understandable attitude is itself an excessive reaction to judicial error.

A changed judicial treatment of public employee unionism soon reflected the impact of the sustained criticism. The most significant decision is the often cited 1951 Connecticut *Norwalk Teachers'* case.[18] That decision swept aside the arguments employed in an earlier day to prevent collective bargaining entirely and held that teachers had a right to organize and that school boards were empowered to bargain with a union and embody a settlement in a collective agreement.

A more permissive attitude was also demonstrated in actions taken by other branches of government. No matter what the formal

18. *Norwalk Teachers Association* v. *Board of Education of City of Norwalk*, 138 Conn. 269, 83 A.2d 482 (1951).

legal structure seemed to dictate, many mayors, selectmen, and school boards began to bargain seriously with unions of their employees. Resolutions of municipal legislative bodies recognized unions, and other resolutions established terms and conditions of employment that in fact formalized bargains struck after arm's-length negotiations with unions. And municipal ordinances establishing formal procedures to govern collective bargaining were enacted.

State statutes began to appear in the late 1950s, the bulk of legislation coming after 1965. Executive Order 10988, promulgated by President Kennedy in 1962 and providing for collective bargaining with federal employees, imparted some momentum. While the order sharply limited the scope of bargaining, did not permit strikes, and had no legal effect on state governments, it has served as the legitimating federal imprimatur on the principle of collective bargaining by public employees.

The state statutes are quite varied in both general structure and specific detail as the tables in Appendix A demonstrate. They are generally marked, however, by two common features. The first is a peaceful procedure, with appropriate administrative machinery, for determining questions of recognition. To be sure, recognition under some statutes is at the public employer's option and not mandatory. But even limited procedures serve to establish collective bargaining as an appropriate labor policy for public employment.

The second common feature of these statutes is an impasse procedure to be invoked when a public employer and union cannot agree upon the terms of a new contract. Because most legislation prohibits resort to the strike—the ultimate impasse mechanism in the private sector—impasse procedures are essential parts of public employment statutes. But where strikes are barred, existing impasse procedures generally are limited to mediation and fact finding, procedures that, while useful in helping the parties reach an accord, do not provide for final resolution of a continuing impasse. They do not, therefore, ensure a settlement, and in too many situations they have not avoided strikes.

Increasingly, however, the force of the criticism of the early judicial treatment of public employee unionism is being felt, and an increasingly permissive attitude toward strikes as an impasse mechanism is apparent. Indeed, Hawaii and Pennsylvania have recently enacted statutes permitting some strikes by public employees without corresponding measures reducing the vulnerability of the political processes to them.[19] The view that collective bargaining can be fully transplanted to the public sector (with variations perhaps for strike-created emergencies) is, unfortunately, gaining steadily.

Any discussion emphasizing legislation at the state level must end with a caveat. Although trends toward uniformity are discernible, there is an ad hoc quality about the legal structure surrounding public employee bargaining today, even in those states with comprehensive statutes. Where no such statutes exist, the legal structure is composed of a crazy-quilt of local executive orders, resolutions, ordinances, civil service statutes and procedures, and other state statutes establishing or affecting terms and conditions of employment. Where statutes do exist, the legal structure is by no means uncomplicated. While a comprehensive statute may endorse bargaining, other legislation—most frequently civil service statutes—may in fact resolve a large number of matters that seem traditional subjects of bargaining. The existence of a state statute governing bargaining and establishing formal procedures for it, moreover, by no means guarantees that parties at the local level will not work out their own ad hoc arrangements. There is evidence, for instance, indicating that unit determination and recognition procedures are sometimes agreed upon by the parties outside the framework of the comprehensive state statute.

The State of Bargaining

A description of the law, however, by no means reveals the actual state of bargaining in the public sector. Bargaining relationships vary enormously from place to place and the formal legal structure is only one variable affecting them. Bargaining may occur, for example, in a jurisdiction in which an opinion of the state attorney general holds that it is illegal. And occasionally the

19. The Hawaii statute, Act 171, L. (1970), may be found in *Government Employee Relations Report,* No. 51, Reference File 2011; the Pennsylvania statute, S.B. 1333, L. (1970), is in *GERR* No. 51, RF 4711.

parties ignore the formal procedures provided by state agencies and state statutes and make up their own.

There is reason to believe that in many places bargaining is in an embryonic state. Unions are frequently led by part-time local members who are amateurs when it comes to negotiations. Where that is the case, the unions may be relatively ineffective because they do not systematically establish their goals and the priorities among them. In other cases, the unions are not fully organized and cannot depend on all their members responding to a strike call. As a result, the full impact of public employee unions has not yet been revealed, and accordingly, some observers may be dangerously underestimating the extent to which the unions will skew the political process once they have professional guidance and are fully organized.

There can be little question, however, that militancy among public employees is growing. Public employee work stoppages in government have increased dramatically since 1958. The number of public sector strikes rose from 15 to 409 between 1958 and 1969. During the same period the number of workers involved in strikes went from 1,720 to 159,400, while the man-days idle during the year increased from 7,510 to 744,600 (see Appendix B).

Dollars and cents issues are not the only target of union pressure. Police unions are increasingly concerned with matters of discipline relating to the relationship of their members to various groups in the community. Social workers are concerned with the content of the programs they administer, while teachers' unions bargain over student discipline, decentralization of the governance of schools, and curriculum content. Disputes over such issues often contain the seeds of racial and ethnic conflict and exacerbate the already aggravated problems of urban government.

If the unions are in many cases inexperienced, the public employer, nevertheless, is often worse off. Collective bargaining involves a radical change in public personnel policy and the typical municipality with no previous experience is not well geared to meet the challenges it poses. When initially faced with public employee unionism, municipalities all too often entrust to their regular personnel—for example, the city attorney—full responsibility for handling the problems created by public employee unionism. Often these persons are totally inexperienced in such matters and respond in ways that guarantee future problems. Some are halfhearted about recognition and bargaining and thereby increase union militancy for no particular reason, since in most places a nonrecognition policy cannot be maintained in the face of any substantial pressure. Others are unwilling to run political risks and see little at stake in recognizing a union. They want to seem agreeable and reasonable and thus often recognize inappropriate units and permit supervisory employees to be included in such units. The excessive number of recognized bargaining units in New York City amply demonstrates the extent to which the mistakes made by an agreeable but inexperienced administration will affect the long-run course of bargaining and urban government.

Just as the unions are gaining more experience and are looking to professional assistance, so too are public employers attempting to rationalize their labor relations policies. The hiring of professionals and the establishment of formalized procedures are becoming more common and represent major steps in the right direction. The public employer, however, remains highly vulnerable and it is doubtful whether the degree of rationalization achieved in the private sector can ever be achieved in the public. One important hurdle is the structure of municipal government itself, which is frequently characterized by fragmented and overlapping authority. Changes in the structure of government are not easily achieved and there may well be countervailing considerations that make such changes undesirable. Another hurdle is the fact that municipal politics and public employee bargaining cannot be separated. This increases the maneuvering and posturing that accompany bargaining and tends to make a large number of short-run considerations of excessive importance. It also increases the number of constituencies whose demands must be accommodated as part of any settlement.

The Importance of Racial Issues

Because public employee bargaining cannot take place in a nonpolitical context, it often touches society's most sensitive nerves. The frequency with which racial considerations affect public sector bargaining is a notable, if regrettable, contemporary example that must be given explicit recognition. Dr. Martin Luther King's presence in Memphis was caused by a strike that had polarized that city along racial lines. The school decentralization dispute in New York City was viewed by many as a Jewish-black confrontation, and the issue of a police civilian review board invariably pits a largely white police force against a hostile black citizenry. In some places a work stoppage may well be viewed as an act of the entire black community, as in Jackson, Mississippi, which experienced a strike of all its black municipal employees.

A number of factors have combined to make racial considerations critical to public employee bargaining in many urban areas. The black community has turned increasingly to government as a source of employment. It seems almost universally the case in urban areas that the percentage of municipal employees who are black is on the rise. The employment relationship is always of great importance to the individual, and, if it is a troubled one, it may be looked upon as a prime cause of what seems a generally unsatisfactory existence. Black employees of a municipality have thus, on occasion, identified employment problems with race or discrimination problems generally. Public employee unionism among blacks, moreover, provides a convenient vehicle for community organization as well as a symbol for unity and action in the black community.

The contexts in which the race issue seem most frequently to crop up can be identified. First, members of the black community may develop hostility to a group of white employees with whom they have frequent contact. Welfare workers, policemen, firefighters, and teachers all seem vulnerable targets of racial hostility. Where the employee group is unionized and contains few blacks, the problem is exacerbated. And even where some blacks are employed, hostility may exist between them and their co-employees, as is amply demonstrated by the organization of all-black unions within particular police forces.

A second context, and one likely to increase in importance, is hostility between black workers and white supervisors. Such a subordinate relationship is often viewed by blacks as a symbol of discrimination and, where the black workers are members of a union, bargaining may be affected. The third context is where black workers are organized and the dominant political forces represent the white community, as in the Memphis and Jackson cases. These can develop into particularly aggravated disputes when recognition of the union is denied by the municipality. In such circumstances, a strike for recognition of the black union may be viewed as a strike for recognition of the black community.

The fourth context overlaps with the others. When the black community feels strongly about the desirability of certain governmental policies, which in turn affect the services provided by public employees, resistance to the establishment of such policies by a predominantly white union can lead to a racial confrontation. It is evident, of course, that any interest group in the society may find itself at odds with a public employee union. Where the dispute has racial overtones, however—and in large urban areas that will frequently be the case—it can place a particular strain on the social fabric.

The Role of Legislation

A final word should be said about comprehensive public employee bargaining laws. The unions, understandably, are often a prime force behind the enactment of such statutes. These statutes seek to protect and encourage organization among the unorganized, and no doubt they do provide a moral and legal imperative in that direction. However, a comprehensive statute generally is not enacted until union organization is substantial. In one sense, therefore, organization seems as much a cause of legislation as an effect.

What is easy to overlook is that such legislation is also helpful to the municipal employer. Municipal employers gain from the lack of such legislation only when they are determined to refuse to recognize a union. Where that is not a feasible policy or where, as seems frequently to be the case, the public employer is agreeable to recognition, legislation is quite useful to it. A prohibition on strikes by public employees is more acceptable if embodied in a statute protecting organization and requiring recognition and bargaining than if it emanates from a judge who has the power only to prohibit the strike and not the power to compel recognition. Legislation also focuses the attention of municipal authorities on problems they ought to consider. A statute setting out criteria for unit determination can encourage municipal employers to look to their long-run interest and not recognize units based solely on the extent of organization. Had such statutes been more prevalent at an earlier time, we might today be less concerned with the problems of unit fragmentation.

A judgment as to whether public employee unions or public employers benefit more from state statutes is thus very difficult to make. There is no way to know how much organization has come about because of the existence of state statutes. It does appear, however, that the absence of a statute has led inexperienced municipal employers into error on many occasions.

A mandatory recognition procedure need not, however, be wholly unqualified. Some public employees have responsibilities that, if properly fulfilled, may put them in conflict with persons who also belong to unions. Police may be called upon to keep peace in labor disputes in the private sector. And supervisors may be the first line of authority in the enforcement of collective agreements in the public sector. Where such a conflict of interest exists, public employees ought not to be represented by a union that has in its membership persons whose interests may conflict with their responsibilities. Police ought thus to be represented only by police unions and supervisors by a union that does not represent nonsupervisory employees.

Beyond advocating the establishment of mandatory recognition procedures, all that can be said with assurance about the proper role of law in public employment is that there is no one "right" law. Indeed, a diversity of structures must be created. Those structures should be designed with two principal problems in mind: the strike and the scope of bargaining. Portions of this book consist of a discussion of those two problems. A number of mechanisms and structures, some complementary, some mutually exclusive, will be suggested. Which are appropriate for adoption by a particular city must be determined by political judgments on a large number of variables. No one structure, no one mechanism, can be recommended for all municipalities.

Federal Regulation

A recent decision of the United States Supreme Court indicates that federal power to regulate the relations between local governments and their employees exists.[4] But the existence of a power is not by itself the justification for its exercise. That depends on a demonstration of federal responsibility and a congressional capacity to fashion workable policies. It would appear that the structuring of collective bargaining by local governmental units is a matter of very low priority on the federal agenda, and that desirable structures are best attained by local regulation. Federal legislation seems, therefore, inappropriate.

4. *Maryland* v. *Wirtz*, 392 U.S. 183 (1968).

There are many important differences between the private and public sectors in terms of federal responsibility. Some involve legal history,[5] others reflect the hope of the sponsors of the Wagner Act (National Labor Relations Act) that it would be an antidepression measure.[6] The most important difference, however, stems from the nature of competitive markets. In the private sector, firms compete in the sale of their products across state lines. To permit widely varying labor policies among the states might benefit those firms operating where the law favored unionism least. Not only would that disrupt competitive relationships; it would also limit the effectiveness of laws in other states designed to encourage collective bargaining. If collective bargaining were to become a favored policy, it had to be formulated at the federal level so that competitive pressures would not destroy it.

No such pressures exist in the public sector. New York City teachers are not paid less because of competition from Philadelphia's school system. Municipal employers simply do not compete in an interstate product market that effectively prevents some states from adopting collective bargaining as a policy because others do not.

When an issue is a matter of low federal priority, considerations of federalism dictate that governmental action be left to state or

5. When Congress enacted the Norris-LaGuardia Act in 1932, 47 Stat. 70 (1932), and the National Labor Relations Act in 1935, 49 Stat. 449 (1935), it was acting against a history of federal regulation of collective bargaining. By applying the Sherman Antitrust Act to unions in *Loewe* v. *Lawlor,* 208 U.S. 274 (1908), the Supreme Court had imposed a federal regulatory scheme on union activities. See R. Winter, Jr., "Collective Bargaining and Competition: The Application of Antitrust Standards to Union Activities," 73 *Yale Law Journal* 14, 30–38 (November 1963). That the rules imposed were largely judge-made did not matter. The point was that they could not be changed by state legislatures but only by Congress. And, for better or worse, that body was irrevocably plunged into the debate over the legitimacy of collective bargaining in the private sector. No such historical background exists as to public sector unions.

6. In 1935, the nation was still in the Great Depression, and some believed that an economic cure might be found in devices intended to increase the purchasing power of lower income groups. As the preamble to the act attests, 29 U.S.C. § 151 (1964), believers in the "purchasing power" theory thought collective bargaining such a device. Whatever one thinks of "purchasing power" theory—and we don't think much of it—it may be effectively pursued only at the federal level. Collective bargaining by public employees, however, is not generally thought of as an antidepression device, and even if "purchasing power" devotees were to be shown some sympathy today by informed opinion, that particular call for federal action seems muted.

local initiative. One can claim more, however, than that municipal public employee bargaining should have a low priority on any agenda for congressional action. One can claim that intervention at the national level would be positively harmful. Federal legislation or regulation necessarily tends to a uniform rule. In the case of public employee unionism, uniformity is most undesirable and diversity in rules and structures virtually a necessity.

Consider just two important examples, although many more exist. It has been stated here that recognition ought to be mandatory on the part of the municipal employer. But that duty alone necessarily involves the enforcement tribunal in the bargaining of the parties. Just as the National Labor Relations Board cannot avoid imposing some minimal duty to bargain as part of the duty to recognize a union,[7] so too a tribunal enforcing a municipality's obligation to recognize must determine whether it is in fact bargaining with the union and making a good faith effort to reach an agreement. Even so minimal an intrusion entails involvement in matters that may be sensitive issues of local government. Complicated fiscal structures, local budgetary practices, charter limits on taxes, state restrictions on tax increases, statutes designating how certain services are to be performed, and so forth, may severely limit the power of municipal bargainers to negotiate in a fashion deemed essential as well as traditional by the union.[8] And when that is the case, the union will quite naturally turn to an enforcement tribunal for an order to bargain on the grounds that it has not been truly "recognized." Equally intractable is the question of who "bargains" for the "employer" with, for example, a teacher's union in a typical small town: the first selectman, board of selectmen, town meeting, board of finance, or board of education? That question must be resolved before a legal duty to recognize can be effectively enforced. If the tribunal is a federal one, uniform rules as to the structure of local governments may be the result of such litigation. It understates the case more than a little to say that resolution of such issues at the federal level would be undesirable.

Consider also whether strikes ought to be permitted. The argu-

7. H. Wellington, *Labor and the Legal Process* (Yale University Press, 1968), pp. 49 ff.

8. See C. Rehmus, "Constraints on Local Governments in Public Employee Bargaining," 67 *Michigan Law Review* 919 (March 1969).

ment is made in subsequent pages that appropriate structures can be created in which strikes of a nonemergency nature should not be illegal. Essential to the establishment of such structures is the adoption of devices that reduce the vulnerability of particular municipal political processes to such strikes. What measures will accomplish such a reduction clearly will vary from municipality to municipality and no uniform rule ought to be imposed.

State and Local Regulation

The role for state legislation seems considerably larger than for federal, although perhaps not as large as that for the municipalities. Subordinate governmental units, such as towns, counties, and cities, derive their power from the state. Many of the functions performed by lesser governmental units that seem prone to unionization are already performed under significant state regulation. Education, welfare, and health services are frequently provided under a blend of state and local control. Limiting tax structures may have been imposed by a state legislature. And, as a matter of history and tradition, state responsibility for seeing that local governmental functions are performed without interruption has always been substantially greater than that of the federal government.

State regulation, moreover, promises a more flexible approach than national legislation. State officials are likely to be more sensitive to problems of local government than federal officials, and legislation that proves inappropriate can be modified more easily at the state level than at the national. Many of the limitations that constrain municipalities in bargaining with unions are the result of restrictions imposed by the state. And within a particular state, a common history gives some assurance that the diversity in local governmental structures will be less than that among states.

Nevertheless, considerable room ought to be left for local regulation and experimentation. The variables are so numerous that comprehensive legislation even at the state level may introduce unwise uniformities. The strike question, for instance, largely turns on the vulnerability of local political structures. The availability of adequate measures to reduce that vulnerability will vary from place to place as will the need to permit strikes rather than resort to other kinds of impasse procedures. Some devices, such as partial operation schemes, necessarily must be worked out on a community-by-community basis. The scope-of-bargaining issue will be of different orders of magnitude in different communities. In the absence of some imperative dictating one rule for all, such matters can be left to local regulation.

The difficulty with state abstention, however, is that municipal inaction may result in labor crises that cannot be ignored by state officials. There is room, therefore, for state legislation that encourages municipal regulation tailored to the needs of the particular community, but that also provides the legal structure minimally necessary for effective bargaining.

The state first should establish a mandatory recognition procedure. As to every other provision, a lesser governmental unit should be free to opt out of the state scheme and provide its own mechanisms. The state law should make strikes illegal and provide post-impasse procedures. Local governments might, however, permit various kinds of strikes, provide different impasse procedures, redefine mandatory subjects of bargaining, establish procedures for the resolution of nonmonetary issues, and so on. Such a statutory scheme, with areas of concurrent power, both encourages local initiative and inventiveness and guards against the dangers of local inertia.

Also, a state level agency with dual functions ought to be created. First, it should be empowered to enforce the applicable provisions of the state statute and to implement the impasse procedures. Second, it should be available to take on functions delegated to it by municipal regulation. Thus, if a municipality decided to permit nonemergency strikes, the task of determining whether an emergency existed might rest with this agency. Or, if the municipality desired to adopt impasse procedures that varied from those of the state statute, this agency could be empowered to administer them.

The value of such an agency stems not only from the experience and specialized skills it would gain but also from the fact that it would be neutral so far as municipal labor disputes were concerned. This is essential, for many of the devices suggested in subsequent pages would best be implemented by a neutral rather than by a party to the dispute.

The Governing Variables

In order to tailor a public employee bargaining law to serve best the needs of a particular municipality, an almost infinite number of factors must be considered. And largely political judgments as to the relative weight to be given to each factor must be made by those responsible for local governance. What follows is only a catalog of the more important variables.

The functions that local government performs must be considered in determining what kind of collective bargaining structure should be erected. The number of employees who are potential union members, the kinds of services they provide, the reliance of the community on these services, their essentiality in terms of maintaining public health and safety, the extent to which the character of particular services may become politically controversial, and the ability of the local government to shed certain functions all have a bearing on the form various provisions of the law ought to take.

The nature of local governance in a structural and operational sense is also of great importance. The extent to which political power is centralized or diffused, the visibility of budgetary decisions, the shape of the tax structure, the way particular unionized services are funded, and the financial and legal relationships with larger political units all have implications for decisions as to the scope and structure of bargaining, the nature of ratification by the public employer, and the strike question.

Size is also a major factor. In small towns, the claims on government will differ from those in a large city. It may be easier for concerned citizens to form ad hoc interest groups—for example, taxpayer organizations—that can critically scrutinize the demands of public employee unions and publicize the budgetary effects of wage settlements.[9] Moreover, where the public employee has a

9. The publication of individual salaries has stirred a reaction in one smaller city; see p. 198.

personal relationship with those who rely on his services—as he often does in smaller communities—he may feel less inclined to disappoint that reliance by striking. Where these circumstances exist, the political process may not be significantly endangered by public employee strikes.

The homogeneity of the political entity's population is yet another factor. A homogeneous population makes politically explosive confrontations over nonmonetary issues unlikely; thus, the law can focus on the resolution of wage disputes. Where social, ethnic, and racial heterogeneity exists, however, it may be necessary to establish procedures through which other interest groups can become involved in bargaining over disputed political matters.[10]

The nature and history of the bargaining relationship are also important to legal structure. Expectations created by existing practices ought not be disturbed, or relationships that actually work restructured, except for fundamental reasons. This may mean, for instance, that where a very high degree of militancy among union members exists, the goal of protecting the political process from disproportionately powerful unions might better be achieved by a structure that reduces the vulnerability of the political process to strikes than by one that prohibits strikes altogether.

Finally, the attitude of the community generally toward collective bargaining must be weighed. Where the prevailing ethos is hostile to unions, a number of options ranging from a total prohibition on strikes to mere reliance on hostility to unions are available. Where the ethos is different and significant segments of the community feel strongly about the importance of the right to strike, structures permitting nonemergency strikes, and reducing the vulnerability of the political process to them, may be more appropriate.

A diversity of structures, then, seems not only inevitable but desirable. A later chapter will suggest a number of alternative directions public employee bargaining laws might take. Choice

10. The racial composition of the disputants is clearly an important factor governing the explosiveness of a dispute. In Memphis and Charleston the employees were predominantly black, while the political forces dictating the employers' response were white. The New York decentralization dispute, on the other hand, involved predominantly white employees and issues of community control over schools in predominantly black neighborhoods.

among structures depends on essentially political judgments, weighing the factors sketched above. Whatever structure a public employee law takes, however, the existence of collective bargaining will have important implications for the role of municipal government.

CHAPTER FOUR

Collective Bargaining and the Role of Government

One of the touchstones of the debate between modern-day liberals and conservatives is the question of what functions government may properly undertake. At one end of the political spectrum are those who, because of their belief in individual freedom as a value in itself and as a means to achieve the greatest good for the greatest number, and because of their profound skepticism about the ability of government to perform in a controlled and efficient manner, would limit government strictly to areas where large social cost is clearly involved. At the other end are those who are more sanguine about the ability of government to achieve stated ends and who believe that the total quantum of individual freedom need not be reduced by a large governmental role in restructuring society along egalitarian lines.

We decline to join the debate over these issues, not only because they are somewhere in the great beyond so far as this book is concerned, but also because we have no desire to terminate prematurely an otherwise pleasant collaboration. The relevance of collective bargaining in the public sector to the role of government, however, must be considered.

Bargaining as a Constraint on Governmental Functions

Local government presently performs an extraordinary range of functions: health (inpatient, outpatient, at-home care, preventive, educational);[1] education; sanitation (sewers, refuse collection); housing; transportation (streets, trucks, autos, buses, subways, airports); utility (water, gas, electric); social (babysitting to social work); clerical; police; fire; recreational (parks, zoos, museums); food (in government buildings). Among those employed in providing these services are skilled, unskilled, and professional persons directly involved in each service, and support personnel who perform custodial and maintenance functions. Some of these occupations—for example, refuse collection—are especially subject to labor disputes.[2] And it seems clear that the sum of the problems a municipality faces grows substantially as these services are unionized. The time, energy, and resources expended by the municipality on collective bargaining matters increase along with unionization. In addition, political difficulties multiply quickly. Only a lucky politician, or one with a very divided opposition, can survive a series of strikes that inconvenience his constituents.[3]

An increase in the number of unionized services, moreover, aggravates the difficult question of parity or relative wage rates.[4] Government employees engaged in one service are neither ignorant of nor indifferent to the wage scales in other services. Transit workers, sanitation workers, policemen, and firemen formulate their demands with an eye to what the others have extracted through bargaining. It is no coincidence that the most militant postal workers' local is in a city where the ratio of mailmen's wages to comparable municipal employees had recently been

1. Among the kinds of employees involved are nurses (practical and registered), doctors of various kinds, orderlies, public health specialists, elevator operators, maintenance workers, and so forth.

2. Memphis, Atlanta, New York, and Cincinnati have had notable disputes.

3. Mayor Lindsay's career was clearly endangered by such a series of disputes. His ability to avoid a preelection school strike through a handsome settlement, as well as his good fortune in facing two candidates who split the opposition vote and were unattractive to those most alienated by his handling of the decentralization dispute, may have accounted for his victory.

4. Relative wage rates also create difficult problems in the private sector. Railroads and newspapers are examples. See L. Reynolds and C. Taft, *The Evolution of Wage Structure* (Yale University Press, 1955), pp. 19 ff.

drastically altered to the mailmen's detriment.[5] The spread of unionization in a city thus makes all settlements harder to achieve.

Finally, public employee labor disputes too often polarize society by raising delicate political issues in ways that reduce the area of permissible compromise and compel political leaders to appear to make decisions on ethnic or racial grounds. The recent labor disputes in Memphis, Charleston, and New York are paradigmatic cases.

This is not to say that the unions are right or wrong on the underlying merits of any issue. It is to say that the answer to the question of whether a particular function is appropriate for government depends in part upon the growth of public employee unionism. Refuse collection, for example, seems highly susceptible to unionization. Whether it should be continued as a municipal function, contracted out to a private employer, or left entirely to free enterprise should no longer be determined without considering the inescapable problems that flow from collective bargaining.[6] Indeed, many functions presently performed by local governments should be reconsidered in the light of emerging public employee unionism.

To the extent that public employee unionism is a factor in determining what functions a municipality ought to perform, we believe it always operates in the direction of limiting the role of government. For although a number of constructive suggestions can be made as to legal structures that will help to prevent a distortion of the political process, one must be realistic. Many statutory schemes will fail; many will have only limited effect. That being the case, where the appropriateness of the government's performing a function is in doubt, the fact of public employee unionism should encourage government to decline to undertake it or to cease to perform it.

5. Because employers and industries in the private sector face different demands for their products and different cost structures and have different abilities to substitute capital for labor, it is easy to overestimate the importance of "pattern-setting" in the private sector. Where nonprofit employers are involved, however, as in the public sector, pattern-setting may be more prevalent.

6. Warren, Michigan, has, in fact, contracted this function out to a private firm. In San Francisco, refuse collection is done by private employers who, during the 1970 general strike by public employees, continued their operations, thus reducing the potential magnitude of the emergency.

The Value of Interposing a Private Employer

The traditional view, however, is that collective bargaining is not a factor tending to limit government's role because the nature of the function involved is such that it makes little difference whether a public or private employer performs it.[7] A strike inconveniences the public neither more nor less because refuse collection remains the municipality's responsibility rather than that of a private employer. The inconvenience caused by the strike will create political pressures on the mayor to achieve a settlement in either case. The source of the funds to be used in the settlement is the municipal budget whether the function is performed directly by the city or is contracted out to private employers. The same is true even when private enterprise carries out the function without a government contract; then, pressure for a settlement may generate pressure for a governmental subsidy.

It is true, of course, that contracting functions out to private employers will not return collective bargaining to a state identical with the private sector's paradigm, where the product market substantially limits union bargaining power.[8] On the other hand, contracting out, all other things being equal, is preferable to retaining a function that has been unionized. There are several reasons why this is so.

First, while there have been few general (or almost general) strikes by public employees, there have been some. A recent one in San Francisco was made less unbearable because that city does not collect refuse. The garbage men are unionized but they did not join the strike.

Second, a private employer is better organized to resist union demands than a political subdivision. The organization of a private business is directed largely to one end: the maximization of profits. While there may be internal conflicts over policy, and policy may be formulated only after a series of internal bargains, the hierarchical structure of a firm permits a final decision binding all those within it.

7. See generally J. Burton, Jr., and C. Krider, "The Role and Consequences of Strikes by Public Employees," 79 *Yale Law Journal* 418 (January 1970).

8. See Chap 1, pp. 15–17, 32.

Public employers are organized for totally different purposes. There is a division of power between state and local levels, and within each level there are complex organizational arrangements designed to divide functions and allocate power in a way that creates a system of checks and balances. The principal purpose of these structures seems to be to encourage division and weakness, or at least to prevent omnipotence. As a result, a united front by a public employer in a labor dispute frequently is impossible; each affected group or political unit within the government will have a different perspective on the dispute and will pursue its interest in the matter individually. This fact has not been lost on the unions. Two of the principal adversaries in a recent New York City sanitation dispute, for example, were the mayor and the governor. And, for a time, in Hartford, Connecticut, the firefighters' union held such effective power in the city council that it eschewed the legal role of exclusive bargaining representative in order to avoid negotiating with a relatively obdurate executive.

The organization and motives of a private employer, then, seem better suited to countervail union power than those of a public employer. The threat of unemployment as a result of increased benefits, moreover, is greater in private employment. The profit motive creates an incentive to resist wage demands and to place capital elsewhere if the return is too low. The private employer is better able to substitute capital for labor as a result of a change in the relative costs of those factors of production.

To be sure, the one-step removal of government from the performance of functions does not solve the problem of the disruption of essential services by a strike. However, there has been considerable experience in dealing with the emergency strike problem in the private sector and there is reason to believe that, given the right balance of political forces, appropriate legal structures can be erected that will approach a tolerable solution to that problem.[9] Furthermore, transforming an emergency strike by public employees to one by private employees has an important additional advantage. Governmental intervention becomes neutral intervention. The mayor is not a party to the dispute with the

9. See H. Wellington, *Labor and the Legal Process* (Yale University Press, 1968), pp. 269–97.

interest of a party in the outcome. This is the case in two important respects. First, the government need not seem to intervene as the adversary of the union, the position it inevitably adopts when it is the employer. Second, the appearance of neutrality gives political leaders more breathing space vis-à-vis those constituents who are inconvenienced by the strike and are clamoring for a settlement. When the government is the employer, it appears to the public to have the power to settle immediately. One step removed, it appears able to achieve a settlement only by bringing two other parties together. The price of a service, moreover, will reflect costs directly where a private employer is involved and will not be hidden in an unintelligible municipal budget. This increased visibility of the costs of a settlement will also reduce the pressure on political leaders to settle. Great pressure there will be, but of a different order nevertheless.

Contracting out is not the sole alternative. We have discussed it as if it were because our case is weakest where a function is merely contracted out rather than shed entirely.

Contracting out suffers from the fact that some pressure will inevitably develop to increase the monetary size of the government contract in order to settle a dispute. Although the pressure on the budget will probably be less than if the government were the formal employer, it may neverthelesss be enough to skew the political process undesirably. Shedding the function entirely solves that problem and, since the consumers of the services may be free to choose among entrepreneurs, might create a more competitive situation than would occur under a contracting out scheme.

It may be argued, however, that the poor, having now to purchase the service, will be penalized by such a solution. This does not follow. The impact on the poor depends in part, of course, on the nature of the shed service. It also depends on whether the excess sums public employees would have extracted, if the government were the formal employer, will not now benefit the poor either through direct subsidies or improved municipal services. Moreover, the poor pay taxes both directly (regressive sales taxes) and indirectly (property taxes reflected in rent and increased costs of goods). In this role they are interested in seeing municipal services obtained as cheaply as possible.

To the extent, however, that the poor are disadvantaged, the government might subsidize the purchase of the service through vouchers to eligible individuals or families, as many on both the political right and left are now suggesting with regard to education.[10] During a strike, there would, of course, be pressure on government to increase its subsidy in order to permit the payment of higher wages. The visibility of the cost of increasing the subsidy, however, is apt to be greater, and thus arouse greater opposition, than that of merely changing a contract. And if non-subsidized consumers can limit their purchase of the service, a pressure to resist union demands will be generated.[11]

Public employee unionism, therefore, is a force restraining expansion of the role of government. *Other considerations being equal,* it is a force requiring government to decline new functions or to shed those it already has.

In no circumstances will government shed its labor problems by shedding functions. As a third party, government will have a role to play in helping to resolve disputes. And try as it might to shed functions or contract out, it must remain the employer in many, many areas. What labor relations law should be in those areas requires a close look at some rather specific problems. Part II examines a cluster of problems that relate most closely to what is traditionally called organization and the establishment of collective bargaining. The first problem in that cluster is the constitutional protections enjoyed by public employees.

10. See, for example, M. Friedman, *Capitalism and Freedom* (University of Chicago Press, 1962), pp. 85 ff.

11. Refuse collection again is an example, for frequently there may be ways in which individuals can dispose of their refuse other than by hiring a contractor.

PART TWO

Organization and the Establishment of Collective Bargaining

CHAPTER FIVE

The Right to Join a Union

It was Holmes, of course, who insisted that "the life of the law has not been logic: it has been experience." Yet the great jurist loved his logic; and he was particularly enamored of the proposition—true beyond doubt in a static universe—that the greater includes the lesser. Holmes was also rather taken with the epigram; and his own glitter in the pages of the Massachusetts and United States Reports. But since good epigrams often make bad law, and no logic can rise above its premises, Holmes occasionally offers less guidance than one anticipates from the great.

Consider his celebrated opinion in *McAuliffe* v. *City of New Bedford*.[1] The petitioner—it was a mandamus proceeding—was a former police officer in New Bedford, Massachusetts. He had been dismissed from the force after a hearing for having engaged in political solicitation and canvassing during two elections of the previous year.

Speaking for a unanimous court, Holmes unleashed one of his more enduring and less endearing epigrams. "The petitioner," he said, "may have a constitutional right to talk politics, but he has no constitutional right to be a policeman." He went on, "There are few employments for hire in which the servant does not agree to suspend his constitutional right of free speech, as well as of idleness, by the implied terms of his contract. The servant cannot

1. 155 Mass. 216, 29 N.E. 517 (1892).

complain, as he takes the employment on the terms which are offered him."[2]

Had Holmes been dealing with private employment, that statement might pass muster. The rights granted by the First Amendment impose duties on the federal government, and on the states through the due process clause of the Fourteenth Amendment. No duties of a First Amendment variety devolve on a private employer, however, unless they are imposed by common law or legislative fiat. Of course, Holmes knew the reach of the First and Fourteenth Amendments, and indeed, in the next sentence of the *McAuliffe* opinion, qualified (took back perhaps) what he had just said: "the city may impose any *reasonable condition* upon holding offices within its control."[3] This is to adopt one mode of legitimate constitutional inquiry: Is the city's rule a reasonable interference with the petitioner's constitutional right to talk politics? If not, if it is unreasonable, then he has a right to reinstatement, which would mean that this petitioner, in this situation, does have exactly what Holmes said he did not have, "a constitutional right to be a policeman."

One might have anticipated that Holmes would then set out to unpack the concept of a "reasonable condition." But in fact he seems to have believed in his epigram and its logic. The no-politics rule was reasonable, Holmes asserted, and no elaboration was necessary or even worthwhile.

McAuliffe was not centrally a right of association case, and it was not a decision of the Supreme Court of the United States, but Holmes' cleverness seems to have misled that Court in subsequent association cases of the early 1950s.[4] *McAuliffe* invites judges to analyze governmental restrictions on public employees' First Amendment rights in a curious way; that is, as if public employees were different from everyone else; as if, with respect to public employees, government is especially empowered to restrict the political and civil rights the rest of us enjoy. This must be rubbish. The government may not be a saint, but it cannot be the devil either. It must have power to impose restrictions—and it

2. 155 Mass. at 220, 29 N.E. at 517–18.

3. *Ibid.* (emphasis added).

4. See, for example, *Adler* v. *Board of Education of the City of New York*, 342 U.S. 485 (1952).

makes as much sense to talk in terms of reasonable restrictions as in any other terms—but it makes no constitutional sense to have a different presumption of reasonableness where the restriction is directed at employees from the one that prevails where the restriction is directed at some other class. Government, as employer, has legitimate interests that may justify restrictive rules; so too does government as protector of national defense, collector of revenue, dispenser of welfare, fighter of crime, and maintainer of order. There is just no reason for placing the employment function in a class by itself.

In recent years the Supreme Court has recognized this.[5] It has, moreover, spoken frequently of the right of association as a part of the First and Fourteenth Amendments.[6] Although the court has not told us much about the right of association as a concept, it does deserve some attention.

The Right of Association

Whether the history of the United States and the sociology of its people are better understood in terms of cleavage or consensus is a contemporary intellectual issue of ancient lineage. Concern with the effects of cleavage on the survival of the American republic is as old as the nation itself. And, paradoxically, insistence on the right to band together freely in factions also was heard from the beginning. Thus, Madison in the Tenth *Federalist* worried about factions, found the "latent causes of faction . . . sown in the nature of man," in the "zeal for different opinions concerning religion, concerning government, and many other points," and most importantly, in "the various and unequal distribution of property," accepted factions as therefore inescapable in a free society, and argued that the structure of the republic would keep them in check.[7]

5. See, for example, *United States* v. *Robel,* 389 U.S. 258 (1967); *Keyishian* v. *Board of Regents,* 385 U.S. 589 (1967); *Shelton* v. *Tucker,* 364 U.S. 479 (1960).

6. *Ibid. NAACP* v. *Alabama ex rel. Patterson,* 357 U.S. 449 (1958); *NAACP* v. *Button,* 371 U.S. 415 (1963).

7. Henry Cabot Lodge (ed.), *The Federalist* (G. P. Putnam's Sons, 1888), pp. 53–54.

And Tocqueville stressed the counterpoint:

In our own day freedom of association has become a necessary guarantee against the tyranny of the majority. . . .

No countries need associations more—to prevent either despotism of parties or the arbitrary rule of a prince—than those with a democratic social state. In aristocratic nations secondary bodies form natural associations which hold abuses of power in check. In countries where such associations do not exist, if private people did not artificially and temporarily create something like them, I see no other dike to hold back tyranny of whatever sort, and a great nation might with impunity be oppressed by some tiny faction or by a single man.[8]

Organizations based on mutual economic interests, such as trade associations or labor unions, are paradigms of associations, factions, or—as they are usually called today—interest groups. Such groups are absolutely necessary to the survival of political democracy in the United States. They are the means by which individuals make claims upon government; thus they are important to the structure of our federal system. These groups collect, create, and transmit the economic desires of their members to other interest groups; thus they are vital to political, economic, and social organization.

Many claims made by many interest groups are self-serving and, if granted, would be contrary to national welfare. But that is not the point. The point is that unless individuals can freely band together to advocate whatever they please, we shall not have democracy. We may have efficiency. We may, if we fall into the hands of a lucky, wise, reasonable, talented, and capable king, have a golden age of totalitarianism. If, however, we prefer democracy, either because we think that most kings will be deficient, or because we value freedom for its own sake, we badly need a right of association; and it is best that it be lodged in the Constitution. That, indeed, is where the Supreme Court has placed it:

Effective advocacy of both public and private points of view, particularly controversial ones, is undeniably enhanced by group association, as this Court has more than once recognized by remarking upon the close nexus between the freedoms of speech and assembly. . . . It is beyond debate that freedom to engage in association for the advancement of beliefs and ideas is an inseparable aspect of the "liberty" assured by the Due Process Clause of the Fourteenth Amend-

8. Alexis de Tocqueville, *Democracy in America,* eds. J. P. Mayer and M. Lerner (Harper & Row, 1966), p. 177.

ment, which embraces freedom of speech. . . . Of course, it is immaterial whether the beliefs sought to be advanced by association pertain to political, economic, religious or cultural matters, and state action which may have the effect of curtailing the freedom to associate is subject to the closest scrutiny.[9]

State Interest in Control

Whatever may be the constitutional power of the state to control freedom to associate, its power to control group action is a different—if ultimately related—matter. For the state must be in a position to protect itself and its citizens from oppression by private groups. Some regulation is surely permissible where organizations dedicated to violence are concerned. And the due process clause does not prevent the state from controlling the activities of trade associations or labor unions. In the absence of federal statutory law, the strike, for example, if it is coercive, may be barred; for that matter, so may the establishment of wages and working conditions through collective bargaining.

In the private sector, strikes have not been generally prohibited, as they have in the public. Indeed, in the public sector, attempted restrictions on the right of association rest in large part on a fear of strikes by organized employees. Yet it has been argued, with respect to strikes that do not create a threat to public health and welfare, that the equal protection clause of the Fourteenth Amendment forbids a state from distinguishing between public and private employment. If employees in the private sector may strike, so may public employees.[10] This argument is without merit. The test, under the equal protection clause, is whether the distinction between public and private employment is rational. And it plainly is, for all of the reasons rehearsed in Chapter 1:

9. *NAACP* v. *Alabama ex rel. Patterson,* 357 U.S. 449, 460–61 (1958).

10. *Anderson Federation of Teachers, Local 519* v. *School City of Anderson,* 251 N.E. 2d 15, 21–23 (Ind. Sup. Ct., 1969), rehearing denied, 254 N.E. 2d 329, cert. denied, 90 S. Ct. 2243 (1970) (dissenting opinion of Chief Justice R. De Bruler). The case involved contempt for failure to comply with a strike injunction. The strike was held by the majority to be illegal at common law. The dissent accordingly did not deal directly with the legality of a ban on strikes by public employees under a comprehensive public employment statute. Its reasoning, however, would seem to reach that situation so long as private sector employees are free to strike. Language in the dissenting opinion, however, points in the other direction.

because of the relative inelasticity of demand for public services and the relative vulnerability of the municipal employer, strikes in the public sector have effects different from strikes in the private. The Constitution surely does not prevent the states from taking these very real differences into account.[11]

This fact does not necessarily mean, however, that the health and welfare consequences of a strike are unimportant when it comes to calculating the interest of the state for the purpose of determining whether it may limit an individual's right of association. A police strike dramatically reduces people's safety; a strike by teachers does not. State interest in preventing strikes by police officers is, therefore, substantially greater than in preventing teachers' strikes. If it can be reasonably inferred that the incidence of strikes increases as municipal employees organize—and it seems clear that it can[12]—the state has a stronger case in restricting union membership for its police than it does for its teachers.

Moreover, since the police are called upon to maintain order in labor disputes, it may be thought that if the police are in a union —particularly an AFL-CIO union—their loyalty will be divided. Avoidance of a potential conflict of interest thus can be seen as an additional state interest in some situations, one that requires attention in deciding whether a state may impose restrictions on its employees' rights of association.

But recent judicial decisions make it doubtful whether any state interest is sufficient to justify rules wholly preventing membership in a labor organization. And this is so even if the limitation is placed only on particular employees and runs only to affiliated unions, or to unions advocating the strike.

11. Some strikes by some public employees may not have "effects different" from some strikes by some private employees. But this, of course, does not render unconstitutional the public-private distinction. See generally G. Gunther and N. Dowling, *Cases and Materials on Individual Rights in Constitutional Law* (8th ed., Foundation Press, 1970), pp. 989–1004. No classification system is perfect. The public-private one is better than most. See *Postal Clerks* v. *Blount*, 76 *Labor Relations Reference Manual* 2932 (D.C. Cir., 1971), affirmed by the Supreme Court of the United States, Oct. 12, 1971.

12. Organization of government employees has increased substantially in the last decade or so—from some 915,000 in 1956 to some 2,155,000 in 1968—and the growth continues. Strikes accompanied this growth: from 15, involving 1,700 workers in 1958, to 251 and 200,120 workers in 1968. Advisory Commission on Intergovernmental Relations, *Labor-Management Policies for State and Local Government* (1969), p. 5; U.S. Bureau of the Census, *Statistical Abstract of the United States, 1970* (1970), p. 239; Appendix B, below, Table B-1.

The Emerging Law

Four recent cases have struck down governmental restrictions upon the right of public employees to join unions. In *Atkins* v. *City of Charlotte*,[13] a three-judge District Court held "unconstitutional as an abridgement of the freedom of association protected by the First and Fourteenth Amendments" a North Carolina statute providing that:

> No employee of the State [or subdivision thereof] shall be, become, or remain a member of any trade union, labor union, or labor organization which is, or may become, a part of or affiliated in any way with any national or international labor union, federation, or organization, and which has as its purpose or one of its purposes, collective bargaining [with a governmental employer] with respect to grievances, labor disputes, wages or salary, rates of pay, hours of employment, or the conditions of work of such employees.[14]

"The flaw in it," said the court, "is an intolerable 'overbreadth' unnecessary to the protection of valid state interests."[15]

McLaughlin v. *Tilendis*[16] was a decision of the Court of Appeals for the Seventh Circuit, holding that a cause of action under the Civil Rights Act of 1871[17] was made out by a public school teacher who alleged that he had been dismissed because of his association with a local of the American Federation of Teachers. While at trial, said the court, the defendants "may show that [plaintiff was] engaging in unlawful activities or [was] dismissed for other proper reasons . . . the complaint sufficiently states a justifiable claim,"[18] for "teachers have the right of free association, and unjustified interference with teachers' associational freedom violates the Due Process clause of the Fourteenth Amendment."[19] The court noted, moreover, that no state legislation made union membership illegal. This, the court reasoned, indicated that "no paramount public interest" of the state warranted the limiting of plaintiff's right of association.

13. 296 F. Supp. 1068 (W.D., N.C., 1969).
14. N.C. Gen. Stat., §§ 95–97 (1965).
15. 296 F. Supp. at 1075.
16. 398 F.2d 287 (7th Cir. 1968).
17. 42 U.S.C., § 1983.
18. 398 F.2d at 290.
19. *Id.* at 288.

The same reasoning was relied upon by the Eighth Circuit in *American Federation of State, County, and Municipal Employees* v. *Woodward.*[20] *Woodward* was similar to *McLaughlin;* but the plaintiffs were manual laborers and not teachers. For these purposes, however, this made no difference.

The fourth case, *Letter Carriers* v. *Blount,*[21] was a decision of a three-judge district court holding a federal statute and oath to be in violation of the First Amendment. Both statute and oath attempted to prohibit postal employees from asserting the right to strike against the government and from joining any union known by the employee to assert such a right.

The opinions in all four cases are guarded; no suggestion is made that in proper circumstances, and if done in the proper way, a state lacks power to place some restraints on its employees' associational rights. Nor would the rhetoric of relevant Supreme Court opinions justify a different approach. For while the constitutional test has been phrased in a number of ways, the right of association has never been stated as an absolute.

The Supreme Court has said:

> Only the gravest abuses, endangering paramount interest, give occasion for permissible limitation. It is therefore in our tradition to allow the widest room for discussion, the narrowest range for its restriction, particularly when this right is exercised in conjunction with peaceable assembly.[22]
>
> . . .
>
> Of course, it is accepted constitutional doctrine that these fundamental human rights are not absolutes. . . . The essential rights of the First Amendment in some instances are subject to the elemental need for order without which the guarantees of civil rights to others would be a mockery.[23]
>
> . . .
>
> Whether there was "justification" [for imposing restriction on the right of association] turns solely on the substantiality of [the state's] interest.[24]
>
> . . .

20. 406 F.2d 137 (8th Cir. 1969).

21. *Letter Carriers* v. *Blount,* 72 *LRRM* 2591 (Dist. Ct., D.C., 1969). The case, which invalidated portions of 5 U.S.C., § 7311 Supp IV, 1969, is not being appealed. *Government Employee Relations Report,* No. 326 (Sept. 7, 1970), p. A-10.

22. *Thomas* v. *Collins,* 323 U.S. 516, 530 (1945).

23. *United Public Workers (C.I.O.)* v. *Mitchell,* 330 U.S. 75, 95 (1947).

24. *NAACP* v. *Alabama ex rel. Patterson,* 357 U.S. 449, 464 (1958).

In a series of decisions this Court has held that even though the governmental purpose be legitimate and substantial, that purpose cannot be pursued by means that broadly stifle fundamental personal liberties when the end can be more narrowly achieved. . . . The breadth of legislative abridgement must be viewed in the light of less drastic means for achieving the same basic purpose.[25]

However the test for determining constitutional validity is phrased, the Court increasingly has tended to find restraints on association unconstitutional. Cases do survive that point in the other direction,[26] and what's to be is still unsure,[27] but a case like *United States* v. *Robel*[28] leaves little room for state limitations on the right of public employees to join unions.

Robel involved the constitutionality of a section of the Subversive Activities Control Act, which provided that when a Communist-action organization is under a final order to register it shall be unlawful for any member of the organization "to engage in any employment in any defense facility."[29] Robel, a member of the Communist party (the party was under a constitutionally valid final order to register), was employed at a defense facility, continued his employment, and was indicted for doing so.

Declining to construe the section narrowly, the Court held it to be an unconstitutional abridgment of the right of association protected by the First Amendment. It contains, said the Court, "the fatal defect of overbreadth. . . ." "It is made irrelevant to the statute's operation that an individual may be a passive or inactive member of a designated organization, that he may be unaware of

25. *Shelton* v. *Tucker,* 364 U.S. 479, 488 (1960).

26. *United Public Workers of America* v. *Mitchell,* 330 U.S. 75 (1947) (upholding the Hatch Act, which imposes restrictions on the political activities of federal employees) has not been distinguished to the point of extinction, as has *Adler* v. *Board of Education,* 342 U.S. 485 (1952). See *Keyishian* v. *Board of Regents,* 385 U.S. 589 (1967). Cf. *New York ex rel. Bryant* v. *Zimmerman,* 278 U.S. 63 (1928).

27. "Apart from their sweeping redevelopment of the law of freedom of association, the most striking characteristic of the line of cases leading up to *Robel* [see below, n. 28] was the consistent and increasingly vehement dissents by the same four members of the Court. If there is any area of First Amendment protection which is peculiarly vulnerable to modification on account of recent or impending changes in the personnel of the Court, it is obviously this area of freedom of association and civil disabilities." N. Nathanson, "Freedom of Association and the Quest for Internal Security: Conspiracy from Dennis to Dr. Spock," 65 *New York University Law Review* 153, 177–78 (1970).

28. 389 U.S. 258 (1967).

29. 50 U.S.C., § 784 (a)(1)(D).

the organization's unlawful aims, or that he may disagree with those unlawful aims."[30] And earlier cases had made it clear that "mere knowing membership without a specific intent to further the unlawful aims of an organization is not a constitutionally adequate basis, . . ."[31] and that "legislation which sanctions ["imposes any disqualification or disability"[32] as a result of] membership unaccompanied by specific intent to further the unlawful goals of the organization or which is not active membership violates constitutional limitations."[33]

In ruminating about the application to public unions of the law of association developed in cases like *Robel,* one might suppose that a state is free, if it acts in a sufficiently precise manner, to protect its legitimate interests by limiting government employment to nonunion or equivocal union members (that is, passive members or members who disagree with an unlawful goal of the organization). A legitimate state interest is certainly the protection of health and welfare; and, since strikes by police and firemen would threaten health and welfare, presumably a narrowly drawn statute could cover such employment. The language of the *Robel* opinion may also be thought to suggest that less pressing state interests—protection against nonemergency strikes by public employees, conflict of interest, and so forth—can legitimately support a carefully drafted statute.

In the text of the *Robel* opinion, the Court explains what it is doing:

> Our decision today simply recognizes that, when legitimate legislative concerns are expressed in a statute which imposes a substantial burden on protected First Amendment activities, Congress must achieve its goal by means which have a "less drastic" impact on the continued vitality of First Amendment freedoms.[34]

A long footnote describes what the Court says it is not doing, namely, balancing governmental interest against constitutional rights:

30. 389 U.S. at 266.

31. *Keyishian* v. *Board of Regents,* 385 U.S. 589, 606 (1967).

32. Nathanson, "Freedom of Association," p. 175.

33. *Keyishian* v. *Board of Regents,* 385 U.S. 589, 606, 608 (1967). See also *Elfbrandt* v. *Russell,* 384 U.S. 11 (1966); *Aptheker* v. *Secretary of State,* 378 U.S. 500 (1964).

34. 389 U.S. at 267, 268.

> It has been suggested that this case should be decided by "balancing" the governmental interests expressed in [the statute] against the First Amendment rights asserted by the appellee. This we decline to do. We recognize that both interests are substantial, but we deem it inappropriate for this Court to label one as being more important or more substantial than the other. Our inquiry is more circumscribed. Faced with a clear conflict between a federal statute enacted in the interests of national security and an individual's exercise of his First Amendment rights, we have confined our analysis to whether Congress has adopted a constitutional means in achieving its concededly legitimate legislative goal. In making this determination we have found it necessary to measure the validity of the means adopted by Congress against both the goal it has sought to achieve and the specific prohibitions of the First Amendment. But we have in no way "balanced" those respective interests. We have ruled only that the Constitution requires that the conflict between congressional power and individual rights be accommodated by legislation drawn more narrowly to avoid the conflict.[35]

If no balancing at all is to go on, then any legitimate state interest is as good as any other: strikes by teachers are indistinguishable from strikes by policemen.

But, of course, the Court cannot mean this. Some balancing must take place and it probably makes little difference whether the "substantiality" of the state interest—to use a word the Court has used—is considered directly, as it sometimes has been,[36] or indirectly, by measuring "the validity of the means adopted by [a legislature] against both the goal it has sought to achieve and the specific prohibitions of the First Amendment."[37]

There is, however, substantial doubt whether even a carefully drawn statute aimed at the associational rights of policemen or firefighters can survive constitutional attack after *Robel*.[38]

35. *Id.* at footnote 20.

36. See n. 24, above, and accompanying text.

37. 389 U.S. at 268, n. 20. Compare G. Gunther, "Reflections on *Robel:* It's Not What the Court Did but the Way That It Did It," 20 *Stan. L. Rev.* 1140 (June 1968), with "Comment, Less Drastic Means and the First Amendment," 78 *Yale Law Journal* 464 (January 1969).

38. The Alabama Firefighters statute, Title 37, Ch. 8, Art. 7, § 450(3) (Supp. 1969), is an insufficiently careful attempt at such a statute. It provides:

> (1)—No person shall accept or hold any commission or employment as a fire fighter or fireman in the service of the state or of any municipality in the state who participates in any strike or asserts the right to strike against the state or any municipality in the state, or be a member of an organization of em-

The reason is not that state interest in deterring strikes threatening a community's health and welfare is less than it is in preventing revolution by force and violence; rather, that the cost of such deterrence in terms of First Amendment rights is so much greater. The principal goal of the Communist party is overthrow of the government by force and violence. Advocacy of this is protected to some extent by the clear and present danger standard or by some other standard of similar effect but different name. But the important point is that the goal of the party is not served, to any substantial extent, by advocacy of change in the laws of the land. And effective advocacy of change in the law is not enhanced by association with an organization that does not have such change as its goal.

One goal of some unions is, when necessary, to strike; and to do so even if the law forbids strikes. This goal, of these unions, is plainly promoted by advocacy aimed at changing the law. Such advocacy is protected, either absolutely or very near thereto. And since "effective advocacy of both public and private points of view, particularly controversial ones, is undeniably enhanced by group association,"[39] restraints on individuals associating with unions have a far greater effect on protected speech than would similar restraints directed against individuals associating with the Communist party.

Moreover, other goals of unions are perfectly legal. They represent their members by bringing political pressure on public employers to improve terms and conditions of employment, in lobbying for legislation endorsing and protecting their role as collective bargaining agents, and by appealing to the public to support them

ployees that asserts the right to strike against the state or any municipality in the state, knowing that such organization asserts such right.

(2)—All fire fighters serving the state or any municipality in the state either as paid firemen or as volunteer fire fighters who comply with the provisions of this section are assured the right and freedom of association, self-organization, and the right to join or to continue as members of any employee or labor organization which complies with this section, and shall have the right to present proposals relative to salaries and other conditions of employment by representatives of their own choosing. No such person shall be discharged or discriminated against because of his exercise of such right, nor shall any person or group of persons, directly or indirectly, by intimidation or coercion, compel or attempt to compel any fire fighter or fireman to join or refrain from joining a labor organization.

39. *NAACP* v. *Alabama ex rel. Patterson,* 357 U.S. 449, 460 (1958).

in the pursuit of these goals. Such activity is explicitly political and must be protected in a free society. The right of an individual to join such an organization in order to share and participate in these activities and the fruits they bear is located somewhere near the core of the constitutional right of association. Restraints on union membership interfere with these protected rights. Restraints on membership in the Communist party do not, for the party does not have these goals.

If, then, any prohibition on union membership substantially interferes with legitimate First Amendment rights of public employees, *Robel* would seem to suggest that a state "must achieve its goal by means which have a 'less drastic' impact."[40] Those means probably must be directed at collective bargaining or the strike itself, and not at prior association.

One goal, however, might arguably be achieved by restrictions on association. Where the association entails a conflict of interest between the employment responsibilities of the public employees and the interests of other members of the union, a prohibition on that *particular* association perhaps can be imposed by a carefully drafted statute. Restricting police membership to police unions, or stopping supervisors from joining unions to which their subordinates belong, may not in any major way infringe on their associational rights. The fruits of associational activities are available in other organizations, while the valid goal of the state—elimination of the conflict of interest—can be effectively attained only by limiting the right to join certain unions. This restriction may seem, therefore, sufficiently narrow.

Even here, however, *Robel* can be read to call for a narrower regulation. Membership in a larger union may enhance the associational activities of a political nature in which the individual police officer or supervisor desires to engage by increasing the resources available to support his claims. And there is available the alternate course of permitting the municipal employer to refuse to recognize as bargaining agents for police or supervisors unions that entail a conflict of interest.

The ultimate constitutional resolution of these questions by the Supreme Court cannot be predicted. No matter what the Court

40. 389 U.S. at 268.

does, however, it seems unwise for a state to attempt to limit union membership that does not entail a conflict of interest. First, the right of association is too important. Second, it is hard enough to make the case for the strike ban, to persuade doubters that it is fair. To have also to show the fairness of a ban on membership is to ask too much for too small a gain. Prudence dictates a different course, no matter what content the Supreme Court may ultimately give to the right of association.[41]

41. Neither prudence nor the First Amendment, however, dictates that a state refrain from requiring a union to affirm, as a condition precedent to certification as a bargaining representative, that it does not assert the right to strike. *Rogoff* v. *Anderson*, 310 N.Y.S. 2d 174 (N.Y. App. Div., 1970), aff'd, 28 N.Y. 2d 880 (N.Y. Ct. App., 1971), affirmed by the Supreme Court of the United States, October 12, 1971.

CHAPTER SIX

Representation Elections, Recognition, and Union Security

Prudence dictates more than that government not attempt to prevent its employees from joining a union, when no conflict of interest would be created. In an earlier chapter,[1] it was concluded that the establishment of a state agency empowered to enforce mandatory recognition procedures was prudent, indeed, in some situations, essential. The procedures themselves ought to include provision for unit determination (which employees—if a majority wants a union—should be represented by the bargaining agent), elections (method, counting procedures, timing, and so forth), and certification of representatives. For the most part, the private analogy is satisfactory, although the timing of elections and the form of recognition may call for special rules, and a subsequent chapter[2] suggests some departures in criteria for unit determination.

1. See pp. 50–51, above.
2. See Chap. 7.

Procedures in the Absence of Legislation

Where there are no statutory guidelines, the parties themselves must work out their own procedures for determining recognition issues. In a typical case, the union and the public employer agree upon the unit—often the one requested by the union and based entirely on the extent of organization—and "recognition" is evidenced formally, if at all, by various legislative or quasi-legislative measures such as school board resolutions or municipal ordinances. Even where there are statutory guidelines, ad hoc recognition procedures are often employed. A county attorney in a midwestern state that has a comprehensive public employee law informs us that informal methods are employed "although at some point they [we] make a formal recognition of sorts. But the decision or process of recognition is informal and unwritten. There is simply an effort to see if the union represents a majority in an appropriate unit."

There are also helpful private institutions available to those operating without the benefit of legislation. The American Arbitration Association (AAA) has established a center for dispute settlement that offers public employers and unions services similar to those a state board would provide. The AAA is prepared to determine appropriate units, conduct representation elections, and mediate disputes. Another approach is for the parties to accept by contract National Labor Relations Board (NLRB) rules of procedure for recognition cases.[3]

The development of informal procedures is perhaps best exemplified by education. A legal counsel for a municipal school district has written that orginally (in 1964) the school board determined the unit. The AAA conducted the election in school gymnasiums or other areas away from administrative offices. The general supervisor of procedures was a "neutral third party," whose expressed goals were full participation in the election and full integrity of the election proceedings. Places on the ballot for the competing unions and "no representation" were determined by flipping a coin; observers had to be eligible to vote; and plans

3. R. McLaughlin, "Collective Bargaining Suggestions for the Public Sector," 20 *Lab. L.J.* 131, 132–33 (1969).

were made for a runoff election between the two highest choices if no one received a majority.[4] More often, however, school boards unilaterally determine the election units and procedures. "Even in those cases where a moderator was called in to make a determination," concluded Robert Doherty in 1966, "in most instances, as the documents will show, certain matters had been predetermined by the school board."[5]

State departments of labor (and, on occasion, other state agencies) frequently fill the void and help the parties with their recognition problems even though they lack statutory authority to do so. A state labor commissioner has indicated that he will conduct a representation election for a public employer upon request even though an opinion of the state attorney general concluded that public employers do not have to negotiate with or enter into agreements with unions of their employees.

Such a haphazard approach to recognition procedures is not altogether satisfactory, however, and comprehensive legislation at the state level, enforced by a state agency, seems desirable. Municipal employers eager to get along with unions petitioning for recognition have tended to acquiesce in units that are not well tailored to local governmental structures or that result in excessive fragmentation.[6] Unit determination is an area in which the experience of a state agency can be most helpful in avoiding such mistakes.

Where the employer views collective bargaining more apprehensively, if not hostilely, mandatory state procedures affecting other questions are also useful. Unilateral determination by the employer may lead to an uneasy bargaining relationship and continued strife over representational questions. When a specialized state agency acts as a neutral adjudicative body, such issues, even if resolved unfavorably to the union, may be put to rest and not haunt the bargaining relationship in the future.

4. See Robert E. Doherty, "Determination of Bargaining Units and Election Procedures in Public School Teacher Representation Elections," 19 *Industrial and Labor Relations Review* 573, 581–84 (1966). In Connecticut, the ballot for teacher elections is horizontal. Generally the CFT is on the left, the CEA on the right, and "no organization" in the middle.

5. *Ibid.*, p. 574. See also M. Lieberman and M. Moskow, "Representation and Recognition Procedures," in their volume, *Collective Negotiations for Teachers: An Approach to School Administration* (Rand McNally, 1966), p. 196.

6. See pp. 98–102, below.

State and Local Agencies

Although most of the recently enacted laws establish public employment relations commissions, some leave procedures up to the local employer.[7] Typical of the most effective agencies is the Wisconsin Employment Relations Commission (WERC), which is composed of three full-time members appointed by the governor (one every two years for six-year terms). It is an independent administrative agency like the NLRB, has nine professionals on its staff, and a budget currently running about $350,000 a year.[8] Between 1962 and 1968 the WERC held some 369 municipal representation elections involving over 47,000 employees.[9]

The Michigan Employment Relations Commission (MERC) also has three members and a professional staff consisting of seventeen mediators, four trial examiners, and two election officers.[10] During fiscal 1967–68, the commission conducted 182 public-sector representation elections, 139 of which were consent elections and 43 commission ordered, including 12 involving cities, 12, noneducational school employees, 11, hospitals, and 4, counties. Eighty-nine of the 182 were school board elections (67 involving noneducational personnel), 46 involved municipal employees, 28, hospitals, and 14, county employees.[11] The New York Public Employment Relations Board (PERB) has three permanent members too, and not only determines units and conducts representation elections itself but approves and oversees the procedures of twenty-seven "mini-PERBs" supervising labor relations between public employers and some 70,000 public employees. The PERB has fifty-three employees in three main offices (Albany, New York City, and Buffalo) and had a budget of $983,598 for fiscal 1968–69.[12]

7. See, for example, Cal. Gov't Code, Sec. 3507 (West Supp. 1971), Bureau of Nat. Affairs, *State Labor Laws*, Vol. 4, sec. 14, p. 219.

8. M. Slavney, "Experiences with Current Substantive Practices in Administering Wisconsin Public Employee Labor Relations Statutes: Wisconsin," in H. Anderson (ed.), *Public Employee Organization and Bargaining* (Bureau of National Affairs, 1968), p. 71; see also WERC, *Thirtieth Ann. Rep.* (1968).

9. *WERC, Thirtieth Ann. Rpt.*, p. 54.

10. "MERC Annual Report," in *Ann. Rep. Mich. Dept. Labor* (1967–68), p. 71.

11. *Ibid.*, pp. 77, 80.

12. New York State Public Employment Relations Board, *Year One of the Taylor Law* (State of New York, 1968), pp. 20, 27.

The New York City Office of Collective Bargaining (OCB) is independent of the PERB and, in addition to its three impartial members, has two city and two labor members. During 1968, its first year, the OCB handed down 80 decisions on unit determination and union representation, held 13 representation elections, and closed out a total of 124 cases.[13] "Measured by its impact on stabilizing labor relations," wrote Mayor Lindsay on August 1, 1969, "the OCB has fully demonstrated its effectiveness and the need for its continued operation in New York City."[14]

State and Local Board Procedures

The Taft-Hartley Act is generally the model followed by state statutes, and agency procedures are generally variants of NLRB procedures. All the state commissions that proposed legislation might have acknowledged, as did the Illinois Commission, that "[t]he recommendations made here with respect to election procedures have been largely derived from the rules and practices developed over a period of years under the national Labor Management Relations Act."[15] The decisions of some state boards frequently cite NLRB and federal labor case law as support for a particular decision.

The rules of the New York PERB[16] are typical of the major state agencies. There must be a 30 percent showing of interest by employees in a union before the PERB will hold a representation election,[17] with a 10 percent showing necessary for an intervenor to gain a place on the ballot.[18] The petitioning union must prove that membership in the union is for the purpose of representation

13. New York City Office of Collective Bargaining, *First Annual Report* (1968).

14. J. Lindsay, "Report Submitted Pursuant to Chapter 24, Laws of 1969," p. 2.

15. Governor's Advisory Commission on Labor-Management Policy for Public Employees, *Report and Recommendations* (1967), p. 21.

16. Public Employment Relations Board, *Rules of Procedure,* in 1 PERB, Par. 200 et seq. For a detailed discussion of PERB procedures see J. Crowley, "The Resolution of Representation Status Disputes under the Taylor Law," 37 *Fordham Law Review* 517 (May 1969).

17. PERB, *Rules of Procedure,* Sec. 201.3(a).

18. *Id.,* Sec. 201.6(i) (1). See *Smith* v. *Helsby,* 72 *Labor Relations Reference Manual* 2464 (N.Y. Sup. Ct., N.Y. County, 1969).

in collective bargaining.[19] Proof that has been accepted includes notarized membership lists and cards, dues deduction cards, and membership application cards. If two unions have proof for the same employees, the board ignores the evidence entirely. Also, such evidence must be dated not earlier than one year prior to the filing of the certification petition.[20]

Elections for the bargaining representative are by secret ballot and a place for "no union" is on the ballot. Runoffs are held between the two top choices. To win, a union must receive a majority of the valid ballots cast.[21] While the PERB can overturn mini-board certifications,[22] it will uphold the local board if it has acted within the spirit and parameters of the Taylor law.[23]

The PERB (as is the case with other state agencies and the NLRB) also has rules attempting to impart stability to established bargaining relationships, while allowing employees to change their minds about who should represent them. The statute provides that a recognized or certified employee organization is entitled to a period of unchallenged representation,[24] and the agency will take account of an existing collective agreement in determining when a petition to unseat an incumbent organization is timely. (This is called a contract bar rule.) A petition to unseat generally is filed by another union on the ground that the established union no longer represents a majority of employees. The PERB rules protect the established union from challenges for a period of from eight to thirty-two months depending on such factors as the budget submission date of the employer and the provisions in the collective agreement.[25]

In Wisconsin the labor statute has no explicit requirement for a

19. PERB, *Rules of Procedure,* Sec. 201.6(h) (1) (1967). See Crowley, "Representation Status Disputes," p. 531.

20. Crowley, *ibid.,* pp. 531–33.

21. PERB, *Rules,* Sec. 201.6 (j).

22. See *City of Ogdensburg and Teamsters Local 687 and Civil Service Employees Association, N.Y.,* PERB Case No. C-0056, in *Government Employee Relations Report,* No. 254 (July 2, 1968), p. B-1.

23. "Petition on Behalf of Local 237, International Brotherhood of Teamsters: N.Y.S," PERB Case No. I-0007 (Feb. 7, 1969), in *GERR,* No. 286 (March 3, 1969), p. B-5.

24. PERB, *Rules,* Sec. 208(c).

25. *City School District and Schenectady Federation of Teachers,* PERB Case No. C-0352 (April 11, 1969). in *GERR,* No. 295 (May 5, 1969), p. B-6; *GERR,* No. 294 (April 28, 1969), p. E-1.

showing of interest in representation elections; the WERC, however, instituted the 30 percent rule in 1968 in order to avoid frivolous petitions.[26] In entertaining petitions challenging representation status, the WERC will consider such factors as (1) the presence or absence of a current agreement, (2) the presence or absence of current active negotiations, (3) budgetary deadlines, (4) statutory deadlines, (5) whether the current bargaining agent is certified or recognized, (6) how long the bargaining agent has been certified or recognized, and (7) the employer's bargaining history.[27] Where a bargaining agent is negotiating with the employer, the commission allows "insulation" for "meaningful bargaining" before permitting a challenge: a petition must be filed either sixty days before negotiations begin or, in some situations, eight months before the employer's budget submission date.[28]

Unit determinations of the New York PERB—unlike those of the NLRB—are reviewable.[29] The PERB, however, cannot restrain negotiations being conducted between parties appealing its determination.[30] Massachusetts and Connecticut courts do not follow this approach but—adopting the federal model—will review the unit determination only as part of a review of an unfair practice charge, generally a refusal to bargain.[31] The reasoning of the Connecticut court reveals its reliance on private sector precedents. "Since it was well established by . . . 1964 that the federal act precluded not only direct appeals but all immediate judicial review of certification proceedings, the General Assembly in 1965 could hardly have omitted provision for direct appeal from such proceeding and at the same time have intended to grant such a right in an act which it so closely structured and worded after the federal act."[32]

26. See *Wauwatosa Board of Education* v. *Wisconsin Employment Relations Commission*, aff'd, 69 *Labor Relations Reference Manual* 2241, No. 8300-A (1968) (Wisconsin Cir. Ct., 1968).

27. *City of Menominee*, WERC No. 8730, October 1968.

28. *Teamsters Local 242*, WERC No. 8622 (July 23, 1968), *GERR*, No. 266 (Oct. 14, 1968), p. B-5 (Commissioner Rice dissenting).

29. *Civil Service Employees Association (CSEA)* v. *Helsby*, 2 PERB, para. 2-7002 (App. Div., 1969), aff'd, 2 PERB, para. 2-7007 (N.Y., 1969).

30. *CSEA* v. *Helsby*, 70 *LRRM* 3273 (App. Div., 1969).

31. *City Manager of Medford* v. *Massachusetts State Labor Relations Commission*, 353 Mass. 519, 521–24, 233 N.E. 2d 310, 312–14 (1968).

32. *Town of Windsor* v. *Windsor Police Department Employees Association*, 154 Conn. 530, 538, 227 A. 2d 65, 68–69 (1967).

State board hearings are also similar to NLRB hearings. In Wisconsin, for example, the hearing examiner may administer oaths, issue subpoenas, rule on offers of proof, and receive relevant evidence, question witnesses, take depositions, and regulate the "time, place and course of the hearing."[33] As in most other administrative hearing procedures, "hearings, so far as is practical, shall be conducted in accordance with the rules of evidence and official notice."[34] The hearing officer may "rule upon offers of proof, receive relevant evidence and exclude irrelevant, immaterial, or unduly repetitious evidence."[35]

The principal conclusion is that election procedures in the main do not raise serious problems of policy, and that, once a state public employee relations agency is created, such procedures can be quickly and easily fashioned on the basis of private sector analogy. There are, however, two issues of significance that call for somewhat different treatment in the public sector.

Timing of the Election

The timing of an election ought of course to be affected by the date of the last election and the term of any existing collective agreement. There seems no reason to run elections more than once a year and no cause not to fashion reasonable contract bar rules.

The nature of the public employer's budget compels further specification as to timing.[36] Public employers generally must submit their budget on a fixed date. Bargaining, if it is to be effective, must begin well before that date. It would be wise, therefore, to create a rule, as the Wisconsin board has,[37] that forbids the holding of an election within a certain period of time before the

33. Wisc. Adm. Code, Sec. ERB 10.18.

34. *Id.*, § 10.16 (2).

35. *Id.*, § 10.18 (3).

36. Arvid Anderson has written, "Depending on the scope of bargaining, the budget deadline may be more important in determining the timing for a representation election than any other factor." "Selection and Certification of Representatives in Public Employment," in T. Christensen (ed.), *Proceedings of New York University's Twentieth Annual Conference on Labor* (Matthew Bender, 1967), p. 295.

37. See n. 27, above.

budget submission date; and, since bargaining right after that date seems rather pointless, for some period thereafter. Thus, elections in the public sector ought to be restricted to a fixed period of time between budget submission dates.

Recognition

Although a significant number of agreements with public employee unions now provide that the certified or recognized union shall be the exclusive bargaining representative, it has not been uncommon in public employment for individuals to retain membership in rival unions that sometimes have certain consultation rights. But the trend is toward genuinely exclusive recognition throughout the public sector. Many, perhaps most, of the agreements we have seen—whether or not from a state with a public employment statute—contain an exclusive recognition clause.

Among the major state legislation, New York's Taylor law mandates exclusive representational status for a certified or recognized union,[38] and the public employee laws of New Jersey,[39] Michigan,[40] Connecticut,[41] Massachusetts,[42] and Wisconsin[43] (state but not municipal) all provide for exclusive bargaining by the majority union. The California law does not provide for exclusive representation, and teachers' unions in California must operate under a statutory proportional representation scheme.[44] Judicial decisions are following the trend. The Wisconsin Supreme Court, for example, has held that although the Wisconsin municipal bargaining law is silent on the matter, a certified majority representative shall be the exclusive bargaining agent for all teachers in the unit.[45] And in the federal-public sector, formal and informal recognition have been abandoned by executive order in favor of exclusive recognition.[46]

38. 1 PERB, Par. 1-208, § 208 (c) (Taylor Law).
39. N.J. Stat. Ann. § 34: 13A-5.3 (Supp. 1970).
40. Mich. Comp. Laws Ann. § 423.211 (West 1967).
41. Conn. Gen. Stat. Rev. § 7-468 (b) (Supp. 1969).
42. Mass. Laws Ann. §178H (3) (Supp. 1970).
43. Wis. Stat. Ann. § 111.83 (Supp. 1970).
44. Cal. Educ. Code, § 13085 (West Supp. 1970).
45. *Board of School Directors* v. *WERC,* 42 Wis. 2d 637, 168 N.W. 2d 92 (1969).
46. Executive Order 11491, § 7; 3 C.F.R. 191, 195–96 (1969).

Multiple recognition is alleged to lead to serious problems such as an increased possibility of strikes and leapfrog bargaining by rival groups. Some believe California's Winton Act,[47] for example, invites union rivalry by providing for negotiating councils composed of representatives from rival organizations, representation being proportional to membership strength among the teachers.

Debating at length the merits of the exclusivity principle as against proportional or multirepresentation hardly seems worth the effort. Majority rule in the private sector appears to have set an irresistible example and the stakes do not seem to be of such significance as to justify extensive analytical brooding over the inevitable. One exception to the exclusivity of the bargaining representative's power, however, does seen justified.

When public employees seek to bargain over the noneconomic aspects of political or policy issues, far more is at stake than the collective bargaining relationship. In a subsequent chapter,[48] means by which interested groups in the community can inject their views and positions into the bargaining process are discussed. This is necessary both to preserve the political process from excessive union power and to insure that the merits of important issues are fully exposed before they are resolved. For similar reasons, employees who dissent from their union's position on such issues ought not to be foreclosed from pursuing their case outside the political processes of that union. It is in the long-run interest of the community as a whole to know in detail the judgment of its employees on such issues—most particularly in the case of professionals—and not to get only a version thoroughly strained and severely narrowed by debate within the union. To be sure, the union's bargaining position often will represent accurately the full judgment of the employees involved. Nevertheless, the process of deciding which demands to pursue, and the resolution of conflicting positions within the union, may produce a distorted picture of the views of many employees on important public policy issues, views that ought to have an airing.

47. Cal. Educ. Code § 13085 (West Supp. 1970), construed in *California Federation of Teachers* v. *Oxnard Elementary Schools,* 272 C.A. 2d 514, 77 Cal. Rptr. 497 (Cal. Ct. App., 1969).

48. Chap. 9.

How this is to be accomplished is not entirely clear. One might attempt to define in advance those kinds of issues likely to raise the problems discussed above. That, however, may be difficult. More feasible, perhaps, would be to grant public employers the right at any time to consult with any employee or group of employees about his or their views on the nonbudgetary aspects of matters of governmental policy, whether or not those matters are issues in, or likely to arise during, bargaining. To be sure, this runs risks, but the state enforcement agency can be empowered to enjoin such consultation if it finds that it is a ruse designed to undermine the bargaining agent generally (not on its position as to a particular issue) rather than to collect relevant information about the views of employees on important policies relating to their jobs. The nature of the issue involved, the controversy surrounding it, the employees consulted, and so forth, would be relevant to that finding, and in the typical case would expose an attempt to misuse the public employer's right to consult.

Union Security

Closely related to exclusive representation is the issue of union security: if the union is the exclusive representative should it be permitted to enter into a union or agency shop agreement with the public employer calling for the discharge of all who refuse to pay dues (union shop) or a fee for representation (agency shop)?[49]

The agency shop has been adopted with increasing frequency recently and has often survived legal challenges to its validity.[50]

49. An agency shop may be defined more precisely as a security arrangement in which employees are not required to join the union but are required to pay an amount equal to the initiation fee and regular dues. A fee for representation, or a service fee, might be less than the initiation fee plus regular dues. There are two other common types of union security arrangements that are more nearly voluntary. One—prevalent in the public sector—is the check-off: the employer deducts from the payroll dues of union members and remits them to the union. The other is a maintenance of membership agreement: all members must maintain union membership (and remit dues) during the term of the contract.

50. Those interested in the details of the subject should read "Impact of the Agency Shop on Labor Relations in the Public Sector," 55 *Cornell Law Review* 547 (1970). See also *Tremblay* v. *Berlin Police Union,* 108 N.H. 416, 237 A.2d 668 (1968). Under the Hawaii statute, Act 171, L. 1970, Sec. 4(a): "The employer shall, upon receiving from an exclusive representative a written statement which specifies

Yet, where statutes are not clear, legality is uncertain. In Michigan, for example, the original advisory commission appointed to inquire into public employee bargaining recommended the authorization of those union security provisions permitted by the National Labor Relations Act.[51] Although the final Michigan law is silent on the issue, Chairman R. Howlett of the Michigan Labor Relations Commission held in his opinion in *Oakland County Sheriff's Department* (concurred in by member L. Walsh, thus making it the majority opinion) that the agency shop is a mandatory subject of bargaining under the Public Employment Relations Act.[52] Several Michigan circuit courts have held that the agency shop is legal, but the issue has been put in doubt by the State's Court of Appeals, and is not likely to be finally resolved until the Michigan Supreme Court addresses the question.[53]

A number of developments clearly indicate that some form of union security is likely to become relatively common in the public sector. In some parts of the country, collective agreements are apt to contain either a union or agency shop clause. Connecticut is an example. The Massachusetts legislature has passed an agency shop law permitting the agreement in Boston and Suffolk County.[54] The Boston-Suffolk law is unique in providing that the agency shop exists only during the life of the contract; the fee is to be proportionally related to the cost of bargaining and contract administration; and the agreement must be ratified by a majority of those in the unit. Mayor Lindsay has promised to grant the agency

---

an amount of reasonable service fees necessary to defray the costs for its services rendered in negotiating and administering an agreement and computed on a pro rata basis among all employees within its appropriate bargaining unit, deduct from the payroll of every employee in the appropriate bargaining unit the amount of service fees and remit the amount to the exclusive representative."

51. The National Labor Relations Act permits check-off, maintenance of membership, agency, and union shop agreements.

52. Oakland County Sheriff's Dept., Michigan Labor Mediation Board, 1968; *GERR*, No. 227 (January 15, 1968), pp. F-1 to F-14.

53. See *Government Employee Relations Report*, No. 352 (June 8, 1970), p. B-14. The Wayne County Circuit Court has held, in a case involving the city of Detroit, that only the Detroit Civil Service Commission can discharge employees and that therefore the commission must approve and be a party to an agency shop agreement. *Nagy* v. *City of Detroit*, 71 *LRRM* 2362 (1969).

54. Mass. Acts 171 (1969), Ch. 335, §§ 1 and 2.

shop to New York City unions if they join the Office of Collective Bargaining and if the state legislature gives its approval. "Experience has taught us," the mayor is quoted as saying "that stable labor relations are closely tied to union security. The agency shop will contribute stability by strengthening the majority representative in a collective bargaining unit. And it will reduce the abuses practiced by unions on nonmembers to dramatize the disadvantages of remaining outside the union."[55] Several months later, Albert Shanker said the UFT had been promised the agency shop if any other union was granted the right (the UFT is not under mandatory OCB jurisdiction).[56] In a message to the legislature asking it to bring the nonmayoral agencies under mandatory OCB coverage, the mayor specifically requested power to enter into agency shop agreements.[57]

Even though union security continues to be a controversial subject in the private sector, such agreements are believed by many to be beneficial to bargaining in the public sector. The claims are that the majority union will not have to fear continually a minority organization and that the unit itself will be protected to a greater extent from balkanization. As Eli Rock puts it:

> Even if a union succeeds in winning recognition in a large unit employees in that unit are generally not required to become members of the union. The relative lack of union security clauses in the collective bargaining agreements of the public service assures that, to a degree unparalleled in the private sector, dissident small-unit groups are able to maintain their separate identities and to prolong the battle for break-off from the larger group's exclusive bargaining agent.[58]

The union security issue in the public sector seems overblown in the sense that it is fundamentally the same issue, with the same merits or demerits, as in the private sector. In both sectors there are, to be sure, important unresolved questions: To what extent may a union require actual membership, rather than merely the tender of dues, under a union shop agreement? To what extent may a union use compelled dues money for purposes that are not

55. *GERR*, No. 286 (March 3, 1969), p. B-7.

56. *New York Times*, June 25, 1969, p. 26.

57. J. Lindsay, "Report Submitted Pursuant to Chapter 24, Laws of 1969," pp. 9–10.

58. E. Rock, "The Appropriate Unit Question in the Public Service: The Problem of Proliferation," 67 *Mich. L. Rev.* 1001, 1005 (1969).

obviously germane to its collective bargaining activities?[59] And what is a reasonable fee for representational services?[60] These are problems of union security generally. No special dimension results from the fact that a union represents public rather than private employees.[61]

In our judgment, so long as the tender of a fee is all that can be required by a union security agreement, the stirring issues of principle—such as they are—disappear in the face of the "free rider" contention that has been accepted as arguably valid in the private sector.[62] While some employees will object to being forced to "purchase" the union's representational services, just as some object to being forced to "purchase" health insurance or a pension as a condition of employment, what is at stake is not a unique issue of freedom. The issue is one of union power and labor stability. Those who don't like union security agreements in the private sector ought to be equally hostile to their institution in the public; those who are receptive to them in the private sector ought willingly to accept their extension.

59. See *International Association of Machinists* v. *Street,* 367 U.S. 740 (1961); *Brotherhood of Railway and Steamship Clerks* v. *Allen,* 373 U.S. 113 (1963). The question has been raised under the Michigan Public Employment Relations Act; see *GERR,* No. 374 (Nov. 9, 1970), p. B-14.

60. See the approach of the Hawaii statute, n. 51, above.

61. It might be thought that the public-private distinction is important because federal constitutional protections apply to the public sector and not the private. But in *this* area, the Supreme Court seems to have rejected the distinction, extending the First, Fifth, and Fourteenth Amendments to private as well as public employees. *International Association of Machinists* v. *Street,* n. 60 above; *Railway Employees' Dept.* v. *Hanson,* 351 U.S. 225 (1956). See generally H. Wellington, *Labor and the Legal Process* (Yale University Press, 1968), pp. 239–66.

62. By virtue of § 14(b) of the Taft-Hartley Act, a state may prohibit union shop agreements in private employment.

CHAPTER SEVEN

Determining the Appropriate Election Unit

The concept of an election unit is related to the concept of an exclusive representative. Where there is no single designated representative, where the employer deals with each union as the representative of all employees who for the moment adhere to it, there is no need for an official determination of which employees shall decide by majority vote upon a single representative for all. However, when the law, or an agreement of the parties, stipulates one body as exclusive representative for purposes of bargaining or consultation,[1] it becomes essential to define with precision the constituency represented. And when representative status is to be conferred only after a determination of the desires of the employees involved, the group defined may properly be called an election unit.

Election units should be distinguished from bargaining units even though they are often identical and frequently parade under the same name. Election units are functionally what their name implies: carefully defined groups of employees within which a formal registration of opinion is taken. Bargaining units, on the

1. This is true whether the body is one union or a council on which unions attain membership through a proportional representation scheme, as is the case under the California Teachers' Statute. Bureau of National Affairs, *State Labor Laws*, Vol. 4, sec. 14, p. 221 (as amended, October 1970).

other hand, define the group affected by the process of negotiation. An election unit usually constitutes the minimum bargaining unit that may be derived from it. But where a union has organized several election units, or several unions negotiate in coalition, bargaining generally takes place on behalf of all the units combined and the distinctions between them are of little importance, the unit of significance being the combined whole. The composition of election units, therefore, necessarily influences bargaining and its impact, both because they may become bargaining units and because they limit the combinations that may emerge.[2]

The Significance of Election Units

Unit determination plays a large role in both the private and public sectors in influencing which, if any, union will be chosen as a bargaining representative, the power structure of bargaining, the ability of various groups of employees to affect directly the terms and conditions of their employment, and the peacefulness and effectiveness of the bargaining relationship. These are important matters, to be sure, but in the private sector the margin for error seems rather large. While any particular decision may have important consequences for the parties involved, the shape of collective bargaining and the economy as a whole are influenced substantially more by underlying forces at work in the labor movement and the society than by the total impact of National Labor Relations Board decisions on election units. Even if one were able to reverse every one of its truly disputed decisions, the likely effect on collective bargaining would in no sense be considered radical.[3] An industry here or there would be hindered or helped, a bargaining relationship come into being or disappear, a particular business survive or dissolve. But collective bargaining and the economy as a whole would remain basically the same.

In the public sector, however, there is reason to believe that unit determination may be important to the future of collective bargaining and of local government itself. First, if bargaining

2. This discussion oversimplifies the possibilities by ignoring multilevel bargaining. Where that occurs, employees may be included in several election and bargaining units.

3. See generally C. Summers and H. Wellington, *Cases and Materials on Labor Law* (Mineola, N.Y.: Foundation Press, 1968), pp. 511–48.

units are not finely tailored to governmental structure, the bargaining relationship may be unstable and volatile, with the result that neither labor peace nor effective government is attained. From the union's point of view, bargaining may seem an exercise in frustration. Finding someone on the management side with whom to bargain, and then finding someone else to administer the resulting contract for management is often a serious hurdle. It is, as put by one government executive, the task of finding someone able to say, " 'I will' or 'I won't' instead of 'I can't.' "[4] Herbert Lahne, a long-time student of unit determination problems in the federal public sector, has elaborated on the quotation:

> This question of who can say yes or no, and on what issues, is often complex and poorly defined even within an agency, to say nothing of issues on which even the agency, rightly or wrongly, alleges a legal incapacity to act, referring the union to the Civil Service Commission, the General Accounting Office, and so forth. Both small and large units have this trouble, but again it is more acute for the small units because they are frequently established at lower organizational levels of the hierarchy to which the delegation of authority (whatever it is) is least.[5]

Lahne was writing about the federal service, but the problem exists in virtually all governmental entities. It is, put simply, the need to tailor the unit carefully in light of the differences between the delegation of managerial authority in the public and private sectors:

> Not only do many decisions made by private management at a low level reach higher counterpart levels in the Federal hierarchy for decision or review within the particular agency, but other segments of the government outside the agency itself may become involved. The unions must not only find an effective path to the seats of authority and decision within each agency but, having once reached this goal, they will have to find the means to reach the executive policy and rulemakers for the Federal service as a whole.[6]

From the employer's viewpoint, failure to tailor the unit carefully is also undesirable. Eventually the union will not be put off by claims of lack of authority. Decisions that should have been reached in an atmosphere of reasoned discussion will be made in

4. Quoted by H. Lahne, "Bargaining Units in the Federal Service," 91 *Monthly Labor Review* 37, 38 (December 1968).

5. Lahne, pp. 38–39.

6. *Ibid.*, p. 39.

the most aggravated circumstances. Important policy matters may be wrongly resolved and the crisis may cause government itself to be restructured in undesirable ways. Another outcome of frustrated bargaining may be the usurpation of authority by lower echelon officials attempting to buy peace in their departments. While this may avoid a visible crisis, it may also prevent effective, coordinated, and intelligent bargaining—and government—by those genuinely responsible for the destinies of the municipality.

Unit determination can affect municipal government adversely in yet a second way, a way visibly demonstrated by the results of public management's all too frequent failure to consider its implications when public employee unions first emerged as a force to be reckoned with. Faced with demands for recognition, inexperienced municipal officials often determined the unit solely on the basis of the extent of union organization. Given the haphazard growth of unionism in this area, the result has been the creation of a large number of small, competing units of employees engaged in very similar, if not identical, occupations, and sharing what would in the private sector be called a "community of interest." As Arvid Anderson has noted, the damage is usually done before it is realized: "It is only when the public employer is subsequently confronted with the impact of . . . excessive fragmentation of a bargaining unit, that it begins to realize the significance of the unit determination."[7]

Balkanization, of course, is not unknown to the private sector; witness the railroad and newspaper industries.[8] These industries, however, suggest instability and decline; surely no one would look to them as examples of how collective bargaining should work. They serve rather as models of tangled and endless bargaining, frozen occupational differentials, wholly obsolescent (not to say ridiculous) work practices, and perpetual strife. Fragmentation and the problems associated with it, however, are not nearly so widespread in the private sector as in the public.

In Wisconsin, for example, where municipal craft (and profes-

7. A. Anderson, "Selection and Certification of Representatives in Public Employment," in T. Christiansen (ed.), *Proceedings of New York University's Twentieth Annual Conference on Labor* (Matthew Bender, 1967), p. 282.

8. See L. Reynolds and C. Taft, *The Evolution of Wage Structure* (Yale University Press, 1955), pp. 19 ff.

sional) employees are in separate units,[9] public sector organization and the fragmentation of units have gone together.[10] WERC Director Slavney says that this has fostered competition by unions both for members and in bargaining:

As an example of the extremes to which fragmentation of units may result because of the present statutory procedure, the City of Milwaukee has the following separate bargaining units: Department of Public Works (consisting of 11 bureaus), Building Inspection, Election Commission, Harbor Commission, Health Department, Museum Board, Public Library, and Tax Department, all represented by District Council 48, AFSCME, AFL-CIO, and its appropriate local. In addition, there . . . [are separate units] . . . of Nurses, Psychiatric Personnel, Physicians and Dentists, and Engineers and Architects, all represented by professional organizations. Further, the employees in the Division of Operations, other than craft in the Bureau of Municipal Equipment, are presently represented by the Teamsters, who recently won an election wherein the employees carved out the unit and selected the Teamsters as their representative. The Garbage Collection Laborers, whose classification was changed just the other day to Truck Loaders, Combustible, [sic] are represented by the Laborers. The units range in size from approximately 2,800 employees in the Department of Public Works to four employees in the Election Commission.[11]

In Michigan, one even finds single employee units.[12] Such fragmentation easily leads to uneven and irrational benefits between similar groups of employees. As the Taylor Committee Report warned:

An employee organization may seek to negotiate, for the special benefit of its own members, modifications or supplementations to the terms which are supposed to apply to a more comprehensive group of employees such as all employees of the State, or a city, or town, or

9. Wisc. Stat. Ann., § 111.70 (4)(d) (West Supp. 1971).

10. A. Thompson, *Unit Determination in Public Employment* (New York State School of Industrial and Labor Relations at Ithaca, Public Employee Relations Reports, No. 1, 1968), p. 10; M. Slavney, "Experiences with Current Substantive Practices in Administering Wisconsin Public Employee Labor Relations Statutes: Wisconsin," in H. Anderson (ed.), *Public Employee Organization and Bargaining* (Bureau of National Affairs, 1968), pp. 68–69.

11. Slavney, p. 69. Milwaukee has nevertheless done well because it has intelligently organized itself as an employer for bargaining. See pp. 129–30.

12. See, for example, *Our Lady Queen of Angels Church,* MLMB 1966, 63 *Labor Relations Reference Manual* 1021; *Roostertail, Inc.,* 1968 L. Op. 147; *Laborers Local 1098,* 1968 L. Op. 152. One also finds single employee units in Wisconsin, for example, *City of Whitefish Bay,* WERC 6160, November 1962. *Contra, Town of Ashburnham School Committee,* Mass. LRC Nos. MCR-326, 375; *Government Employee Relations Report,* No. 255 (July 15, 1968), p. B-4.

county. The result is that a crazy quilt of salary and wage and welfare benefits structure can emerge. This creates conflicts over alleged inequities because of the disturbance of relationships among sub-groups of employees. This produces problems for the executive officers who must maintain satisfactory and just employee relations among all groups of employees in the units for whose management they are responsible. It also produces problems for individual employees whose career interest might suggest the desirability of transfer from one job to another within the more comprehensive employing unit. To such transfer, obstacles would be presented by the differential negotiated wages, benefits, seniority, retirement provisions, etc. among the sub-units.[13]

Grave problems are created not only by the results reached but also by the process of fragmented bargaining itself. The existence of a large number of bargaining relationships necessarily diverts municipal leaders from other urgent problems and imposes substantial bargaining costs on the public employer. Furthermore, the unions involved will tend to compete with each other and to settle only when the concessions each extracts seem acceptable in light of all the other settlements. Long and tortuous negotiations may result and no one settlement may in fact be final until all others are. To the employer, therefore, such bargaining involves one total package, to be viewed as a whole but which must be put together through a number of bilateral negotiations with different adversaries, each of which would like to use its power over the employer to extract more than the others. The difficulties are obvious, as is the intractability of the occasional dispute in which each of two unions will accept neither parity with, nor subordination to, the other.

Experience has clearly shown the desirability of avoiding fragmentation. In contrast to the chaotic situation of New York City, the single large unit for nonuniformed employees in Philadelphia has been called "near Utopian." The same commentator, however, noted that "New York City, while it is an extreme case, probably is more representative than Philadelphia."[14]

Unit determination in the public sector, therefore, contains pitfalls of a nature more serious than those found in private employ-

13. Governor's Committee on Public Employee Relations, *Final Report* (State of New York, 1966), p. 24.

14. E. Rock, "The Appropriate Unit Question in the Public Service: The Problem of Proliferation," 67 *Michigan Law Review* 1001, 1012, 1015 (March 1969).

ment and calls for the application of somewhat different procedures and policies.

State Legislation

Existing state legislation is marked by great variations in the general standards provided for unit determination. The Minnesota statute directs the decision maker to:

take into consideration, along with other relevant factors, the principles of efficient administration of government, the principles and the coverage of uniform comprehensive position classification and compensation plans in the governmental agency, the history and extent of organization, occupational classification, administrative and supervisory levels of authority, geographical location and the recommendations of the parties.[15]

New York's Taylor Act, on the other hand, is less specific:

(a) the definition of the unit shall correspond to community of interest among the employees to be included in the unit;

(b) the officials of government at the level of the unit shall have the power to agree to, or to make effective recommendations to other administrative authority or the legislative body with respect to, the terms and conditions of employment upon which the employees desire to negotiate; and

(c) the unit shall be compatible with the joint responsibilities of the public employer and public employees to serve the public.[16]

And Michigan law seems merely to delegate the issue to its labor board by instructing it to:

decide in each case, in order to insure public employees the full benefit of their right to self-organization, to collective bargaining and otherwise to effectuate the policies of this act, the unit appropriate for the purposes of collective bargaining.[17]

The statutory variations in specific unit inclusion and exclusion for particular kinds of employees are equally great. The Connecticut statute, for example, dictates that there "be a single unit for each fire department consisting of the uniformed and investigatory employees . . . and a single unit for each police department consisting of the uniformed and investigatory employees."[18] Wiscon-

15. Minn. Stat. Ann., § 179.52 (West Supp. 1971).
16. N.Y. Civ. Serv. Law, § 207 (McKinney Supp. 1970).
17. Mich. Comp. Laws Ann., § 423.213 (1966).
18. Conn. Gen. Stat. Ann., Title 7, § 7-471(3) (Supp. 1970).

sin law, to the apparent detriment of public employers, permits a separate unit for each craft where the employees desire it.[19] And other states have similar, and proper, provisions as to professionals, while many specifically address the question of the supervisory employee.[20]

A particularized examination of the application of the general criteria and detailed statutory provisions would not be useful in further illuminating the underlying problems. The state statutes rely too heavily on private sector analogies and take insufficient account of the unique features of the public sector. What does emerge, and is worthy of further discussion, is that there must be a departure from private sector approaches and criteria for unit determination.

Criteria for Unit Determination in the Public Sector

The National Labor Relations Board long ago held that a bargaining unit need only be *an* appropriate unit rather than *the most* appropriate unit.[21] Even though state public employee relations statutes seem greatly influenced by the private sector analogy and do not explicitly nullify this long-standing rule, the feasibility of its use in the public sector has been challenged and, in one case, denied. The New York Public Employee Relations Board has held that the public sector calls for greater selectivity in unit determination and that, under the Taylor law, it would direct elections only in *the most* appropriate unit.[22]

One need not agree with the precise formulation of the New York ruling to perceive that it moves the law in a wise direction. To be sure, there are cases in which the differences between one unit and another are so small in terms of important policies that choosing one as the most appropriate seems pointless. In such

19. See n. 9 above.

20. Connecticut is an example; see n. 18 above, at § 7-471(2). See also pp. 113–14, 156–57, below.

21. *Morand Brothers Beverage Co. et al. and Distillery Rectifying and Wine Workers International Union of America, A.F.L.*, 91 N.L.R.B. 409 (1950).

22. *County of Rockland*, 1 PERB, para. 1-430 (1968). See generally J. Crowley, "The Resolution of Representation Status Disputes under the Taylor Law," 37 *Fordham Law Review* 517 (1969).

circumstances the rule formulated by the New York tribunal seems overstated; a ruling that either unit is appropriate would be sensible. Nevertheless, the New York rule is an attempt to take account of an important difference between the public and private sectors. The margin for unit determination error in the private sector is much greater. There are usually so many criteria with relevance in a disputed case that no one result is clearly better than all alternatives. Nor can one say that one or two criteria are in all cases more important and should always be weighed more heavily than others. Thus it is that one can look at the total impact of disputed National Labor Relations Board unit determinations and conclude that different decisions would have had little effect on the shape of collective bargaining or the economy.

In the public sector, however, there are considerations of such importance as to deserve priority over other criteria relevant to unit determination. The diffusion of employer authority and the tendency of unions to seek small units, which, in their sum, constitute excessive fragmentation, are matters—given their frequency and impact—of the greatest importance. The margin for error is less, the situations where one unit is preferable to all alternatives, more. Accordingly, the standards embodied in a public bargaining statute should distinguish between those primary criteria that are to weigh heavily and those secondary ones that may govern only in close cases.

PRIMARY CRITERIA

History. Where a history of separate representation by a particular union exists, either as to a group of employees or a particular craft, the case for a separate unit is rather strong. One goal of collective bargaining in both the private and public sectors is industrial peace, a purpose unlikely to be well served, no matter what the apparent merits of a more inclusive unit, if employees are not permitted to be represented by the union they regard as their natural and traditional representative. Where the building trades have organized their particular crafts in the public sector, for example, it would be a dangerous, if not futile, exercise to attempt to impose departmental or functional units that deprived such crafts of the opportunity to choose their traditional representative. And where a municipality has a history of successful bargaining with a particular group of general, rather than craft, employees, it would be a mistake to disrupt that relationship without some clear and overriding purpose.

This is not to say by any means that established units should never be disregarded. If bargaining has not been successful or attachment to a union is not particularly strong, and if other primary criteria indicate the desirability of change (and where they do, bargaining will generally not have been successful), new units ought to be fashioned. The need for such change, however, should be clearly demonstrated.

The Locus of Employer Authority. As discussed earlier, bargaining with a governmental official who lacks authority to bind his principal can be frustrating indeed to a union. And it occurs all too often. Unlike his private sector counterpart, the negotiator for a municipality may not even have the authority to discuss some matters relating to important terms and conditions of employment. This frequently means that the union must bargain at several levels of government.

> [Consider] the case of an employee unit composed of the professional employees of the welfare agencies of a city. The corresponding employer unit with respect to determining and administering many of the terms of employment is the Welfare Department. The "employer" executives with whom negotiations are carried on are the Superintendents of the several Welfare services and ultimately the Commissioner of Welfare. It is within their authority to negotiate about the working rules, the provision of facilities, services, equipment, and other aspects of the working environment not involving major expenditures with respect to such items. They are also likely to be the "employers" with respect to the administration and supervision of working routines and relationships, the handling of grievances, and the administration of discipline. But [there is] another stratum of employer, whose chief executive, the city manager or mayor, holds the administrative authority with respect to an overall personnel policy for all employees of the city, with respect to the determination of costly city-wide benefits of various sorts, and wages, and concerning decisions as to the distribution of city funds among various uses (buildings, streets, sewers, new schools, payrolls for the several departments, etc.). But even that chief executive can only recommend such a distribution and the budget required to meet the expenditures involved. His budget proposals must be submitted to the next stratum of "employer," the legislative body which is responsible for approving the overall budget and for levying

the taxes with which to balance income with expenditures. If the negotiated items include any which have been mandated by state law or if they involve any modification of local or state civil service provisions, there is a further level of decision-makers who must approve the settlement.[23]

Bargaining in the upper echelons of government takes many forms. Each union, representing a unit of employees, may bargain individually or in a coalition. Sometimes one union may be dominant, and the agreement it reaches with the higher authorities will, as a matter of custom, be accepted by the remaining unions. Still other patterns have occurred. An interesting one exists in the Post Office, for example, where three sets of units function: a national unit to resolve national questions; a regional unit for regional questions; and 24,000 local units.[24] In such a situation an employee may be represented by rival organizations at each level of government.

How the problems of fragmented authority within government should be managed in a particular municipality or other governmental entity depends, of course, on a large number of variables. In the next chapter these variables will be discussed in some detail and ways suggested for the public employer to organize itself for effective bargaining. It seems clear, however, that with respect to unit determination a balance must be struck by the state labor board between units so small that the employee representative will not have access to personnel with authority to determine substantial matters affecting employment, and units so large that particularized local or individual issues cannot be easily resolved. Put another way, the unit must not be too small to correspond to a governmental body with enough authority over conditions of employment to make bargaining worthwhile. Nor should it be too large. It should not cover too many relatively autonomous government departments or branches. For if it does, important localized issues may be difficult to discover or resolve, and, indeed, the upper echelons of government may not have authority over them. While the former danger has proved in practice to be the more frequent—principally because unions seeking organizational foot-

23. Governor's Committee on Public Employee Relations, *Final Report* (State of New York, 1966), p. 26.

24. See Rock, "Appropriate Unit Question," pp. 1008–10.

holds tend to request smaller units—there may be cases in which separate units, bargaining at various levels, are superior to an all-inclusive unit.

One final matter must be mentioned. The size and constitution of bargaining units are clearly related to the scope of the subject matter to be negotiated. If there are restrictions on the scope of bargaining, or if certain procedures are prescribed for the resolution of controversial nonmonetary issues—and Chapter 9 suggests such restrictions and procedures—the determination of the unit must take them into account. Under no circumstances should unit size limit the effectiveness of such statutory requirements.

Balkanization. The final primary criterion is the goal of avoiding excessive proliferation of bargaining units; this entails keeping three ends in mind. First, unnecessary bargaining costs—increased bureaucracy, diversion of time, and so forth—ought not be imposed on public employers. The more units there are, the larger these costs are likely to be. Second, units must be fashioned with a view to creating or maintaining a rational and comprehensive wage structure within government. As the Taylor Committee noted, balkanization can lead to "a crazy quilt of salary and wage and welfare benefits." Third, competition between unions in different units ought, where possible, to be avoided. To be sure, this is frequently not feasible, since the existence of more than one bargaining unit drawing on a single budget inevitably invites comparisons, and parity has long been an issue among many traditional units such as police and fire. Nevertheless, where it is possible to avoid such competition, units ought to be fashioned to that end.

The implications of a policy of avoiding excessive unit proliferation are greatest for the nonsupervisory employees in those departments or agencies directly responsible to the executive. Where a governmental body has relative functional autonomy and is not in the direct chain of command of the executive branch, the case for a separate unit is stronger. Thus it is, among other reasons, that hospitals, school systems, police and fire departments properly constitute separate functional units. Generally, each of these departments is under the direction of a separate board or commission with a certain amount of independent authority. Many of the costs of bargaining, therefore, will not fall directly on the executive, who in any event may not have the power to bargain over issues within the purview of the governing board or commission. Within the direct chain of command of the executive branch in large cities, however, are a number of departments and agencies with little independent functional power and little occupational or craft differentiation among the involved employees. The establishment for such employees of separate units along functional lines has been the most frequent error of those municipalities now paying the high costs of needless proliferation. And excessive homage to occupational craft differences, as in the case of Wisconsin, discussed earlier,[25] has led to similar results. To avoid balkanization, therefore, there must be a strong presumption against separate functional or occupational units within those departments and agencies in the direct chain of command of the executive branch. This presumption should be rebuttable only by a clear showing that other unit determination criteria require a different result.

There are many hopeful signs that the law is moving in the direction of preferring the wider and more inclusive unit. The Wagner Commission in Illinois urged in its final report that "fragmentation of units should be avoided and that mere extent of organization by employees should not be controlling in a unit finding."[26] A report of the California State Personnel Board similarly recommended that "to avoid excessive fragmentation of units, which is neither in the State's nor the public interest, the statute [that the board was proposing] provides that: '(1) Insofar as practicable, the unit shall be the largest feasible which is consistent with maintaining a community of interest; and (2) the extent to which employees have organized shall not be the sole criterion.' "[27] And recent federal unit arbitrations, as well as New York Public Employee Relations Board decisions, have generally favored the wider unit. President Johnson's Review Committee on Employee-Management Relations in the Federal Service similarly urged that "an appropriate unit should be one that promotes

25. See pp. 100–01, above.

26. Governor's Advisory Commission on Labor-Management Policy for Public Employees, *Report and Recommendations* (State of Illinois, 1967), p. 19.

27. California State Personnel Board, "A Proposed Approach for Formalizing Employer-Employee Relations in the State Civil Service," *GERR*, No. 285 (Jan. 24, 1969), p. E-4.

effective dealings and efficiency of agency operations."[28] This suggestion was implemented in President Nixon's Executive Order 11491.[29] New York City's Office of Collective Bargaining chairman reports that the office's Board of Certification has attempted in every unit determination case to combine job titles—including new job titles that did not exist in the original unit—and thereby facilitate the formation of larger bargaining units.[30]

SECONDARY CRITERIA

Community of Interest. Community of interest is probably the most frequently mentioned standard for unit determination. It is also the most open-ended, in that it may refer to anything from a history of successful negotiations to the ability to exercise the right of representation effectively. It is used here in three senses. First, where a group of employees is working within a unified compensation structure—for example, a single pension fund or the same salary classification ladder—the case for an all-inclusive unit seems strong. Quite apart from the fact that primary criteria usually call for a single unit in such cases, the existence of the unified benefit structure is evidence of administrative feasibility and of the ability of the employees involved to act concertedly.

Second, where employees work under a common set of procedures relating to hiring, firing, and the handling of grievances, the case for a single unit is again strong. The existence of these procedures also suggests administrative feasibility and a unity of interest on the part of the employees.

In the normal case these two factors will work in the direction of larger units. The third factor is a countervailing one. Where there are great occupational differences, in terms of the nature of the functions performed by an employee and the kind of education, training, and experience required for job applicants, where there is a strong sense of a separate trade or craft (no matter what objective observers might conclude), and where there is little

28. *GERR*, No. 280, Spec. Supp. (Jan. 20, 1969), p. 9.

29. Sec. 10(b). See *GERR*, No. 320, Spec. Supp. (Oct. 27, 1969), p. 7.

30. See also *GERR*, No. 305 (July 14, 1969), p. B-2 (OCB accretion policy); OCB Press Release, July 22, 1969, also in *GERR*, No. 306 (July 21, 1969), p. B-7 (announcement that no more departmental bargaining certifications shall be issued).

movement from one occupation to another, the case for a separate unit will be powerful and must be balanced against competing considerations.

Freedom of Organization and Representation. In the typical case it is not likely that the freedom to be organized and to be represented effectively would weigh heavily against what seemed the appropriate unit under the criteria discussed above. By and large, the existence of a community of interest will be consistent with this freedom and, indeed, usually guarantee its effective exercise. Nevertheless, there are two situations in which it should be weighed against other criteria.

First, there may be occasional occupational classifications in which the employees have little say over the bargaining done on their behalf because they represent a very small part of a large unit. This is, it must be noted, more a matter of numbers than of sharp craft differences or of a significant conflict of interest with the other groups in the unit. A unit in which the different occupational classifications have relative parity in numbers gives all a chance to participate, while a unit dominated by one large group may leave minorities with little voice. Unit determination in such circumstances is a delicate business, for it requires that the tribunal find as a fact that one group will dominate, and either that this domination will be harmful to smaller groups or that the discontent of those groups will outweigh the benefits of the more inclusive unit. One would anticipate that such cases will be extremely rare, both because the absence of sharp craft differences gives some insurance against discrimination and minority discontent, and because other criteria ought usually to prevail.

Second, there may be cases in which occupational differences, not themselves of decisive importance, ought nevertheless to be recognized because of underlying ethnic, racial, or other hostilities among the employees involved. It is a fact of life, particularly in public employment, that occupational classifications frequently tend toward relative ethnic or racial homogeneity. As a result, hostilities at large in the society may surface as hostilities between occupations in public employment. Where that is the case, an inclusive unit can lead to more rather than less strife, by eliminating any chance of a consensus within the union as to its bargaining position. A dissident group that feels excluded from the bargaining process will not be inhibited by the legal structure regulating bargaining. Wildcat strikes may result, and management will find it difficult to bargain with the minority group since it must by law deal with the exclusive bargaining representative. Where such a situation seems likely—and it will not be frequent—and the tribunal finds that hostility between the employees in identifiable occupational classifications would disrupt the bargaining relationship, separate units ought to be permitted. It perhaps needs to be said that this is not to encourage segregation, for the case posited assumes its existence. Segregation cannot be eliminated by the establishment of a single unit. Indeed, such a unit would not only have unfortunate consequences for bargaining but might result in the unfair representation of the numerically smaller group.

One final word about the utilization of the extent of organization as a standard for unit determination. In the private sector the National Labor Relations Board takes it into account as an element of the calculus.[31] In the public sector, however, it seems inappropriate. Its sole function is to encourage unionization and, while there may be good reason to permit collective bargaining by public employees, the complications it introduces into the political process seem sufficient to dispel any notion that it ought to be affirmatively encouraged. Since a history of successful bargaining will generally permit a separate unit, the principal significance of extent of organization is in cases when the union is seeking an organizational foothold. Thus, it is nothing but a device to override the primary criterion of avoiding excessive proliferation. Indeed, one prime source of the fragmentation that now exists in many cities is the early use of extent of organization as the principal unit determinant.

CRITERIA FOR SPECIFIC KINDS OF EMPLOYEES

Professionals. In the private sector, the case for permitting professionals to have an absolute right to a separate unit rests principally upon the belief that retention of their separate occupational identity is necessary, and that they have unique interests that might be infringed upon if separate units were not permitted. These considerations seem applicable to the public sector.

There is yet another reason, however, why professionals in the

31. See Labor Management Relations Act, 1947, § 9(c)(5).

public sector ought to be entitled to their own unit. The public sector faces a critical problem in bargaining over nonmonetary issues, since these often involve controversial political matters traditionally resolved through the political process. Either the scope of bargaining must be limited or procedures established that preserve the political process from excessive political power. Professionals in the public sector—teachers, welfare workers, and so on—are likely to be interested in policy questions relating to the nature of the services they provide, and any properly run department will, in any event, solicit the judgment of its professional staff as to how its functions should be performed. As a consequence, controversial nonmonetary issues are particularly likely to arise in collective bargaining by professionals. To have them raised in a bargaining unit containing nonprofessionals as well as professionals runs the risk of having the issues skewed or obscured. The internal processes of a union may compel compromises over such matters between the professionals and nonprofessionals, and those who bargain for the union may not be able to make the professional case in a persuasive manner. It is in the public interest to see such issues raised and dealt with clearly and articulately. A separate professional unit seems best suited to that end.

Supervisors. With respect to the inclusion of supervisors in a unit with nonsupervisory employees, or the creation of supervisory units, it is the public employee unions that desire a departure from the private sector analogy, for supervisors are explicitly excluded from coverage by the Taft-Hartley Act.[32] The public sector union's case for inclusion touches basic issues only obliquely. First, it is argued, with merit, that supervisors in the public sector are frequently not actual supervisors. Titles conferred on public employees often overstate the actual responsibilities and discretion that go with the job. The delegation of actual authority is haphazard and job titles and organizational charts do not accurately reflect the locus of authority over terms and conditions of employment. Second, it is argued, again with merit but less relevance, that those with supervisory positions have often worked their way up through the ranks, participated actively in professional and union affairs, and have held, and hold, union offices.

Notwithstanding these arguments, the case for excluding supervisory employees—those with real authority, that is—from the

32. *Ibid.*, §§ 2(3) and 2(11).

collective bargaining law is overwhelming. Municipalities are frequently not well organized for collective bargaining and never will be if they cannot create positions with effective responsibility for the administration of collective agreements. Such positions must necessarily be filled by persons who identify with, and are part of, management, not by those who are unionized, whether or not the union is exclusively supervisory. Nor can such responsibilities be carried out by persons who are members, much less officers, of the other party to the contract, as might occur when supervisors are in a unit with regular employees. Indeed, the creation of such positions and the delegation of supervisory power are likely to constitute a principal change in municipal structure as a consequence of collective bargaining. The law should not discourage this trend by permitting the holders of these positions to organize or be in units with nonsupervisory employees.

To be sure, the exclusion of supervisors requires judgments as to the existence of actual supervisory authority and not pro forma obeisance to titles. That, however, is no insuperable task, as the Wisconsin Employee Relations Board has demonstrated by establishing satisfactory criteria to be considered in deciding whether an employee is a supervisor. WERB looks to:[33]

(1) The authority [of an individual] to effectively recommend the hiring, promotion, transfer, discipline, or discharge of employees.

(2) The authority to direct and assign the work force.

(3) The number of employees supervised, and the number of other persons exercising greater, similar, or lesser authority over the same employees.

(4) The level of pay, including an evaluation of whether the supervisor is paid for his skill or for his supervision of employees.

(5) Whether the supervisor is primarily supervising an activity or is primarily supervising employees.

(6) Whether the supervisor is a working supervisor or whether he spends a substantial majority of his time supervising employees.

(7) The amount of independent judgment and discretion exercised in the supervision of employees.

Such criteria, or similar ones, can be easily applied to determine the existence of actual supervisory authority and to exclude those individuals exercising it from unionized units.

33. Slavney, "Administering Public Employee Labor Relations Statutes," p. 65; "Wauwatosa Board of Education," WERC 6219-D (September 1967); "Racine City," WERC 8330 (December 1967).

PART THREE

Bargaining in the Public Sector

CHAPTER EIGHT

Organizing the Public Employer for Bargaining

While the public and private sectors share the difficult and important problem of determining the appropriate election unit, the public sector alone faces the often frustrating question of deciding which branch or branches of local government should represent management, and what the internal allocation of management functions for collective bargaining should be. If one attempts to resolve this question by asking who the public employer is, he will find that answers vary from local government to local government.

At common law, the identifying marks of an employer were that: (1) he selected and engaged the employee, (2) he paid the wages, (3) he had the power of dismissal, (4) and he had power and control over the employee's conduct.[1] It might be supposed, therefore, that the executive branch, responsible as it is for the administration of a city, would perform all four of these functions. This often is not the case. The legislative branch usually must approve all transactions with monetary consequences and sometimes there is an independent board of finance that also must give approval. Thus, at least one other part of the local government will share the wage-paying function of an employer. In addition, in many communi-

1. *American Jurisprudence*, Vol. 53 (2d ed.; Rochester: Lawyers Cooperative Publishing Co., 1970), "Master and Servant," sec. 2, p. 82.

ties, independent commissions or boards rather than executive departments run important city services such as schools or parks. A commission may perform all the functions of an employer, or all except providing the needed money for wages and fringe benefits. Moreover, a municipal or county civil service commission may have an important role in fixing wages, hours, and conditions of employment.

Each branch of local government has different goals; each is subject to different pressures. And unless curative legislation can be enacted at the local or state level, each may participate in the collective bargaining process in ways that vastly complicate the formation and administration of collective agreements between a city or county and its unionized employees.

Forms of Local Government

The fragmentation of the powers of municipal employers reflects the extensive system of checks and balances that exists in local governments. To start with, most such governments observe the principle of separation of powers between the executive and legislative branches. This separation, which began around 1820 with the popular election of mayors, apparently stems from the traditional American regard for the federal system.[2]

Throughout most of the nineteenth century the power of the executive was slight relative to the legislature. Perhaps this manifested the spirit of the frontier and of Jacksonian democracy, with its skepticism of politicians and government itself. At any rate it was tolerable, for the functions of city government were few. As this changed, toward the end of the nineteenth century, a movement developed to strengthen the executive branch by increasing the appointive powers of mayors.[3]

Today there is wide variation among cities in the allocation of power between executive and legislature. If the mayor has greater authority than the council, a "strong mayor" form of government is said to exist; if less, it is called a "weak mayor" form.[4]

2. E. Banfield and J. Wilson, *City Politics* (Harvard University Press, 1963), pp. 78, 79.

3. *Ibid,* pp. 79, 80.

4. *Ibid.* The following description of weak mayor, strong mayor, and city manager forms relies on C. Adrian, *Governing Urban America* (McGraw-Hill, 1955), pp. 180–206.

WEAK MAYOR FORM

In a typical weak mayor city, the elected legislative body both legislates and administers. The mayor is not weak because he lacks policymaking power. Usually he can recommend legislation, preside over the legislative body, and veto council action. He is weak because he lacks administrative authority. He has very limited appointive power and may not have removal power. Moreover, the annual budget usually is prepared by a committee within the legislative branch. Thus, employer functions are performed by the legislative body and by relatively independent commissions.

Because the weak mayor system makes no provision for administrative leadership, it is not a common form for large communities. Indeed, the only major cities with a government resembling the weak mayor form are Los Angeles and Milwaukee.

STRONG MAYOR FORM

In a typical strong mayor city, administrative responsibility is concentrated in the hands of the mayor, while policy making is a joint function of the mayor and the legislative body. The mayor generally appoints and dismisses department heads without legislative approval. He is responsible for implementing policy and coordinating the efforts of the various city departments.

The mayor is also responsible for preparing the annual budget and for administering it once it has been approved by the legislature. However, the council must approve the budget and only occasionally does the mayor have power to veto changes it may make. And in some cities, both monetary and nonmonetary terms of an agreement with a union must be approved by the legislative body.

CITY MANAGER FORM

Early in this century a movement started, aimed at improving the quality of local government by making the chief officer of a municipality a trained professional. This resulted in the city manager form of government, which gives administrative authority to the professional manager. He is hired by the elected council, which is the policymaking body, and he serves at the council's pleasure.

The manager does not take orders from individual councilmen but from the council as a collective body, and then on policy matters only. If the manager has the confidence and respect of the council, he may run the city with little interference. If, on the other hand, the council is divided, he may not be able to venture beyond the routine.

This form of local government has been popular among reform-minded city planners. However, since it does not usually provide a strong chief executive officer, only a few large cities are under this plan.

COMMISSION FORM[5]

Still another relatively common form of government is the commission plan. The city is run by a small number of commissioners who are elected on a nonpartisan basis. The notable feature of this plan is the dual role of the commissioners. Each serves individually as the head of an administrative department of the city, and collectively the commissioners function as the city's legislative body. Accordingly, there is no separation of powers: the commission both legislates and administers.

All the functions of an employer are performed by each of the administrative departments, save only the allocation of funds, which is done through the commissioners acting as a legislature. Because of this and other weaknesses, this form of government is on the decline, although close to 400 cities were still under this plan in 1956, and many counties operate under similar forms.

INDEPENDENT COMMISSIONS AND BOARDS[6]

No matter what the form of government, most sizable cities and many smaller ones have boards, commissions, agencies, and councils that perform functions for the city but that have little or no formal connection to the legislative or executive branches. Typical examples are a board of education, board of finance, or a civil service commission.

5. See generally, C. Kneier, *City Government in the United States* (Harper, 1957), pp. 286–301.
6. See Banfield and Wilson, *City Politics*, pp. 81–84.

During the nineteenth century, when reformers were eager to keep certain city functions out of the hands of party machines, the practice was to create a large number of entirely independent boards and commissions—sometimes twenty or thirty. Some of these were established by the state and some by the community itself. Many eventually became city departments under the mayor or council, but quite a few are still only loosely tied or not tied at all to the legislative or executive branches.

Commissions often are involved in labor relations either because they employ workers to carry out their duties—a school board—or because they serve as a check on the executive and legislature—a civil service commission. In either case, the involvement of one of these boards further fragments management's authority for collective bargaining.

Fragmentation of Management Authority and Collective Bargaining

While an extensive system of checks and balances at the local level is useful for many purposes, it often makes collective bargaining difficult. Each governmental body is likely to have different goals, to be responsive to different pressures, and thus to view its interests on any given labor issue differently. If the collective bargaining process at the local level were essentially an economic one with economic constraints, the fragmentation of managerial authority might not be too great a problem, for the market would discipline decision making. But the process is primarily political, with political constraints, and fragmentation can lead to a number of undesirable results. In any given case results are determined by the complex of political and structural factors at work. The general picture is best seen through a number of particular examples.

WARREN, MICHIGAN

Consider first a situation where each relevant governmental body feels that union support is politically necessary. Such a situation can arise in a community where labor is a particularly strong political force and all the elected and appointed officials want credit for being "good to labor." Since each body in the wage-fixing process will desire to give labor something, the size of the union package will be importantly influenced by the number of bodies involved.

Warren, Michigan, before 1965, illustrates this situation. Warren is a strong mayor city. The mayor and city council are elected. Each year the mayor presents a budget to the council, which can change it in whole or part; and the mayor has no veto power over changes.

Prior to 1965, representatives of the unions would discusss labor matters having monetary consequences with the mayor before he made his budget recommendations. The unions subsequently would use these recommendations as their starting point in dealing with the council. If the mayor proposed a 3 percent increase, the unions would always ask for 1 to 2 percent more from the council. And since the council wanted credit for giving city employees wage increases, it would always raise the mayor's recommendations. Indeed, one city official stated that the council informally had asked the mayor not to offer any wage increases to the unions so that the council would have greater flexibility in dealing with the unions. However, the mayor never acquiesced since he too wanted credit for granting wage increases.

HARTFORD, CONNECTICUT

"Bypassing" is likely to take place when a union is unable to obtain a concession it wants from one of the bodies involved in the bargaining process. If the executive is obdurate and the city council must ultimately approve any collective agreement, the union may approach friendly members of that body in an attempt to get them to put pressure on the executive or to take other action that will assist the union in achieving its bargaining goals.

Perhaps the most extraordinary example of this phenomenon may be found in the labor history of Hartford, Connecticut. Hartford has a city manager, who in 1955 accepted the recommendation of consultants that the city bargain collectively with its unionized employees. The city manager, the personnel director, and department heads sat down with employee representatives (who were union officials in cases where a department was more than 50 percent organized) and worked out a comprehensive pay plan. The plan was embodied in a memorandum of understanding signed by all the parties.

This memorandum was the basis for an ordinance presented to the city council. However, to their complete surprise, the city negotiators discovered that the representatives of the police and fire unions, who had signed the memorandum, had approached individual councilmen and had persuaded a majority of them to increase the police and fire departments' pay scales above those previously agreed to in the memorandum of understanding.

The problems have continued since then, and not even the passage of the Municipal Employee Relations Act in Connecticut solved them quickly so far as the firefighters local of the International Association of Fire Fighters (IAFF) was concerned. Until recently, the IAFF local refused to seek official recognition, because doing so would require it to obey the statute and bargain exclusively with the city manager rather than the city council, where the firefighters had tremendous political influence.

Thus, in 1967—an election year—negotiations in Hartford were conducted between the policemen's local and the city manager and between the manager and the American Federation of State, County, and Municipal Employees (AFSCME) locals. The city manager, in an effort to force the firefighters to seek recognition under the statute, decided not to include any wage or fringe increases for firemen in his budget recommendations. Moreover, he asked the council not to bargain with the IAFF. The IAFF then requested the manager to reduce the firefighters' work week from 56 to 42 hours. He refused to talk with the union representatives unless they agreed to seek formal recognition and not to bargain with the city council in the future. The union refused, went to the council with their proposal, and it was approved. (The approval took place one week prior to the municipal elections.)

The city manager was outraged. He publicly claimed that the council action was equivalent to increasing the firefighters' wages by 17 percent since there was no possibility of hiring enough additional men to implement the resolution without having all present firemen work at least eight hours overtime per week. This proved to be a major strategic mistake, for negotiations with the police and AFSCME locals had not been terminated. The statement, combined with considerable campaign rhetoric about law and order, forced the city manager to agree to a 17 percent wage increase for the policemen—much larger than he had been prepared to offer originally.

As soon as the policemen were given 17 percent, the firefighters went back to the council, arguing that they were entitled to wage parity. They were able to convince the council to maintain wage parity and they received a 17 percent wage increase in addition to the reduction in hours. Since all firemen continued to work a 56-hour week (getting paid straight time for the first 48 hours and overtime for the excess), their wages went up 34 percent in 1967, according to their local president.

SANTA MONICA, CALIFORNIA

The independent "watchdog" commission, with a voice at some point in the process that fixes the working conditions of city employees, can cause additional difficulties.

Consider the case of Santa Monica, California, which has the city manager form of government. The manager, the top administrative officer, is hired by and reports to the city council. He is responsible for preparing the annual budget and for making recommendations on wages and fringe benefits. The city council has final authority for setting the budgetary expenditures and the tax level. The manager does not make his wage recommendations directly to the council, however. His recommendations first go to the Personnel Board, a quasi-independent agency composed of citizen volunteers. This board has no responsibility for the raising of funds, and if it is responsive to any political pressures they are different from those that play on the manager and the city council.

Some few years ago, the board took the city manager's recommendations and added 2.7 percent in every classification. According to the city manager, the board did not look at any of the supporting data he submitted or consider how the city would pay for the extra increases. The sanitation workers, in their discussions with the manager, had asked for an 8.1 percent wage increase. He had agreed to this request and recommended it to the Personnel Board. The board then voted a 10.8 percent increase to these workers. Once the recommendation had been made the union leaders quickly agreed that it was justified.

The city council ignored the Personnel Board's recommendations and cut the increase for the sanitation workers back to their original request of 8.1 percent. During the confusion at the final city council meeting, many employees thought that the council had reduced the wage increase not by 2.7 percent, but to 2.7 percent; others thought no increase had been approved; some, who knew what was going on, were resentful because the council rejected the recommended increase of the Personnel Board. Many employees thought they had already won a higher increase and were disappointed when the council did not go along. This confusion, which probably would not have occurred if the Personnel Board had not been involved in the process, led to a twelve-day strike.

WAYNE COUNTY, MICHIGAN

Independent commissions that employ workers to perform municipal or county functions, and civil service commissions charged with administering merit systems give rise to some of the most troublesome problems in the area we have been addressing. The situation in Wayne County, Michigan, is classic.

In 1965, Michigan passed a Public Employment Relations Act designed to ensure public employees the right to unionize and to bargain collectively. Unfortunately, the statute makes no attempt to dictate which part of a local government in Michigan is to serve as the "public employer" for collective bargaining purposes.

In Wayne County, both the Wayne County Board of Supervisors and the Wayne County Civil Service Commission believed that it should be the public employer, while the Wayne County Road Commission thought it should be the public employer for its employees.

Wayne County is governed nominally by a 126-man Board of Supervisors, 63 of whom come from Detroit and 63 of whom come from outlying areas. The Board of Supervisors is the legislative body for the county, which lacks an executive branch. The administrative functions pertinent to the county's operations are performed partially by the supervisors, but chiefly by an assortment of elected and appointed officers, officials, boards, departments, commissions, commissioners, committees, bureaus, authorities, facilities, and trustees. According to a Michigan Circuit Court judge, "the structure of the [Wayne County] government is somewhat reminiscent of Winston Churchill's memorable description of Russian foreign policy: 'a riddle wrapped in a mystery inside an enigma.' "

The budget for the county is set by a three-man board of auditors, all of whom are elected at large in the county for six-year terms.

By far the most important operating agency within the county is the Road Commission, which was established by the state legislature to build and maintain the roads in Wayne County. The funds to do this come from the state gasoline tax and the annual state auto license fee. Michigan law also provides that, in the counties with one million or more population, the Road Commission must operate the metropolitan airport. This applies only to Wayne County. The airport is self-financing, and in 1967 reported a profit of $2.5 million before allowances for depreciation.

The state legislature has also ruled that if any county decides to operate a county park system, the road commissioners shall act as the park trustees. The Road Commission receives $1.8 million from the county's general fund to pay for the park system. And the county Board of Supervisors, by resolution, has given the Road Commission responsibility for the county's sewage system, the building and maintaining of water systems, and the county's Economic Development Commission. According to the Road Commission's director, the Board of Supervisors simply recognized that the Road Commission was better able to handle these functions than any other county agency.

The three road commissioners are appointed by the supervisors. Despite this fact, the commissioners are almost completely independent of the supervisors once they have been appointed. A past chairman of the Road Commission was an important labor official, and the supervisors had little or no control over him since he had an independent power base.

The budget of the Road Commission is approximately $100 million per year. Of this, the supervisors appropriate approximately $1.8 million. The other revenue is obtained from the state and from users' fees, primarily from the airport. The Road Commission has absolute authority over its own budget, the supervisors having no power to amend or even approve it. Their control extends only to the $1.8 million they allocate. And the Road Commission has full authority to enter into contracts on its own and is empowered to fulfill its financial commitments.

The county also has a three-man Civil Service Commission whose members are appointed by the supervisors. Until 1965 the Civil Service Commission set the wage rates and fringe benefit levels for all county employees. This included the Road Commission employees. Indeed, all phases of employment, including wages, fringes, recruitment, and promotions, were handled by civil service. The Road Commission made recommendations to civil service on these matters, but recommendations might not be acted upon for some years.

Following the passage of the Public Employment Relations Act, the county was faced with deciding who its employees were and who was to represent the county in its negotiations with these employees. The act places the responsibility for collective bargaining on the "public employer," but it makes no attempt to define that term.

The county's legislative response was to create by ordinance a Labor Relations Board to represent it in all matters involving unionized county employees. The three-member board was composed of one representative of the Board of Supervisors, one from the Civil Service Commission, and one from the Road Commission. It was to conduct all negotiations through an appointed labor relations director. All policy matters were to be decided by a majority vote of the members. The ordinance also provided that, after a contract agreeable to the union and the board had been agreed upon:

> Such contract . . . shall not be binding unless the same shall have been submitted to and approved by the Wayne County Civil Service Commission and concurred therein by the Board of Supervisors and/or the Board of Wayne County Road Commissioners as their respective jurisdiction may appear.

This ordinance has failed to accomplish order. When the secretary of civil service was not named director of labor relations, civil service refused to cooperate, contending that under the Civil Service Act it alone has complete authority and responsibility for the county's employees, including all aspects of the collective bargaining process. And the Road Commission has insisted that it is an independent employer, and as such may determine its labor policy under the Public Employment Relations Act independent of the supervisors or civil service.

The consequences of this fragmentation of managerial authority have made—to understate the case rather considerably—collective bargaining difficult. Each governmental body has blocked the efforts of the other in its dealings with the unions. And litigation has thus far failed to accomplish much. In a suit brought by the Civil Service Commission, the Michigan Court of Appeals has, in effect, declined to resolve the underlying dispute.[7]

The state Public Employment Relations Act, as noted, does not define "employer." Nor does it undertake to accommodate to collective bargaining the functions performed by various governmental bodies. And the court took itself to be "without authority" to bring "judicial order out of . . . legislative chaos."[8] While it seems to us that the court should have done what it declined to do —the issue before it was plainly fit for the judicial process—it also seems that legislative attention to the fragmentation problem is essential if collective bargaining is to be made workable.

Toward Elimination of Fragmentation

These examples suggest that legislation for collective bargaining between local governments and their employees should carefully define the governmental employer and, in so doing, severely curb or eliminate the role of each governmental body save one. Concentration of authority in bargaining seems imperative if municipal and county labor relations are to be efficient. This does not mean, however, that all checks on the governmental branch with major authority should be eliminated. A check in the form of budget approval by the legislature, where the executive is the employer, or in some cases by direct voter approval, may be necessary to curb the power of the unions. This is particularly true in those municipalities that would permit nonemergency work stoppages in ac-

7. *Civil Service Commission* v. *Wayne County Board of Supervisors*, 73 *Labor Relations Reference Manual* 2822 (Mich. Ct. App., 1970).

8. *Ibid.*, p. 2826.

cordance with the legal strike model, to be presented in Chapter 12.[9]

The multiplicity of governmental forms suggests that local experimentation and innovation are necessary. The Milwaukee experience, examined below, is instructive because it shows one successful response to the fragmentation problem in a weak mayor form of government. It may be suggestive also for county governments. Connecticut, on the other hand, provides insights about other governmental forms.

THE MILWAUKEE EXPERIENCE

Milwaukee is one of the largest cities in the United States with a weak mayor form of government, and it has had a relatively long history of dealing with organized public employees. Both the mayor and the members of the nineteen-man Common Council are elected. The mayor does not prepare an executive budget; he makes few important appointments without council approval; he cannot legally terminate the service of an unsatisfactory appointee before that appointee's fixed term expires; and he has no direct administrative authority over department heads.

The budget is prepared by the Board of Estimates, which consists of the mayor, the president of the Common Council, the five members of the council's finance committee, the comptroller, the treasurer, the city attorney, and the commissioner of public works. The Common Council has the final authority to approve the budget.

The mayor's role in the collective bargaining process is extremely limited. Under an ordinance passed by the Common Council in 1965, all responsibility for collective bargaining is placed in a "labor policy committee" of the council. Tentative agreements recommended by the committee can be amended only by a three-fourths vote of the full council. The council also established the position of labor negotiator. The incumbent is appointed by the council, deals directly with the unions, and reports directly to the labor policy committee. The position of labor negotiator is a full-time one.

The negotiating process is as follows:

1. The union submits its contract demands in February.

9. See pp. 190–201, below.

2. The labor policy committee then holds a public hearing to put the union's demands before the public and to hear civic groups.

3. The city, which contacts all department heads and makes extensive use of wage surveys, must make a counter-offer within six weeks.

4. The labor negotiator meets with the labor policy committee at which time they set the limits within which he may negotiate. This generally takes the form of placing a limit on the total increase in costs, leaving the negotiator free to distribute the funds as he deems best.

5. Negotiations with the unions take place in private.

6. When an agreement is reached, the labor policy committee holds another public hearing at which time the agreement is made public for the first time.

7. The agreement becomes final unless three-fourths of the members of the full Common Council vote to reject it.

8. The mayor has the power to veto any agreement, but the veto can be overridden by a two-thirds vote of the Common Council.

Given its form of government, there is considerable merit in the Milwaukee system. The full council, inefficient because of its size, is never really involved in labor negotiations. Agreement reached and approved by the labor policy committee can be overturned only by a three-fourths vote of the council. The negotiator is a full-time professional hired for that express purpose. He is able to bargain in private and, since there is only one chain of command, he finds it relatively easy to get guidelines from his principal. Serving as he does at the pleasure of the council, he is not likely to stray from the guidelines. Moreover, the unions know that when they are bargaining with the negotiator they are dealing with an authorized individual, and that they are unlikely to improve their position by bypassing him and going directly to the mayor or council.

THE CONNECTICUT EXPERIENCE

The Connecticut Municipal Employee Relations Act places responsibility for representing the city government in employee negotiations with the city's chief executive officer, be he elected or appointed.[10] Unless a negotiated agreement conflicts with the city charter or city ordinances or requires funds in excess of those appropriated in a budget already voted on, the agreement reached between the chief executive and the union is binding, and the legislative body has no role at all. Even if one of the two above conditions exists, the legislative body's only power is to accept or reject the agreement in toto. It does not have authority to change any provision in the contract. If the legislative body is dissatisfied with a particular part of the contract, it must veto the entire contract and instruct the chief executive or his labor representative to negotiate a new agreement.[11]

Thus the law deters "bypassing" by preventing the legislative body from voting to give employees larger wage increases than those granted by the executive. The statute, moreover, eliminates the role formerly played by independent boards of finance, which, in Connecticut, have budgetary responsibilities. Now, if an agreement reached by the executive is not rejected by the legislative branch, the board of finance must appropriate the required funds. Note also that the executive and the union can agree to items that supersede the city charter or ordinances, and such agreement will be valid unless disapproved by the legislative body.[12]

Amendments, court opinions, and State Labor Relations Board rulings since 1965 have further clarified the roles of legislative and executive under the Connecticut statute, and indicate some of the problems other states may face in this area.

One of the state board's first problems involved elaboration of the legislature's role in the collective bargaining process. In a case involving the town of Groton, the board found that the acting town manager had committed a prohibited practice by stating during the negotiations that he could make no proposals on money items without obtaining prior approval of the town council. The board stated:[13]

> It is quite understandable that the Chief Executive might be fearful of being repudiated by the legislative body and seek to shift responsibility for making decisions as to terms and conditions of employment

10. Conn. Gen. Stat. Ann., § 7-467 (Supp. 1970).
11. *Id.* at § 7-474(b).
12. *Id.* at § 7-474(f).
13. Conn. SLRB Decision No. 806, May 28, 1968.

to the legislative body. The statute, however, places that responsibility upon him and he cannot, out of political timidness or caution, refuse to fulfill that statutory responsibility. He may, in conducting the other affairs of the Town, act as an errand boy for the legislative council, but he is charged with exercising primary authority and responsibility in the bargaining process. His failure to accept that responsibility and to exercise that authority is a failure to bargain in compliance with the statute.

In a case involving the city of Norwich, the board considered the fundamental "function and responsibility of the legislative body of a municipal employer in approving or rejecting a collective agreement." The board said:[14]

The chief executive of a municipal employer or his designated agent is the bargaining representative, and he is empowered by the statute to sign a binding agreement unless provisions of that agreement conflict with provisions of the City Charter, ordinances or regulations, or unless additional appropriations are necessary to implement the agreement. The legislative body has no role in the bargaining process except where one or both of these exist. However, where one or both of these conditions do exist, the chief executive must make a request for the funds necessary to implement the agreement and for approval of any provisions of the agreement which are in conflict with any charter, ordinance or regulation of the municipal employer. The legislative body must act to accept or reject that request. If the legislative body rejects, then the matter is returned to the parties for further bargaining.

Another problem arose in the *New Milford Highway Department* case,[15] where the legislative body was the town meeting. There, a contract negotiated and agreed to by the Teamsters' local and the community's Board of Selectmen was rejected by the town meeting. Subsequently, the town meeting approved the appropriations necessary to implement the contract, although the appropriations were placed in an unmarked "contingency fund." However, the town refused to make them available.

This, the labor board concluded, constituted a prohibited practice. The board stated that "the Town Meeting . . . rejected the resolution for reasons which were improper ones under the statute" (i.e., anti-union bias), and that the *only* legitimate reason, under the statutory scheme, for a legislative body to reject a duly negotiated contract is "a judgment that the municipal employer could

14. Conn. SLRB Decision No. 790, Feb. 20, 1968.
15. Conn. SLRB Decision No. 740, Feb. 21, 1967.

not afford the raises and fringe benefits called for by the agreement."[16] Since the money had been appropriated in a contingency fund of the annual budget, it was clear that the town could afford the raises.

Although this decision greatly narrowed the role of the town meeting by limiting it to the question of whether the town could "afford" the negotiated settlement, union leaders nevertheless sought to make certain that collective bargaining agreements were not rejected in the future by a town meeting unsympathetic to union demands. To that end the statute was amended in 1967 to read:

> Except where the legislative body is the town meeting, a request for funds necessary to implement such written agreement . . . shall be submitted . . . to the legislative body. . . . Where the legislative body is the town meeting, approval of the agreement by a majority of the selectmen shall make the agreement valid and binding upon the town and the board of finance shall appropriate or provide whatever funds are necessary to comply with such collective bargaining agreement.

Another problem that arose under the original enactment was the length of time allowable for legislative approval of the funds required. No specific time limit was written into the statute. This raised the possibility that a legislative body could use stalling tactics to prevent the implementation of a contract it opposed for some reason.

Indeed, in the *Norwich Public Works* case, the council refused to act upon a contract agreed to by a union of public employees and the city manager. The refusal to act apparently stemmed from alleged conflict between the contract and the merit system rules of the city's Personnel and Pension Board. The State Labor Relations Board found the council's delay in acting upon the contract to be a prohibited practice.[17] However, to prevent any repetition of this problem, the state legislature amended this section by adding the italicized words:

> A request for funds necessary to implement [a] written agreement and for approval of any provisions of the agreement which are in conflict with any charter . . . rule or regulation [etc.] . . . shall be submitted by the bargaining representative of the municipality *within fourteen days of the date on which such agreement is reached* to the legislative

16. *Ibid.*

17. Conn. SLRB Decision No. 764, Sept. 22, 1967.

body. . . . *Failure by the bargaining representative of the municipality to submit such request to the legislative body within such fourteen-day period shall be considered to be a prohibited practice committed by the municipal employer. Such request shall be considered approved if the legislative body fails to vote to approve or reject such request within thirty days of the end of the fourteen-day period for submission to said body.*

A final problem indirectly related to fragmentation concerned negotiations beyond the final date for budget approval. New Haven, for example, had taken the position that once the budget approval date had passed the city could no longer negotiate over provisions for that fiscal year. Consequently, the city could stall beyond the budget approval date and save itself the cost of a year's salary increase. The original wording of the statute did not prohibit this; but in 1967 the statute was amended to read:

> No provision of any general statute, charter, special act or ordinance shall prevent negotiations between a municipal employer and an employee organization, which has been designated or recognized as the exclusive representative of employees in an appropriate unit, from continuing after the final date for making or setting the budget of such municipal employer. An agreement between a municipal employer and an employee organization shall be valid . . . when entered into . . . and signed. . . . Such terms may make any such agreement effective on a date prior to the date on which such agreement is entered.

Although the issue is not faced squarely, an interesting result of the Connecticut statute is that a chief executive apparently has the full power to commit the city to expenditures beyond the current fiscal year so long as the expenditures in the current year do not require funds beyond those allocated in the annual budget. Many contracts will be effective for a period of time longer than the annual budget. The contracts may run anywhere from twelve months to three years. This concentrates more power than would seem desirable in the chief executive.

For example, a mayor might agree to a 30 percent wage increase for policemen over a three-year period—5 percent in the first year, 10 percent in the second, and 15 percent in the third year. In the first year he will have to find only enough money in the budget to cover the 5 percent, and the funds needed for the subsequent wage increases become fixed obligations.

Perhaps the easiest solution would be to make the length of

contracts coincide with the length of the budget. Unfortunately this is often impractical. It would mean that most executive branches would spend too much time negotiating, that the cost of operations would increase, and that labor relations too often would be in an unstable posture. A promising alternative is for the legislature to have power to approve or reject, but not amend, monetary commitments extending beyond the term of the budget. This would serve as a needed check on the executive.

The Connecticut statute, as it applies to independent commissions or boards, also reduces the function of other governmental branches more than would seem desirable. The statute defines a municipal employer as "any political subdivision of the state, including any town, city, borough, district, district department of health, school board, housing authority or other authority established by law." No mention is made of the fiscal status of the body. And section 7-474(d) provides that:

> If the municipal employer is a district, school board, housing authority or other authority established by law, which . . . has sole and exclusive control over the appointment of and the wages, hours and conditions of employment of its employees, such district, school board, housing authority . . . or its designated representatives, shall represent such municipal employer in collective bargaining and shall have the authority to enter into collective bargaining agreements with the employee organization which is the exclusive representative of such employees, *and such agreements shall be binding* on the parties thereto, and *no such agreement or any part thereof shall require approval of the legislative body of the municipality* [emphasis added].

Thus, it would appear that a fiscally dependent agency has the full power to commit funds it is not responsible for raising. Furthermore, the local legislative body does not have even the power to accept or reject a contract. The legislative branch, remarkably enough, has less control over the process when a fiscally dependent board negotiates than when negotiation is by the chief executive. This is unfortunate. While, as a general proposition, commissions that are fiscally independent should not be subject to control by other branches of local government, dependent commissions should. Indeed, perhaps the best solution is for the city's negotiators to have control over the commission's labor relations.

This is not to advocate that the fiscally dependent commission be denied participation in the bargaining process. Members of the commission or its staff should be available for professional advice, just as representatives of a department of public works give professional advice to the chief executive's negotiators when he negotiates with public works employees. But the final responsibility in many cases should be with the chief executive officer.

At the least, the fiscally dependent commission or board should be put in the same position as are the chief executive officer and his representatives in Connecticut: if an agreement requires funds in excess of the total allocated to the commission in the budget, legislative approval should be required.

Conclusions

The appropriate solution to the fragmentation problem varies from place to place. An important element in any situation, however, is to centralize the bulk of authority in one branch of local government. In a weak mayor city, like Milwaukee, or in a county government, this probably means that authority must be placed in the legislative branch. In most of the larger cities, with strong mayor or city manager forms of government, authority belongs in the executive branch, with the legislature performing the functions it does under Connecticut law. As for operating commissions and boards, fiscally independent ones should not be expected to relinquish any of their control over labor relations to the local government. But, at the least, fiscally dependent agencies should be required to get legislative approval for funds committed beyond those allocated to them in the budget of the city. If possible, the city's regular negotiating team should also have the responsibility for collective bargaining for these boards and commissions. The locus of responsibility then will be clear to the unions, to other parts of the local government, and to the public.

CHAPTER NINE

The Scope of Bargaining

No matter how well organized the public employer is for negotiating with the unions, it is likely to encounter scope-of-bargaining issues in negotiation that are politically controversial. Nor will internal organization make these issues tractable. This fact is of great importance, for it threatens to distort the political process and sometimes crops up in ways that can place considerable stress on society—witness the New York decentralization dispute.

The Public Schools and Other Illustrations

Scope-of-bargaining problems in public employment are best illustrated by our schools. In primary and secondary education there are at least three subjects with major educational policy implications that have found, and increasingly are finding, their way into the bargaining process. They are class size, student discipline, and curricular reform.

Of the three, class size is the most "ancient," the subject most regularly negotiated, and the one most clearly related to teachers' working conditions. Bernard Donovan, the former superintendent of schools in New York City, described his ambivalence about the legitimacy of union bargaining over class size when he asked:

> What is class size? Is it a working condition or is it a matter of educational policy? If you think it over, you will find it is a gray area. There are elements in it that have to do with a teacher's working conditions, in terms of load. But there are also elements in it that have to do with the proper number of children that can be handled for a specific type of subject under particular circumstances.[1]

In New York City, collective agreements have addressed questions of class size since 1963. In Chicago the present agreement relates class size to the subject matter taught; in Detroit, to student scores on reading tests. The New Haven contract provides: "No class from Grades 1–12 shall have more than 35 [pupils]. In the school year 1969–1970 no class shall have more than 34 pupils."[2]

The tendency for class size to become a subject of collective bargaining may not be of great concern. While the subject is important to educational policy, it bears directly upon working conditions, and few would argue that smaller classes are undesirable. Moreover, existing physical facilities tend to limit the range of demands a union can realistically make, at least in the short run.[3] Yet, if class size should have rather low priority as a matter of educational policy, and if there are many more important factors in education, all of which compete with class size for too few dollars, then one can legitimately be anxious about the distortion, built into educational policy decisions, that may result from determining class size through collective bargaining.

Little community agreement exists with respect to the role and nature of student discipline in public education; yet student behavior is of increasing concern in many public schools, particularly those located in racially tense urban centers. The deterrent effect of punishment for misbehavior, the educational and rehabilitative goals of disciplinary proceedings, and the safety of teachers and other students are matters of vast importance and items of

1. B. Donovan, "Speaking for Management," in S. Elam, M. Lieberman, and M. Moskow (eds.), *Collective Negotiations in Public Education* (Rand McNally, 1967), pp. 287–88.

2. The Chicago agreement is reproduced in *Government Employee Relations Report*, No. 336 (Feb. 16, 1970), p. 7, § 6(b). For the Detroit provision, see *GERR*, No. 303 (June 30, 1969), p. B-4. The New Haven contract is in *GERR*, No. 287 (March 10, 1969), p. 32 (contracts).

3. However, in Chicago the CTU president has said: "Where no space exists for the increased number of classes [resulting from the reduction in class size], portable classrooms will be employed. . . ." *GERR*, No. 333 (Jan. 26, 1970), p. B-8.

high visibility on many communities' agenda. The teachers' interest in the matter is undeniable; but so is that of the students, the parents, and the rest of the community.

Traditionally, discipline has been the prerogative of management; the superintendent and the school board (generally elected by the community)[4] have set policy. Increasingly, however, student disciplinary problems are becoming, in one form or another, subjects for collective bargaining. Some contract provisions, such as the one in the New Haven agreement, raise no questions of disproportionate control over the decision-making process in this area. The provision, which merely ensures that a teacher injured by a student will receive full salary up to one year while recovering, does not address questions of educational policy.[5]

This is not the conclusion, however, to be drawn from provisions found in other collective agreements. The language in the Huntington, Long Island, contract obviously represents a decision about educational policy. It reads: "Any child designated by a school psychologist as . . . emotionally disturbed shall be admitted to or retained in a regular class only with the consent of the teacher."[6]

In such cities as Philadelphia, Washington, D.C., and Wilmington, Delaware, "the adjustment of behavioral problems" as a "joint responsibility [bargainable issue]" seems well established. In the Wilmington agreement, principals are required to suspend students under circumstances spelled out in the contract and to refer certain types of cases to the police. The agreement also entitles a teacher to call a parental conference or to refer a student to a psychologist without the approval of his principal.[7]

Some negotiated disciplinary provisions may move a school system toward proper educational goals. But the position taken by a union is unlikely to reflect more than what its members believe is good educational policy consistent with their own self-interest. Other groups may have different views and ought to have an

4. "About 15 percent of the boards of education, mostly in large cities, are appointed by the mayor or municipal governing body." M. Moskow and R. Doherty, "United States," in A. Blum (ed.), *Teacher Unions and Associations: A Comparative Study* (University of Illinois Press, 1969), pp. 295, 296.

5. Art. XII, *GERR*, No. 287 (March 10, 1969), pp. 29, 40 (contracts).

6. Art. VIII(g), *GERR*, No. 270 (Nov. 11, 1968), pp. 123, 128 (contracts).

7. Art. V(g), *GERR*, No. 316 (Sept. 29, 1969), pp. 159, 164 (contracts).

opportunity to "make [themselves] heard effectively at some crucial stage in the process of decision."[8] Unhappily, collective bargaining may make that impossible.

When bargaining is over curricular changes, the educational stakes may be even higher. This, coupled perhaps with the fact that curricular matters are less obviously related to conditions of teachers' employment, may explain the relatively slower development of collective bargaining about curricular matters. Yet, as Donald Wollett has testified, "teacher involvement in the development of curriculum and other educational programs is increasingly common."[9] This involvement often touches educational policy at its most sensitive point: programs for underprivileged children.

The More Effective Schools (MES) program of New York City, for example, seeks to improve the education of ghetto elementary students through drastic cuts in class size and a series of specialized services. While MES was not developed in collective bargaining, the United Federation of Teachers had a role in the program's design. In 1967, when the UFT anticipated that MES would be reduced in scope, it sought a specific contractual commitment to the program from the board of education. The bargaining process produced a promise of $10 million to programs in this general field and a tripartite union-administration-community board of governance, with veto power in the superintendent.[10]

The 1969 United Federation of Teachers agreement clearly establishes collective bargaining as a method through which educational innovation is to develop in New York City. In addition to the MES program, the contract requires, for example, that the board of education create yet unplanned preschool centers in fifty elementary schools.[11]

What happens in New York City often sets the pace in other cities. Joint control over curricular matters is taking hold in such

8. R. Dahl, *A Preface to Democratic Theory* (University of Chicago Press, 1956), p. 145.

9. D. Wollett, "The Coming Revolution in Public School Management," 67 *Michigan Law Review* 1027 (March 1969).

10. See I. Klaus, "The Evolution of a Collective Bargaining Relationship in Public Education: New York City's Changing Seven-Year History," 67 *Mich. L. Rev.* 1033, 1047–48, 1060–64 (March 1969).

11. *GERR,* No. 303 (June 30, 1969), p. B-7.

places as Chicago and Washington, D.C.[12] In Detroit and Philadelphia there are beginnings, and in some smaller communities the same trend is discernible.[13]

Scope-of-bargaining problems in public education have their counterparts in other areas of public employment. Consider the police and the issue of a civilian police review board. For the officer and his union, a review board that can determine whether his official conduct was improper is a condition of employment analogous to the handling of discipline and discharge in the private sector. Yet the interest of the community in the civilian review board issue is immense. So, too, are the questions of how many shifts or platoons should be established, whether police are to be required to receive sensitivity training, what such training should consist of, and the use of para-police personnel for special assignments.[14]

Similar problems with similar complexities exist in collective bargaining by firefighters, nurses, and social workers. These are nascent problems with the potential for leading to a confrontation between public employees and other interest groups in the community. In most municipalities this potential is presently obscured, either because there is no real collective bargaining or because collective bargaining is very new.

Where there is no bargaining in a strict sense, there may be various forms of consultation between city management and employee groups. The consultation may be private; it may be at public hearings. The employees and their unions constitute an interest group with access to municipal decision makers similar to that enjoyed by other interest groups in a community. Sometimes the influence of the unions is great, sometimes not. The important point, however, is that, in the absence of bargaining, no formal, legal, institutionalized arrangement for influencing decisions is

12. See *Board of Education and Chicago Teachers Union, GERR*, No. 336, (Feb. 16, 1970), p. 7 (contracts). See generally T. Brunner, "Including Educational Policy Issues in the Scope of Teacher Bargaining: Some Legal and Political Considerations" (unpublished MS, Yale Law School, 1969).

13. Wollett, "Coming Revolution."

14. See generally J. Futch, P. Gewirtz, and T. Humphrey, "Collective Bargaining in the Public Sector: 'Fuzz, Flamers, and Garbage'" (unpublished MS, Yale Law School, 1969).

available for the employee and his union that is different from those available to other groups in the community.

Where the union is undifferentiated from other interest groups, consultation between union and management may be very broad or very narrow in scope. In such circumstances, the influence a union may bring to bear will be determined by the political power it can wield as an interest group active in the political process. This may be a cause of community concern on occasion, but the concern is of a different sort from that addressed here. It is the result primarily of apathy among other groups and skill on the part of the union, rather than of laws that create institutional arrangements designed to increase the power of a particular group.

Where genuine collective bargaining is new, as it is in many cities, the unions are still occupied primarily with recognition, financial terms, and union security. With time they can be expected to press for expansion of the subjects of bargaining, and then the problems will come clearly into focus. When this occurs, the scope of bargaining in the public sector must be regulated in a manner that will adequately limit the role of unions in the political decision-making process. The forms that such regulation should assume depend, in part, on the current state of the law.

Regulation of the Scope of Bargaining

CIVIL SERVICE

In most jurisdictions the law pertaining to the scope of bargaining in public employment not only fails to deal adequately with these problems but often interferes with appropriate collective bargaining by perpetuating an anachronistic civil service system. Civil service or merit systems were established to rationalize the relationship of government and its employees. Mindful of a spoils system with its corrupting influence on the public service and of the need for impartiality and objectivity in the recruitment, promotion, and discharge of government employees, advocates of civil service have been extremely successful in obtaining legislation at the state, county, and municipal levels. Not infrequently, however, the civil service has become encrusted with bureaucratic barnacles, and frequently its administration complicates the achievement of a rational regime of collective bargaining.

Conflict between civil service systems and unionization transcends scope-of-bargaining issues. Indeed, the major task of accommodating the two relates to the pervasive and peculiarly governmental labor problem that was explored in the last chapter; namely, determining who the public employer is. It is not uncommon—as Wayne County demonstrates—for a civil service commission to insist that it, alone or in combination with other agencies, is the public employer for purposes of employee relations. David T. Stanley makes clear the source of difficulty:

> What do we mean by merit systems? We should distinguish them from the *merit principle* under which public employees are recruited, selected, and advanced under conditions of political neutrality, equal opportunity, and competition on the basis of merit and competence. Public employee unions do not question this principle in general and have done little to weaken it, as yet. When we say *merit systems,* however, this has come to mean a broad program of personnel management activities. Some are essential to carrying out the merit principle: recruiting, selecting, policing of anti-political and anti-discrimination rules, and administering related appeals provisions. Others are closely related and desirable: position classification, pay administration, employee benefits, and training. Unions are of course interested in both categories.[15]

Two general types of situation should be distinguished. The first is where there is no legislation mandating collective bargaining and such bargaining is desired by employees. Although unions may have penetrated the decision-making process to varying degrees, generally neither the depth nor the total impact on decisions is as great as where there is legislation.[16] In the absence of legislation the union may have to attempt to influence many different "employers," including a civil service commission, on matters of hiring and firing, promotions, reclassifications, wages, and grievance procedures. Unless the locus of employer authority is in the civil service commission, or the civil service commission is controlled by the mayor or his designee, the unions' task can be

15. D. Stanley, "What Are Unions Doing to Merit Systems?" 31 *Public Personnel Rev.* 108, 109 (January 1970) (emphasis supplied).

16. See generally P. Gerhart, "The Scope of Bargaining in Local Government Labor Negotiations," in *Proceedings of the 1969 Annual Spring Meeting,* Industrial Relations Research Association (1969), p. 545.

frustrating indeed. Nor is it uncommon to find, for example, competing grievance procedures, one established between agency and union, the other administered by the civil service commission.[17]

Where there is legislation for public unions, the problem will persist if the statute is unclear in its definition of the public employer—unless informal accommodations are created.[18] But even if the public employer is defined, the civil service commission may retain most of its statutory powers and undermine collective bargaining over subjects normally considered appropriate for union-management negotiations.

Few states have addressed the role of civil service commissions in the collective bargaining process. Of those that have, the majority appear to resolve conflicts in favor of the commissions. Typical is the Massachusetts statute that states: "Nothing in section . . . 178M [the Right to Bargain statute] . . . shall diminish the authority and power of the civil service commission."[19]

Likewise, the California statute provides:

Nothing contained herein shall be deemed to supersede the provisions of existing state law and the charters, ordinances and rules of local public agencies which establish and regulate a merit or civil service system or which provide for other methods of administering employer-employee relations. This *chapter is intended instead, to strengthen merit, civil service* and other methods of administering employer-employee relations through the establishment of uniform and orderly methods of communication between employees and the public agencies by which they are employed.[20]

The Oregon and Washington statutes also appear to subordinate the collective bargaining provisions to civil service rules and regulations.[21] However, there is some uncertainty among local officials, especially in Washington, as to which statute takes precedence.

17. This has been the situation, for example, in Dayton, Ohio. See generally J. Wender, "Fragmentation of Authority for Collective Bargaining at the Local Level" (unpublished MS, Yale Law School, 1969).

18. See, for example, *Civil Service Commission for the County of Wayne* v. *Wayne County Board of Supervisors,* 73 *Labor Relations Reference Manual* 2822 (Mich. Ct. App., 1970); pp. 125–28.

19. Mass. Laws Ann., Ch. 149, § 178N (Supp. 1970).

20. Ann. Cal. Code, Government, § 3500 (Supp. 1969) (emphasis added).

21. Ore. Rev. Stat., §§ 243.710–.780 (1967); Wash. Rev. Code Ann., §§ 41.56.010–.900 (Supp. 1970).

The Wisconsin law, on the other hand, spells out those items over which a public employer need not bargain:

> Nothing herein shall require the employer to bargain in relation to statutory and rule provided prerogatives of promotion, layoff, position classification, compensation and fringe benefits, examinations, discipline, merit salary determination policy and other actions provided for by law and rules governing civil service.[22]

The Connecticut Municipal Employee Relations Act goes the furthest of any state enactment in limiting the role of civil service commissions. Section 474 (g) provides:

> Nothing herein shall diminish the authority and power of any municipal civil service commission, personnel board, personnel agency or its agents established by statute, charter or special act to conduct and grade merit examinations and to rate candidates in the order of their relative excellence from which appointments or promotions may be made to positions in the competitive division of the classified service of the municipal employer served by such civil service commission or personnel board. The conduct and the grading of merit examinations, the rating of candidates and the establishment of lists from such examinations and the appointments from such lists and any provision of any municipal charter concerning political activity of municipal employees shall not be subject to collective bargaining.[23]

However, the previous subsection states:

> Where there is a conflict between any agreement reached by a municipal employer and an employee organization and approved in accordance with the provisions of [this act] on matters appropriate to collective bargaining, as defined in this act, and any charter, special act, ordinance, rules or regulations adopted by the municipal employer or its agents such as a personnel board or civil service commission . . . the terms of such agreement shall prevail.[24]

Thus, the Connecticut statute excludes from collective bargaining *only* the employment and promotion functions of civil service.

Apart from the employment of new applicants, the "merit principle" probably should be pursued through collective bargaining and not through a civil service system. For present purposes, however, it is important to observe that many governments, through their civil service laws, have placed significant restraints on the scope of bargaining.

22. Wis. Stat., § 111.91(2) (1970).
23. Conn. Gen. Stat. Ann., Title 7, § 474(g) (Supp. 1970).
24. *Id.* at Title 7, § 474(f) (Supp. 1970).

OTHER RESTRICTIONS ON THE SCOPE OF BARGAINING

Legal restraints on the scope of collective bargaining exist in statutes other than those establishing civil service systems. The vast network of state laws may, here and there, affect various aspects of public employment and, because these laws are rarely directed specifically at public employees, they may establish bizarre patterns of regulation.[25] The principal source of law, however, is the public employee labor statutes themselves.

One type of public employee legislation is not directly relevant: the consult, or meet and confer, statute. The obligation such statutes impose on public employers is to consult with the employee representatives rather than to bargain with them. Even some of these do establish guidelines for the scope of required consultation. Contrast, for example, the former California teachers' statute with the Oregon enactment. Oregon confined talks to "matters of salaries and related economic policies affecting professional services."[26] In California, consultation was envisioned over

> all matters relating to employment conditions and employer-employee relations and . . . with regard to all matters relating to the definition of educational objectives, the determination of the content of courses and curricula, the selection of textbooks, and other aspects of the instructional program to the extent such matters are within the discretion of the public school employer.[27]

If, in fact, consultation rather than bargaining were a viable labor policy for a state or municipality, there would be little reason to impose limits on the scope of discussion. Such limitations, however, may be necessary because consultation seems increasingly a position that can be held only temporarily, with collective bargaining frequently replacing it.[28] When the replacement occurs the scope of bargaining will be a battleground, and the outcome may be affected by the positions the parties staked out for themselves at the consultation stage.

Statutes that do impose an obligation on a public employer to bargain often follow the language of the National Labor Relations Act (section 8(d)): the employer is under a duty to bargain over

25. See Wender, "Fragmentation of Authority."
26. Ore. Rev. Stat., § 342.460(1) (1969).
27. Cal. Educ. Code, § 13085 (West 1969).
28. See, for example, Klaus, "Evolution of a Collective Bargaining Relationship."

"wages, hours, and other terms and conditions of employment."[29] Countless decisions of the NLRB and the courts have elaborated this federal requirement. The following may be taken as a too general, but for the purposes sufficiently accurate, summary of that elaboration: The duty is to bargain in good faith—that is, with a sincere desire to reach agreement.[30] It does not, however, require agreement.[31] Nor does it preclude an employer from bargaining in good faith for unilateral control over a matter (pension plans, for example) subject to the duty.[32] Some matters, moreover, are not subject to the duty; that is, the employer need not, if he chooses not to, negotiate about them with the union. These are matters—the price of a product would be a clear example—that have been held not to come within the phrase "wages, hours and other terms and conditions of employment."[33] While most matters unions raise in bargaining arguably fall within that phrase (and arguably should be held so to fall), many matters have nevertheless been excluded by the board or the courts. Indeed, unless a matter is likely to have a significant impact on a unit employee's job interest, it will probably not be subject to the bargaining duty.[34] And the courts have held that some "business decisions" are not within the duty even though they do have a significant impact on employment.[35] The *effect* of the business decision on employees, however, is negotiable.

This body of federal law ought to have little influence on the scope-of-bargaining problem as it develops in public employment, for the underlying problems to which the federal law is a response are very different from those being considered here. In the first place, federal law reflects mainly solutions to issues that arise out of large-scale manufacturing. The legal problems that come before the NLRB involve the effect on employees of the technological

29. See, for example, Conn. Gen. Stat. Ann., Title 7, § 470(c) (Supp. 1969) (duty to bargain in good faith "with respect to wages, hours and other conditions of employment").

30. See, for example, *Reed and Prince Manufacturing Co.* v. *NLRB*, 205 F.2d 131 (1st Cir.), cert. denied, 346 U.S. 887 (1953).

31. 29 U.S.C., § 158(d) (1964).

32. *NLRB* v. *American National Insurance Co.*, 343 U.S. 395 (1952).

33. See *NLRB* v. *Wooster Division of Borg-Warner Corp.*, 356 U.S. 342 (1958).

34. *NLRB* v. *Westinghouse Electric Corp.*, 150 *Decisions and Orders N.L.R.B.* 1574 (1965).

35. See E. Platt, "The Duty to Bargain as Applied to Management Decisions," 19 *Labor Law Journal* 143 (1968).

innovations taking place in industry. The legal problems in the public sector will at times be similar. Teachers may resist technological innovations in the classroom that seem to reduce their role, while police may seek to prevent the use of devices such as vehicle-tracking equipment. Other issues, however, will be the result of social and political change rather than technological innovation and will be of a totally different character.[36]

In the second place, as observed in Chapter 1, the stakes in the two situations are very different. The market disciplines the private sector more directly and insistently than it does the public. Therefore, an expanded bargaining agenda in the private sector means only that unions are trading off benefits in some areas for benefits in others. As noted, this trade-off occurs less frequently in the public sector, and an expansion of the subjects of bargaining may entail an increase in the quantum of union power in the political process.

While it is impossible now to say how state agencies and courts will deal with the phrase, "wages, hours and other terms and conditions of employment," it seems clear, given the lack of further legislative guidance, that agencies and courts are unsuited to their assigned task. Elaboration of this seemingly innocuous phrase will require agencies and courts to resolve issues that are politically, socially, and ideologically among the more explosive in our society; ones that adjudicatory tribunals are institutionally ill suited to resolve. Agencies and courts are not forums in which contesting interest groups should be able to influence decisions through the skillful employment of political pressure. Either the legislature or some multiparty bargaining structure is the appropriate forum for deciding such questions. This does not mean that there is no role for administrative agencies and courts; but if they are to perform properly they need standards and, in this area, fairly specific standards at that.

Some jurisdictions have provided standards. One example is Nevada which, after using the phrase "wages, hours and other terms and conditions of employment," enacted the management's rights clause of Executive Order 10988 that regulated federal employee relations from January 17, 1962, to October 29, 1969. The management's rights provision in its Nevada form provides:

36. See pp. 23–24, 137–42, above.

Each local government employer is entitled, without negotiation or reference to any agreement resulting from negotiation: (a) To direct its employees; (b) To hire, promote, classify, transfer, assign, retain, suspend, demote, discharge or take disciplinary action against any employee; (c) To relieve any employee from duty because of lack of work or for any other legitimate reason; (d) To maintain the efficiency of its governmental operations; (e) To determine the methods, means and personnel by which its operations are to be conducted; and (f) To take whatever actions may be necessary to carry out its responsibilities in situations of emergency.[37]

Even more explicit, perhaps, is the provision in the New York City regulation:

It is the right of the City, acting through its agencies, to determine the standards of services to be offered by its agencies; determine the standards of selection for employment; direct its employees; take disciplinary action; relieve its employees from duty because of lack of work or for other legitimate reasons; maintain the efficiency of governmental operations; determine the methods, means and personnel by which government operations are to be conducted; determine the content of job classifications; take all necessary actions to carry out its mission in emergencies; and exercise complete control and discretion over its organization and the technology of performing its work. The City's decisions on those matters are not within the scope of collective bargaining, but, notwithstanding the above, questions concerning the practical impact that decisions on the above matters have on employees, such as questions of workload or manning, are within the scope of collective bargaining.[38]

The approach of New York City and Nevada seems promising, and the language of the former ("to determine the standards of services to be offered by its agencies") is at least partly responsive to the concerns expressed here. The difficulty with the New York City statute is that the contribution of professional and semiprofessional employees, if it is to be made through the bargaining process, must meet a test that is irrelevant to their professional status. Managerial decisions are not within the scope of bargaining, but questions concerning the "practical impact that [such] decisions . . . have on employees, such as questions of workload or

37. Nevada Local Government Employee-Management Relations Act, chap. 650, L. 1969, § 10.2, reproduced in 4a *Labor Relations Reporter*, 38 SLL 226–33 (1969). The Kennedy executive order may be found in *Federal Register*, Vol. 27 (Jan. 19, 1962), p. 551.

38. "The Conduct of Labor Relations between the City of New York and its Employees," N.Y. City, Executive Order No. 52, § 5C (Sept. 29, 1967).

manning, are within the scope of collective bargaining." This approach can be both too restrictive, where there is no "practical impact," and too liberal, where "the standards of services" plainly do have the necessary impact. In both situations a limited contribution from employees may be desirable. The New York City statute seems more influenced than it should have been by the industrial model of collective bargaining—a model that is appropriate for some municipal employees but not for others.[39]

An approach that is responsive to the underlying problem is found in the Maine public employees' right-to-bargain statute as it applies to public education. Maine requires school boards:

> To confer and negotiate in good faith with respect to wages, hours, working conditions and contract grievance arbitration . . . [and to] meet and consult but not negotiate with respect to educational policies [;] for the purpose of this paragraph, educational policies shall not include wages, hours, working conditions or contract grievance arbitration.[40]

The Maine experiment deserves to be watched with care. In situations where collective bargaining has itself provided for consultation over matters of educational policy, and the two have been employed together as joint methods of ordering, consultation generally either has atrophied or has been a preliminary phase to expand collective bargaining.[41] But because Maine establishes bargaining and consultation by statute, these prior experiences may not foretell the fate of that state's experiment.

THREE SUGGESTED APPROACHES

As alternatives to the Maine statute there are three possible approaches to the scope-of-bargaining question in public employment. First, in addition to collective bargaining over "traditional" subjects, it may be possible, in some municipalities and for some employees, to establish multiparty bargaining over subjects that

39. See City of New York (Fire Department), Office of Collective Bargaining, Decision B-9-68, *GERR,* No. 271 (Nov. 18, 1968), p. G-1. Compare Board of Collective Bargaining 22, Decision 16, *GERR,* No. 280 (Jan. 20, 1969), p. C-1.

40. Chap. 9-A L. 1969, as amended by chap. 578, L. 1970, § 965.1.C., reproduced in 4 *Lab. Rel. Rep. SLL,* sec. 29, p. 218 (1970).

41. See Klaus, "Evolution of a Collective Bargaining Relationship"; Brunner, "Educational Policy Issues."

relate to the nature of the services the employees provide. For example, in education there is good reason to believe that decentralization of educational policymaking is desirable and that orderly community participation in schools is a goal worth pursuing. Whatever the appropriate decentralized unit may be (and it generally should be different from the traditional bargaining unit), multiparty bargaining in the appropriate unit might proceed on some or all matters of educational policy. Where school decentralization exists, the "employer," whether the central school board or mayor, cannot effectively represent the interests of the smaller unit. In such a case, the statute or ordinance establishing the smaller unit, or the collective agreement with the teachers for that matter, might provide for intervention by a specific third party. The third party might be a representative and duly elected community group, for example, parents with students in the school or schools. Determining what groups are sufficiently affected to justify representation, however, is a difficult task as a practical matter and a delicate one as a political matter. Where it seems unwise to undertake that task, the law might nevertheless require that public hearings be held during the course of negotiations and that no contract provision be agreed to unless it has been the subject of such a hearing. Affected groups would thus get the opportunity to publicize their views and rally their political forces in hopes of affecting the bargain.

This may be at a cost, since negotiations are often thought best conducted away from the glare of the public spotlight. It may be a cost worth paying, however, if the views of substantial groups in the community are not represented at the bargaining table. In any event, one can claim for this proposal benefits in areas other than labor relations. Few areas of major public concern will profit more than the public schools from a multiplicity of Brandeisian "chambers of experimentation." For few institutions are more in quest of themselves and more at a loss to discover their identity.

The second proposal looks to the suggestive example of third party bargaining in San Francisco. In that city the Chamber of Commerce has at times become a de facto party to the bargaining between the city and its employees. The ability of the chamber to intervene stems from its ability to submit wage settlements to a referendum. Since a favorable vote is politically assured if the chamber agrees to the settlement, the unions involved have found it to their advantage to make their peace with the chamber as an independent party with an interest in the bargaining.

Analogous structures for the settlement of nonmonetary issues in which other groups in the community feel that they have an interest can be constructed. Intervention by a third party might be permitted on the petition of a certain number of citizens. Or a referendum over an issue might be required on such a petition, thus compelling the unions involved to seek out representatives of opposing interests. These devices may be too permissive to opposing interest groups, however, and too disruptive of the bargaining process. A structure might be created in which a member of the ratifying body, be it the board of aldermen, city council, or school board, can register his conditional dissent as to a particular nonmonetary provision in a contract while voting to approve the whole. If a certain percentage, 20 percent for instance, dissents to a provision, then a referendum will be held on that particular issue but only if a stated number of voters petition for it within a fixed period of time. Otherwise, the contract in toto will go into effect. Such a structure creates a deterrent to the resolution of hotly contested political issues at the bargaining table without concern for the interests of other groups in the society and encourages unions to seek out and bargain with these groups as third parties. A defeat in a referendum may be more damaging than a compromise worked out in advance. And, under this structure, the form of third party intervention and bargaining is left to the parties. The opposing interest groups, moreover, are compelled to work through the political process by exercising influence on their elected representatives. This permits the executive and the union to learn at a relatively early stage what groups are interested and to test the intensity and nature of that interest. And, finally, if agreement is not reached, the decision is left to the voters.

The third proposal is sharply different. It does not create a bargaining procedure for resolving issues with political impact but rather looks to the strict monitoring of the scope of bargaining by governmental commissions. The model is this: (1) A state with a general and comprehensive statute covering public employment, but with a provision limiting collective bargaining to carefully defined subject matters; and (2) the establishment of commissions of disinterested citizens, appointed by the governor, with a continuing charter to hold hearings from time to time, and, where it seems in the public interest, to make proposals to the legislature for special enactments permitting bargaining with respect to specific matters affecting the nature of the service performed by particular public employees. The model envisions a number of commissions, each with responsibility for particular professional and semiprofessional employees. It proceeds from the assumption that some bargaining over some aspects of the nature of the services performed by professional and semiprofessional public employees is desirable, but that the decision on this question should be the result of interactions and accommodations of competing interest groups. The model structures and institutionalizes that process in two steps: before the specialized commission, and then before the legislature. Only after legislation would there be collective bargaining.

All proposals have drawbacks: three-party bargaining makes agreement difficult to achieve; commissions complicate an already cumbersome process. No proposal, quite apart from these drawbacks, can possibly *solve* the underlying problem. But each may make the problem more manageable and contribute to the formation of a better collective agreement.

CHAPTER TEN

Administration of the Collective Agreement

Once a collective agreement is formed it must be administered. And the development of grievance procedures and grievance arbitration machinery is essential to successful administration.[1] Union growth, collective bargaining, and procedures for contract administration are interdependent parts that can exist only together and that have jointly emerged in every successful labor growth period in this century.[2] Grievance procedures culminating in binding arbitration, for example, were a significant element in the first truly successful labor-management accords established in the volatile men's clothing industry during the second decade of the twentieth century.[3] Procedures for contract administration played a similar

1. Grievance arbitration—the use of a neutral third party to determine what an existing contract means or how it should be applied—is to be carefully distinguished from new contract arbitration, the use of third parties to write agreements.

2. See generally R. Fleming, *The Labor Arbitration Process* (University of Illinois Press, 1965), pp. 1–19.

3. See generally E. Morehouse, "Industrial Law in the Making: A Study of the Rochester Clothing Market, 1919–1922" (Ph.D. dissertation, University of Wisconsin, 1927); G. Soule and J. M. Budish, *The New Unionism in the Clothing Industry* (Harcourt, Brace and Howe, 1920); D. Straus, "Hickey-Freeman Company and Amalgamated Clothing Workers of America," prepared for the NPA Committee on the Causes of Industrial Peace Under Collective Bargaining, Case Study No. 4 (National Planning Association, 1949); M. Josephson, *Sidney Hillman: Statesman of American Labor* (Doubleday, 1952).

role in the First World War growth period, while the great surge in private sector organized labor, from 1935 to 1945, led to the almost universal adoption of formal grievance procedures ending generally in binding arbitration.[4]

Contract administration, however, has not been central among the issues arising from the growth of public sector bargaining; by and large it has received distinctly secondary consideration.[5] Legislatures and state and local negotiators understandably have taken the short-range view, attending principally to the more immediate problems of recognition and certification, initial contract negotiation, and methods of resolving impasses. This has meant that public sector grievance procedures have usually relied on the private sector model. Attention has not been turned toward managing the special problems that arise when the employer is a municipality. And some commentators, evidently buoyed by reports of existing public sector grievance procedures providing binding arbitration,[6] advance a conventional wisdom that concludes that private sector procedures should be transplanted intact to the public sector.[7] This view is not wholly erroneous but it may be dangerous. It tends to discount the difficulties of transplant as well as to ignore the fact that grievance procedures in the public sector

4. It is commonly estimated that about 94 percent of all extant collective bargaining agreements in the private sector provide some form of binding grievance arbitration. Bureau of National Affairs Collective Bargaining Negotiations and Contract Service, Vol. 2, § 51, p. 6 (April 2, 1970).

5. But see Pennsylvania Public Employee Relations Act, § 604(5), S.B. 1333, L. 1970, *Government Employee Relations Report*, No. 359, p. E-3.

6. See, for example, J. Ringer, Note, "Legality and Propriety of Agreements to Arbitrate Major and Minor Disputes in Public Employment," 54 *Cornell Law Review* 129–30 (1968); Note, "Arbitration and Agency Shops as Mandatory Subjects of Bargaining," 14 *Wayne Law Review* 1238 (1968). The American Federation of State, County, and Municipal Employees believes that over half of its current agreements provide for the binding arbitration of grievances. Letter from Clare D. Belman, research economist, AFSCME, Oct. 21, 1969.

7. H. Blaine, E. Hagburg, and F. Zeller, "The Grievance Procedure and Its Application in the United States Postal Service," 15 *Lab. L.J.* 725, 726, 734 (1964); J. Welch, "Municipal Collective Bargaining Agreements: Are They Ultra Vires?" 20 *Case-W. Res. L. Rev.* 637, 650 (1969); Executive Committee, National Governors' Conference, *Report of Task Force on State and Local Government Labor Relations* (1967), pp. 5, 22; K. Hanslowe, *The Emerging Law of Labor Relations in Public Employment* (Public Personnel Association, 1967), pp. 29, 32; C. Killingsworth, "Grievance Adjudication in Public Employment," 13 *Arb. J.* (n.s.) 3, 8 (1958); Note, "Arbitration and Agency Shops," pp. 1238, 1239–40; F. Suagee, "Grievance Arbitration in Public Employment," in K. Ocheltree (ed.), *Perspectives in Public Employee*

often are not functioning according to expectations, even where the procedures are most firmly established, namely, among employees who work in jobs similar to those found in private employment.[8]

Administration of the collective agreement in both private and public employment may be broken down for analytic purposes into three problem areas: grievance procedure, arbitration, and individual rights in the collective agreement. Each area has its special difficulties where the agreement is between a union and a local government. These difficulties are rooted in the nature and structure of municipal and county governments and are closely related to some of the problems that arise in the establishment of collective bargaining and the negotiation of the collective agreement.

The Grievance Procedure

Collective bargaining agreements establish the ground rules for the employment relationship. Applying these general rules to particular situations, however, will—no matter how careful the draftsmen have been—raise legitimate questions of interpretation. Nor can the rules deal fully with all employment decisions management must make during contract time. No one can be so foresighted, and no negotiations could survive the attempt. Disputes in the administration of the contract are inescapable and must, therefore, be disposed of in a systematic and orderly fashion. This is attempted in almost all collective agreements through the grievance procedure, a multistep process of dispute resolution.

MANAGEMENT AUTHORITY

One of the cornerstones of a successful grievance procedure is the relationship between the first-line representatives, the union steward or local president and the foreman or first-line supervisor.

Negotiation (Public Personnel Association, 1969), p. 73.

8. See J. Krislov and J. Schmulowitz, "Grievance Arbitration in State and Local Government Units," 18 *Arbitration Journal* (n.s.) 171 (1963); J. Ullman and J. Begin, "The Structure and Scope of Appeals Procedures for Public Employees," 23 *Industrial and Labor Relations Review* 323 (April 1970).

Without daily accommodation of the bulk of the problems brought to these representatives, higher levels of the grievance procedure would become choked. Few grievances should be permitted to go beyond the first line and travel upward toward arbitration. The typical three- or four-step procedure in the private sector resembles a pyramid, fewer grievances surviving each step. Management, in fact, often keeps elaborate figures on lower-level settlement in order to spot a potential source of clogging in the system. The private sector union understands these facts of the grievance procedure too; a union tactic for "getting" an unpopular foreman is to increase the number of grievances coming to him and to refuse to settle them at the first step, purposely sending them to higher management.[9]

But in public employment one is confronted with severe impediments to the establishment of a functioning procedure on the management side. Public management often is weak at the lower levels, while many lower level governmental supervisors—those who would be the first line of managerial authority in the private sector—are themselves active union members. In Detroit, for example, where three levels of supervisors are organized, the personnel director has suggested that the union itself is in a crossfire since it is possible for an employee-steward to represent his own supervisor before higher management, or for a supervisor-steward to represent a subordinate employee. And a firefighters' local in Cincinnati had to hire an attorney to represent it at disciplinary hearings in order to avoid subjecting union officers to charges of insubordination. A genuine grievance system is impossible, concludes a district director of the American Federation of State, County, and Municipal Employees, so long as supervisors are in the union. The development of an effective grievance procedure and a mature collective bargaining relationship, therefore, may depend on implementing the recommendation of Chapter 7 that truly supervisory employees be excluded from the public employee bargaining law.[10]

9. Cf. the chapter entitled "How to Build a Fire under the Foreman," in D. Beeler and H. Kurshenbaum, *How to Be a More Effective Union Representative* (Roosevelt University Press, 1965), pp. 79–84.

10. See pp. 113–14, above.

CIVIL SERVICE

As already seen, the establishment of collective bargaining in a city or county can result in considerable friction with an entrenched civil service commission over the questions of who represents local government for purposes of negotiation and what the scope of negotiation will be. Friction with civil service also can exist in the administration of the collective agreement, for a traditional function of civil service is to provide governmental employees with a structured procedure for appealing discharges. Conflict, however, has generally been resolved, but at the cost of efficiency. Accommodation with civil service is achieved by establishing independent and parallel procedures. And inefficiency is especially high where there are governmental departments, in addition to civil service, with a voice in the outcome.

Consider Boston. There, an employee who is disciplined may resort to four appeals procedures. These procedures are not mutually exclusive; rather, the employee may use them one after the other, until all four have been exhausted. First, the employee is covered by the departmental disciplinary appeals procedures. Normally this means that he has the right to appeal to the department head or the appointing authority. Second, the case can be appealed to the Civil Service Commission. Third, he can appeal the decision of the commission to the local district court. Finally, an employee who has lost may take his discharge to the Retirement Board. Presumably, this appeal exists because an employee has some vested rights in his pension and the Retirement Board is charged with the responsibility for protecting those rights. It may do so by ordering reinstatement.

Thus, in one case, a fire alarm inspector was discharged for a conflict of interest. He had money in a fire alarm installation firm. After losing appeals through the first three procedures, the inspector went to the Retirement Board. It reversed the actions of the Civil Service Commission and of the district court and ordered his reinstatement with back pay.

Another example of competing appeals systems is found in Multnomah County (Portland), Oregon. In all of its negotiated contracts the county has a grievance procedure that is independent of the Multnomah County Civil Service Commission and covers all discipline including discharge. The county charter, however, states that all discharged employees have a right to go to the Civil Service Commission. And, according to the secretary of the commission, whatever has happened before the commission takes jurisdiction is of no concern to it.

Therefore, a discharged employee first may go through the entire negotiated grievance procedure, which ends in a final decision by the County Board of Supervisors or by the Oregon State Mediation and Conciliation Service. He then may receive de novo consideration of his case by the County Civil Service Commission. Moreover, if the decision of the Civil Service Commission is not unanimous, he can appeal again to the county board. Finally, he can appeal the board's decision to the district court.

Detroit also has an inefficient grievance procedure as a result of civil service. Employees there have a right to appeal a discharge or suspension to the Civil Service Commission even after going through grievance arbitration.

It seems clear that there is no reason whatsoever for these parallel procedures except the vested interests of civil service commissions.

POLITICS AND GRIEVANCES

While politics is an integral part of the negotiating process in public employment, it is difficult to assess its role in the resolution of grievances. It is not difficult, however, to assess its legitimacy. Essential as politics is to the making of the bargain, it should have no place in the administration of the contract. Fairness demands evenhanded application of work rules. Indeed, this is a paramount justification for unionization in public as well as in private employment. Yet the ideal is hard to realize.

One story, related by an interviewer, is that the mayor of a Rhode Island city was himself the last step in the grievance procedure. His arbitral excellence was reflected in a decision to reinstate (but transfer) a black truck driver who had allegedly been fired for using "foul" language but whose actual insubordination was, according to the interviewer, political unreliability. The mayor's decision was based on the fact that the man had supported him in the last election *and* had ten more voters in his family. In

Philadelphia a student of labor relations has noted that the "third route" in grievance processing "most frequently employed in the case of a contested discharge is for the employee to exert political influence through his councilman."[11] In Rochester, New York, ward leaders were traditionally used by public employees as their grievance channel, while in Chicago, Mayor Richard J. Daley is still the final step in at least some grievance procedures.

One can expect a decline in the resolution of grievances based on political considerations as collective bargaining gains in acceptance and its processes become better understood. For politicians may welcome contractually established grievance procedures as a way out of intervention. The transitional period may produce abundant unhappiness on the part of some union leaders and others who have benefited from political settlements, but a fair and truly impartial procedure with arbitration should win acceptance among many union members, particularly since the present system cannot provide "equality of pull" among all workers. And it would certainly contribute to public management morale by providing a thick buffer cushioning supervisors from nettling political interference.

Arbitration

The terminal step in most grievance procedures in the private sector is arbitration; and where collective bargaining has established itself in public employment, arbitration is increasingly prevalent.[12] It is adjudication of a dispute by a neutral rather than negotiation by the parties. The latter characterizes earlier steps in the grievance procedure. But accommodation is not foreign to the arbitration process, any more than argumentation in terms of rights established in the contract is alien to the procedure employed in the earlier steps of the process. Yet, because accommo-

11. H. Berger, "The Grievance Process in the Philadelphia Public Service," 13 *Ind. & Lab. Rel. Rev.* 568, 571 (1960).

12. In 1967 394 AFSCME agreements provided for a formal grievance procedure. Of these, 208 provided for final and binding arbitration (Supp. No. 1967-10, *AFSCME Education and Research Guide*, Vols. 1 & 2). The union's research economist estimates that "half or more of our current agreements provide for binding arbitration." Letter from Clare D. Belman, Oct. 21, 1969. See generally Ullman and Begin, "Appeals Procedures."

dation is a part of arbitration, it raises special problems for public employment.

One of private management's major complaints about grievance arbitration is that, because it tends to accommodate interests as well as adjudicate rights, unions frequently gain what they have not been able to win at the bargaining table. The complaint is loudest if it is thought that what the union has gained is at the expense of a management prerogative, particularly one enshrined as a nonmandatory subject of bargaining.[13] Take, as an example, the famous *Warrior & Gulf Navigation Co.* case.[14] An issue for the arbitrator was the contractual legality of contracting work out of the bargaining unit. Management argued that this was, in terms, a management prerogative under the contract and that it was not a matter that the arbitrator could decide at all (it was not arbitrable), let alone decide for the union. At the time, moreover, it might well have been thought that contracting out was not a mandatory subject of bargaining, although, of course, it would be a permissible one.

How frequently arbitrators in fact do what employers say they often do is difficult to judge. But it does happen, because unions press for it and because grievance arbitration involves, to some extent at least, the accommodation of interests as well as the adjudication of rights. Nor, in the private sector, is there much check on the arbitrator. The scope of judicial review has been sharply limited by the Supreme Court.[15]

Whatever one's judgment on the wisdom or unwisdom of accommodation in private sector grievance arbitration, it is dangerous business in the public sector. Because the scope of bargaining has vast social implications in public employment, arbitrators should not be allowed to extend the area of union control through the settlement of grievances. The arbitrator must be given nar-

13. See, for example, address of Francis A. O'Connell, vice president, Employee Relations, Olin Mathieson Chemical Corporation, before the Collective Bargaining Forum, May 19, 1970, in New York City, published in *Collective Bargaining Today,* Proceedings of Collective Bargaining Forum, May 18–20, 1970 (BNA, 1971).

14. *United Steelworkers of America* v. *Warrior & Gulf Navigation Co.,* 363 U.S. 574 (1960).

15. *United Steelworkers of America* v. *Enterprise Wheel & Car Corp.,* 363 U.S. 593 (1960); *United Steelworkers* v. *Warrior & Gulf Navigation Co.,* 363 U.S. 574 (1960); *United Steelworkers* v. *American Manufacturing Co.,* 363 U.S. 564 (1960).

rower boundaries than he is accustomed to in the private sector. This can be accomplished partially in public employee bargaining statutes. Legislation should require clauses in all arbitration agreements that confine the arbitrator to the express terms of the agreement and prohibit him from holding arbitrable any issue that is a specifically prohibited subject of bargaining under state law. A proviso that the arbitrator's opinion must at least set forth its grounds, to facilitate judicial review, would also be appropriate. This review, moreover, should be searching. The private sector practice of judicial deference to the arbitrator on the issue of arbitrability[16] is particularly inappropriate in the public sector and should be rejected by state courts. Grievance arbitration can be very useful in the public sector, but it should not be the institution through which the union extends its area of control over issues that belong to the political process.

Individual Rights in the Collective Agreement

The interest of the individual employee is generally well served in the grievance procedure by his representative, the union. Typically, it is the union that brings the grievance and pursues it through the several steps spelled out in the contract, and, if necessary, on to arbitration. But, as we have learned from experience in the private sector, it would be a terrible mistake to assume that congruity of interests between union and individual always exists. Divergence is possible because of a reasonable disagreement as to what the contract provides, because the interests of the individual and those of a majority of employees do not coincide, because the individual is a political rival of the union president, because he is black and a majority of the union is white, because he is disliked, against union policy, unwilling to do what he is told to do, and so forth. And divergence of interests may occur at any stage of the grievance procedure. The union may decline to process a grievance at all, take it through some steps and drop it, or refuse to go to arbitration.

While potential conflict between individual and union exists at the precontract negotiation stage as well, it is most troublesome

16. *Ibid.*

during contract administration. This may be because at that stage the employee is viewed as having rights that grow out of an existing agreement, rather than amorphous and hard-to-define interests in a yet to be achieved contractual settlement.

Be that as it may, the private sector has developed a bewilderingly complicated and relatively unsatisfactory body of law to deal with the problem.[17] The law is complicated largely because of the complexities in the underlying problem. On the one hand, if collective bargaining is to be an orderly, efficient process that brings stability to labor relations, it is desirable to place the employer in a position where he is able to work out binding settlements with the union, and the union alone. On the other hand, the individual needs protection from the union that fails adequately to represent his interests.

One approach to the problem is to give the individual employee a cause of action against the union if it fails to represent him fairly; but to give him no redress against the employer. Indeed, the duty of fair representation exists in the private sector under federal law. It has, however, been much hedged about. The other approach is to give the employee a direct and individual right in the collective agreement, recognize the fact that this right may undercut efficiency and stability, but recognize also that the effect of this can be grossly overestimated and that institutions have ways of adapting themselves. Federal law recognizes individual rights in the contract. It also hedges them about.[18]

Whatever one's position as to what the law should be in the private sector,[19] it seems clear that in municipal collective bargaining the individual should have access, as an individual, to the grievance procedure, arbitration, and the courts. Without collective bargaining, there is no comparable right in private employment. In public employment such a right generally does obtain and is administered by civil service commissions. While it has been argued that these commissions have no legitimate role in the reso-

17. See generally H. Wellington, *Labor and the Legal Process* (Yale University Press, 1968), pp. 129–84.

18. See *Vaca* v. *Sipes*, 386 U.S. 171 (1967).

19. Compare C. Summers, "Individual Rights in Collective Agreements and Arbitration," 37 *New York University Law Review* 362 (1962), with A. Cox, "Rights Under a Labor Agreement," 69 *Harvard Law Review* 601 (February 1956).

lution of grievances where collective bargaining is established, the protection afforded the individual under civil service should not be lost with their demise. Such protection may be retained by giving the employee generous individual rights in the collective agreement.

Of course, the union's interests must be protected. It should be able to argue for its interpretation of the contract at each level of the grievance procedure, in arbitration, and before the court. Nor, where its antagonistic position is reasonable, should it have to bear the costs of the individual's case.[20] But these are minor and easily resolved difficulties when compared to some of the problems addressed in this chapter, problems that must be faced when techniques of contract administration are transplanted from the private to the public sector. None of the problems discussed here, however, compares in difficulty to either the scope-of-bargaining issue, explored in Chapter 9, or the strike question, to which the remainder of the book is devoted.

20. See generally Summers, "Individual Rights."

PART FOUR

The Strike and Its Alternatives

CHAPTER ELEVEN

The Illegal Strike Model

Distortion of the political process is the major, long-run social cost of strikes in public employment. The distortion results from union's obtaining too much power, relative to other interest groups, in decisions affecting the level of taxes and the allocation of tax dollars. This distortion therefore may result in a redistribution of income by government, whereby union members are subsidized at the expense of other interest groups. And where nonmonetary issues, such as the decentralization of the governance of schools or the creation of a civilian board to review police conduct, are resolved through bargaining in which the strike or threat thereof is used, the distortion of the political process is no less apparent.

It has been earnestly argued, however, that if public employee unions are successfully denied the strike,[1] they will have too little

1. If a strike is illegal, the question arises of what "job actions," short of the full and concerted withholding of services, constitute the proscribed conduct. This will depend in part upon the language of the state public employee bargaining statute. See *Holland School District for the City of Holland, Ottawa and Allegan Counties* v. *Holland Education Association*, 380 Mich. 314, 157 N.W. 2d 206 (1968), for an interpretation of the Michigan statute, Mich. Comp. Laws Ann., § 423.201 (1967). "In *Holland* there was a concerted refusal to work; consequently, once the employment relationship had been established, the court did not have to interpret the facts liberally in order to hold that the refusal was a 'strike'. But in other cases, employee activities short of refusals to work . . . have been broadly construed as strikes. For example, National Education Association 'sanctions' have been held to constitute a strike [*Board of Education of Union Beach* v. *New Jersey Education Association*, 53 N.J. 29, 247 A.2d (1968) (blacklisting of school district

relative power.[2] To unpack the claims in this argument is crucially important. In the private sector, collective bargaining depends on the strike threat and the occasional strike. It is how deals are made, how collective bargaining works, why employers agree to terms and conditions of employment better than they originally offered. Intuition suggests that what is true of the private sector also is true of the public. Without the strike threat and the strike, the public employer will be intransigent; and this intransigence will, in effect, deprive employees of the very benefits unionization was intended to bring to them. Collective bargaining, the argument goes, will be merely a façade for "collective begging."

Initially, it must be noted that even in the absence of unionism and bargaining, the market imposes substantial limits on the ability of public employers to "take advantage" of their employees. Because they must compete for workers with private employers and other units of government as well, public employers cannot permit their wages and conditions of employment to be relatively poorer than those offered in the private sector and still get the needed workers. And, as noted in Chapter 1, the fact that most public employees work in areas in which there are numerous alternative employment opportunities reduces the likelihood that many public employers are monopsonists. Even if they are, moreover, the lack of a profit motive reduces the likelihood that government's monopsony power, if it exists, will be exercised.[3]

In any event, much of the argument about the role of the strike is overstated. First, it exaggerates the power of the strike weapon in the private sector. As argued in Chapter 1,[4] the power of private sector unions to gain comparative advantages, while real, is in-

. . .)] as have firefighters' partial staffing campaigns [271 *Government Employee Relations Report,* B-9 (Nov. 18, 1968)]. Greater definitional problems arise, however, when the alleged strike consists of 'working by the rules' or, in the case of policemen, strict enforcement of the law." "Collective Bargaining for Public Employees and the Prevention of Strikes in the Public Sector," 68 *Michigan Law Review* 260, 264–265 (December 1969).

2. See, for example, D. Wollett, "The Taylor Law and the Strike Ban," in H. Anderson (ed.), *Public Employee Organization and Bargaining* (Bureau of National Affairs, 1968), p. 29; T. Kheel, "Strikes and Public Employment," 67 *Michigan Law Review* 931 (March 1969).

3. See pp. 13–14, 18, above.

4. See pp. 15–17, above.

herently limited by what was there called the employment-benefit trade-off.

Second, the very unionization of public employees creates a powerful interest group, at least in large urban centers, that seems able to compete very well with other groups in the political decision-making process.[5] Indeed, collective bargaining (the strike apart) is a method of channeling and underscoring the demands of public employees that is not systematically available to other groups. Public employee unions frequently serve as lobbying agents wielding political power quite disproportionate to the size of their membership. The failure of the Hartford firefighters, mentioned earlier, to seek formal status as a bargaining agent demonstrates how much punch such organizations can wield. And where a strong local labor council exists, association with it can significantly increase the power of public employee unions. This provides some assurance, therefore, that public employees, even if prohibited from striking, will not be at a comparative disadvantage in bargaining with their employers.

Thus, on the merits, the argument for the strike in public employment is hardly inexorable. But the merits are only part of reality. The attitudes and convictions of public employees and their leaders cannot be put aside. There simply cannot be an effective ban on strikes if public employees believe that they are being treated in a relatively unfair fashion without running the risk of a major political crisis in which the ultimate coercive power of the state must be used on a large scale against its own employees.

If this analysis is correct, a major problem for those designing legislation for labor relations in the public sector is to create institutions capable of achieving a high degree of acceptability. Because most men are greedy and few are deterred by legal norms that, while wise, are hard to explain, nothing may prove wholly effective in the quest to eliminate public employee strikes. If this proves to be the case, the municipal employer will have to be

5. Thus, for example, San Francisco municipal employees did very well without the strike and, indeed, without real collective bargaining for many years. And in New Haven, collective bargaining worked well without the strike or strike threat. In both cities the unions were skillful participants in the political process. Compare R. Dahl, *Who Governs? Democracy and Power in an American City* (Yale University Press, 1961), pp. 253–55.

made less vulnerable to the strike. At any rate, one thing seems sure: lacking institutional arrangements more or less acceptable to all the parties, some strikes are inevitable when collective bargaining leads to an impasse. What follows is a discussion of arrangements that, while they prohibit strikes, provide mechanisms to temper the impact of the prohibition.

Post-impasse Procedures without a Final Settlement Mechanism

In Pennsylvania, Hawaii, and Vermont it appears to be legal for at least some public employees to strike, unless—in the language of the Vermont statute—to do so "will endanger the health, safety or welfare of the public"; and in some other states, such as Michigan, it may prove difficult to obtain an injunction against an illegal strike.[6] However, most states that have addressed the question through legislative act or judicial decision impose a legal prohibition, backed by the injunctive remedy, on strikes by public employees.[7] A number of states that have enacted comprehensive statutes providing for collective bargaining in the public sector, moreover, have developed institutions aimed at making the strike ban effective.

FACT-FINDING WITH RECOMMENDATIONS

Many statutes provide for fact-finding with recommendations or its virtual equivalent, advisory arbitration, when an impasse exists after both bargaining and mediation.[8] Considerable discussion of these post-impasse procedures has appeared lately in the learned journals, and an issue with jurisprudential pretensions has sur-

6. Vt. Stat. Ann., Tit. 21. § 1704 (Supp. 1970); Mich. Comp. Laws Ann., §§ 423.201–.254 (1966); and see *Holland School District* v. *Holland Education Association*, 380 Mich. 314, 157 N.W. 2d 206 (1968).

7. See, for example, Conn. Gen. Stat. Ann, §§ 7-467 to 7-478 (Supp. 1970); Minn. Stat. Ann., § 179.51 (1966); N.J. Stat. Ann., §§ 34.13 A-1 to 34:13 A-9 (Supp. 1970); N.Y. Civ. Serv. Law, § 210 (McKinney Supp. 1970); Wis. Stat. Ann., § 111.70 (4) (Supp. 1970).

8. See, for example, Conn. Gen. Stat. Ann., §§ 7-467 to 7-478 (Supp. 1970); Mass. Ann. Laws, Ch. 149, § 178D (1962), §§ 178F–N (Supp. 1970); Mich. Comp. Laws Ann., §§ 423.201–.254 (1966); N.Y. Civ. Serv. Law, §§ 200–12 (McKinney Supp. 1970); Wis. Stat. Ann., §§ 111.70 and 111.80–.94 (Supp. 1970).

faced.[9] What should fact-finding with recommendations be? Should it be adjudication or adjustment, a judicial process or supermediation? Although these questions are best dealt with in terms of the goals to be achieved by the procedures, some initial misconceptions generated by the manner in which the questions are put must be cleared away.

To ask whether fact-finding with recommendations should be viewed as adjudication through a judicial proceeding is to suggest that fact-finding with recommendations can approximate a typical case in a court of law. It cannot, and for fundamental reasons rooted in the nature of the judicial process. Courts generally decide disputes over rights and obligations in terms of standards knowable to the parties at the time the dispute arose. While this may not mean that there is only one correct resolution of any dispute, it does mean that judges generally have limited discretion in the decision-making process.

Only in a Pickwickian mood would one suggest that a post-impasse tribunal must decide a dispute over rights and obligations in terms of standards knowable to the parties at the time the dispute arose. The issues before such a tribunal are so much more fluid in terms of decisional standards as to be of a totally different order from those faced by judges. The legitimate discretion of the decision maker is enormous relative to that generally accorded judges. In the absence of limiting authoritative instructions—a statute or agreement of the parties—the boundaries of that discretion are fixed by the goals of the procedure, namely, a resolution acceptable to all the parties, including the governmental entity with de facto control of the budget.

9. See J. McKelvey, "Fact Finding in Public Employment Disputes: Promise or Illusion?" 22 *Industrial and Labor Relations Review* 528 (July 1969); W. Gould, "Public Employment: Mediation, Fact Finding and Arbitration," 55 *American Bar Association Journal* 835 (September 1969); J. Stern, "The Wisconsin Public Employee Fact-Finding Procedure," 20 *Industrial and Labor Relations Review* 3 (1966); C. Schmidt, "Observations on the Process of Fact-Finding in Michigan Public Education Teacher–School Board Contract Disputes," in H. Anderson (ed.), *Public Employee Organization and Bargaining*, p. 81; R. Howlett, "Arbitration in the Public Sector," in *Labor Law Developments*, Proceedings, 1969, Southwestern Legal Foundation, Fifteenth Annual Institute on Labor Law, pp. 231, 249; A. Anderson, "The Use of Fact-Finding in Dispute Settlement," paper delivered before National Academy of Arbitrators, in G. Somers (ed.), *Arbitration and Social Change*, Proceedings of the Twenty-Second Annual Meeting, National Academy of Arbitrators, Jan. 29–31, 1969 (Bureau of National Affairs, 1969).

The question of what is an acceptable result depends, of course, on a variety of factors. And there are a number of related ways to view these factors. One is to look at the power configuration within a municipality. Consider what may be the hardest case, namely, where the governmental unit that negotiates does not have effective political control of the budget. If the final budgetary authority[10]—the city legislative body—is not the governmental branch that negotiates—the executive—there is a high probability of contract rejection when the union's political power is substantially less vis-à-vis the legislative body than the executive.

If a post-impasse tribunal's processes are invoked after rejection of a contract by the legislature, the central fact the tribunal must determine, if it is to function effectively, is the existence of the political situation that has been hypothesized. The tribunal's principal task is to help work out an agreement acceptable to union, executive, and legislature. This task does not entail a disinterested and principled quest for "truth"—beyond an accurate assessment of political forces—unless that is thought to be the best tactic for gaining acceptability.[11] Accommodation among the disputants, not the principled application of preexisting standards, is the goal. The job of the post-impasse tribunal is to achieve a contract, and that may mean recommending that employees earn more than the tribunal believes they are "worth" by other arguably relevant standards. Maximizing long-run public welfare in the sense of finding what the services are "worth" or what settlement is "fair" —by looking to the demand for, or supply of, labor or to comparable private sector wages, for instance—is not the job of the post-

10. The final budgetary authority is not necessarily the legislature: "Where the legislative body is the town meeting, approval of the [collective bargaining] agreement by a majority of the selectmen shall make the agreement valid and binding upon the town and the board of finance shall appropriate or provide whatever funds are necessary to comply with such collective bargaining agreement." Conn. Gen. Stat. Ann., § 7-474(b) (Supp. 1970). See also § 7-468(c).

11. Compare Marshall, Report 29, *City of Watertown* v. *International Brotherhood of Teamsters, Local 695* (July 20, 1964), quoted in H. Anderson (ed.), *Public Employee Organization and Bargaining*, p. 15. Recall that we are, by hypothesis, describing a situation where the strike is illegal. Here, we assume also that the unions will obey the law, at least as a general proposition. Accordingly, if there is a distortion of political power in the municipality, it is unrelated to the strike or strike threat. In Chapter 12 we deal with the situation where a strike ban will not work because unions regularly can be expected to break the law.

impasse tribunal. Indeed, the tribunal's quest is always inconsistent with maximizing public welfare in that sense, except for the case in which the balance of political forces fortuitously leads to a result consistent with it.

A second way to approach the question of what factors make a result acceptable is to attend to the institutional arrangements, rather than to the power relationships, that exist in a particular situation. A post-impasse tribunal's role must vary according to whether law or practice makes it difficult for the union to bypass one branch of the public employer, the executive for instance, and "bargain" with another, the legislative body. For where a union is able to choose its ultimate bargaining partner, the post-impasse tribunal may find either itself bypassed or its position undermined. In an earlier chapter it was pointed out that while municipal practices vary enormously, the bypass problem is very often significant.[12]

Finally, but without any suggestion that the subject has been exhausted, the factors affecting the acceptability of a post-impasse tribunal's recommendation may be illustrated by asking whom the tribunal is trying to influence. Several possibilities, of which the following are examples, suggest themselves: (1) Where those negotiating for the public employer have effective political control over its budget, recommendations serve functions similar to recommendations of post-impasse tribunals in the private sector. They may aid the parties by fashioning inventive solutions to the impasse, or they may crystallize public opinion and thus exert pressure toward a negotiated settlement growing out of the recommendations.[13] (2) In the more usual situation, where there is some effective review by a budgetary authority, recommendations may serve the additional function of influencing that authority directly through the persuasiveness and prestige of the tribunal, and indirectly through public opinion.

This brief discussion of the theory of fact-finding with recommendations will now be followed by an examination of its procedures in the practice of some states that employ it.

12. See pp. 121–25, above.

13. See H. Wellington, *Labor and the Legal Process* (Yale University Press, 1968), pp. 284–85.

FACT-FINDING PROCEDURES

The states are truly chambers of experimentation in the field of public employment and collective bargaining. Fact-finding with recommendations, however, is something of an exception, since any variations are generally matters of procedural detail rather than fundamental structure. These differences exist with respect to such questions as: who may invoke the post-impasse procedure and at what point in time; how is the tribunal chosen and who pays for its services; and finally, what is the official attitude toward mediation by the fact-finders?

If, as has been argued, the goal of these procedures is a settlement acceptable to all parties, and if achieving this depends on the several factors outlined, considerable flexibility should be built into any statutory scheme. There is, however, a consideration that places some limits on the degree of permissible flexibility. The post-impasse procedure should not hinder collective bargaining. The major hope for avoiding strikes in the public sector is not the post-impasse procedure but the bargaining process; not the resolution of impasses but their avoidance. Resort to post-impasse procedures, therefore, ought not be so automatic as to become a routine step in the process of reaching a settlement. For if it does, serious bargaining may be deferred until the procedures are invoked, and impasses will also become routine.[14]

It should, therefore, be relatively difficult for the parties to obtain the services of a post-impasse tribunal, and those services should be relatively expensive—but only relatively, because the overriding aim is to achieve a peaceful settlement, not to limit the role of outside intervention. When it can help, the post-impasse tribunal should not be priced out of the market, nor should the parties, for other reasons, fail to use it.

Several states attempt to limit the chilling effect of fact-finding with recommendations by vesting an agency with the task of deter-

14. This phenomenon has occurred in some teacher–school board negotiations in Connecticut. The Connecticut Teacher Negotiation Act, Conn. Gen. Stat. Ann., §§ 10-153(a), (e), (f) (1958), §§ 10-153(b)–(d), (f) (Supp. 1970), provides for mediation after an impasse, and then for advisory arbitration. In some cases, the parties defer serious bargaining because they anticipate arbitration and fear the effect of serious bargaining, with the compromises it entails, on their success in arbitration.

mining, prior to the selection of the post-impasse tribunal, whether a bona fide impasse exists. The agency is normally provided with some criteria as to what constitutes an impasse. In Connecticut, for example, the State Board of Mediation and Arbitration, on receipt of a petition requesting fact-finding from either a municipal employer, a union, or both, must investigate and determine whether, "after a reasonable period of negotiation over the terms of an agreement a dispute" exists between the parties or whether "no agreement has been reached within a reasonable period of time prior to the final date for setting the municipal budget."[15] The Massachusetts statute is virtually identical, and the Wisconsin provisions similar.[16]

In New York an impasse is defined in terms of the budget submission date—"an impasse may be deemed to exist if the parties fail to achieve agreement at least sixty days prior to the budget submission date of the public employer."[17] The Public Employment Relations Board performs much the same screening function under the New York statute as does the Board of Mediation and Arbitration in Connecticut. There are some nuances in the New York statute, however. First, the board, without the request of the parties, may initiate the post-impasse procedure. This seems desirable, for there may be situations where neither party will want to petition the board. On the other hand, a second aspect of the New York statute seems undesirable. Because the confidence of the parties in the post-impasse tribunal may be necessary for it to function successfully, the parties should participate in the selection of its membership. This is not provided for in New York, but it is in a number of other states.[18] The New York statute, however, does explicitly invite the parties to develop through contract their own post-impasse procedures.[19] If there is any truth in the widespread belief that people have more confidence in their own handiwork than in that of others, this explicit invitation makes sense. But there would seem to be no prohibition on contractual

15. Conn. Gen. Stat. Ann., § 7-473(a) (Supp. 1970).

16. Mass. Ann. Laws, Ch. 149, § 178F(7) (Supp. 1970); Wis. Stat. Ann., § 111.70(4) (e) and (f) (Supp. 1970) (municipal employees); Wis. Stat. Ann., § 111.88 (Supp. 1970) (state employees).

17. N.Y. Civ. Serv. Law, § 209, Para. 1 (McKinney Supp. 1970).

18. See, for example, Conn. Gen. Stat. Ann., § 7-473(b) (Supp. 1970).

19. N.Y. Civ. Serv. Law, § 209, Para. 2 (McKinney Supp. 1970).

arrangements of the type encouraged by New York in those states that are silent on the issue.

Several states deal with the problem of compensation for post-impasse fact-finding with recommendations.[20] As we noted, the problem is to make the process expensive enough to encourage settlement without its use, but not so expensive that it will not be invoked when it might prove helpful. A favored solution is to tax the parties equally for the service and to have the fees set by the agency charged with administering the post-impasse procedure.[21]

Several states also deal wisely with the mediation function of the post-impasse tribunal.[22] Recognizing that the goal of the procedure is to achieve a successful resolution of the dispute, they make it clear that the fact-finders are free to mediate.[23] Mediation is not a wise strategy in every situation, but it often can be very helpful. Attempts to separate the fact-finding–recommendation procedure from mediation, as in Michigan, seem misguided.[24]

20. In Connecticut, for example, the memorandum on fact-finding procedure promulgated by the State Board of Mediation and Arbitration provides: "The cost of fact finding, including fees and expenses, will be shared equally by the parties. . . . The fee schedule for days in which a fact finder conducts hearings or devotes to the study, and preparation of his report, is as follows: for cities with a population under 15,000, $100 per day; for cities of 15,000 to 50,000, $125 per day; and for cities of over 50,000, $150 per day. . . . Expenses incurred by the fact finder such as travel, rental of hearing rooms, and other necessary expenses will also be paid by the parties." *Fact Finding Procedure* (State of Connecticut, Board of Mediation and Arbitration, March 1967), p. 3.

21. See, for example, "Massachusetts Rules for Fact Finding," Rule 25, promulgated by the Board of Conciliation and Arbitration (April 3, 1968), reprinted in 4 *Labor Relations Reporter*, 31 S.L.L. 250(k) (1968).

22. See, for example, Conn. Gen. Stat. Ann., § 7-473(f) (Supp. 1970); Wis. Stat. Ann., § 111.88(3) (Supp. 1970).

23. Mass. Ann. Laws, Ch. 149, § 178J(f) (Supp. 1970). In those situations where the parties are unable to reach agreement on monetary issues, they have a tendency to postpone to the post-impasse stage the resolution of nonmonetary issues. Mediation at this point is often helpful in clearing up a number of these unresolved issues.

24. The chairman of the Michigan Labor Mediation Board has stated that board's view that mediation and fact-finding should be separated. "In 1968, we instructed our fact-finders to be judges, not mediators.

"We do not rule out an 'in chambers' settlement if it appears possible. In August/September, 1968, our fact-finders, particularly those with collective bargaining experience, were not always obedient to our instructions. They preferred to mediate. Some of the bargaining teams preferred it that way." R. Howlett, "Arbitration in the Public Sector," p. 249.

THE EFFECTS OF FACT-FINDING

The most interesting and sophisticated studies of the effects of fact-finding with recommendations have come from researchers at the Institute of Industrial Relations at the University of Wisconsin.[25] These studies evaluated post-impasse procedures in terms of what happens to disputes that go to fact-finding, whether it reduces strikes, how the parties view the process, and whether the process is overemployed and does deter collective bargaining. The studies suggest—and others elsewhere tend to confirm[26]—that fact-finding is generally successful.

While any evaluation is difficult because one does not know what would have happened without the existence or employment of the post-impasse procedure, the evidence shows that many disputes are resolved without the issuance of formal recommendations; that recommendations usually are accepted; that while there are strikes after recommendations, they are few; that in most jurisdictions the parties do not resort to fact-finding too frequently; and that, by and large, the parties regard these impasse tribunals as helpful.[27] Criticism exists, to be sure. Nonfinal post-impasse tribunals are no panacea, but expectations realistically set have not been disappointed.

Post-impasse Procedures Providing for Final Settlements

BINDING ARBITRATION: EFFECTIVENESS

Compulsory and binding arbitration is no panacea either. It does not prevent all work stoppages; witness the police strike of October 1969 in Montreal.[28] And it cannot help but chill the bargaining process, to some extent at least. The nature of these

25. See E. Krinsky, "An Analysis of Fact Finding as a Procedure for the Settlement of Labor Disputes Involving Public Employees" (unpublished, 1969); Stern, "The Wisconsin Public Employee Fact-Finding Procedure."

26. See McKelvey, "Fact-Finding," pp. 531–34.

27. See Krinsky, "Analysis of Fact Finding"; Anderson, "The Use of Fact Finding in Dispute Settlement," pp. 8–11.

28. The strike of policemen and firemen in Montreal followed a binding arbitration award granting a substantial wage increase, but refusing an increase that would establish parity with Toronto. Such parity has long been a goal of the police and firefighters' organizations in Montreal. See *New York Times*, Oct. 9, 1969, p. 3.

difficulties with compulsory and binding arbitration often is not fully understood by lawyer or layman.

Compulsory and binding arbitration seeks to prevent strikes in two ways, neither of which is completely successful. First, it attempts to enforce a settlement by application of legal sanctions. Ordinarily this will be enough for all but the aberrational case. And the occasional strikes that still occur sometimes may be prevented if the law responds with very harsh penalties. Such penalties, however, often do not have the support of the community and may stir a feeling of revulsion. In those circumstances they are unlikely to be effective[29] and, in any event, workers willing to accept such penalties can still make a strike effective. Legal sanctions, therefore, do not provide total protection.

Compulsory and binding arbitration, however, seeks to prevent strikes in a second way. Because the strike in private employment is viewed by many as a fundamental right located well within the foothills of the Constitution,[30] there is in some places a corresponding sense that laws against strikes in the public sector are unfair.[31] This attitude—which survives in a fierce state of tension with counter attitudes[32]—emboldens public employees to break

29. The history of the Condon-Wadlin law, Law of March 27, 1947, Ch. 391 (1947) N.Y. Laws 842, as amended, Law of April 23, 1963, Ch. 702 (1963) N.Y. Laws 2432 (repealed 1967), is the classic example. The statute required automatic dismissal of striking employees and a three-year ban on higher pay for any rehired striker, plus a five-year probationary period. In many situations it not only failed to deter strikes but was too harsh to be enforced. See P. Montana, "Striking Teachers, Welfare, Transit, and Sanitation Workers," 19 *Labor Law Journal* 273 (May 1968).

30. The principle is expressed, for example, in § 13 of the National Labor Relations Act, 29 U.S.C., § 163 (1964): "Nothing in this subchapter, except as specifically provided for herein, shall be construed so as either to interfere with or impede or diminish in any way the right to strike, or to affect the limitations or qualifications on that right."

31. "Ultimately, laws depend for their effectiveness upon voluntary acceptance by the vast majority of the decent persons in the groups regulated. Without such acceptance, the police and the courts are powerless to uphold the law, as our experience with prohibition proved. We see another demonstration of this truth when the words on the statute books were defied by a highly respectable, normally law-abiding group—public school teachers. In my view, the teachers were basically right. The law should not forbid them to strike merely because they are public employees." T. St. Antoine, "Public Employees and Strikes," 13 *Law Quadrangle Notes* 13, 19 (Winter 1969).

32. The "counter attitude" is dramatically reflected in the laws of the majority of the states, particularly those states where organized labor is strong and where collective bargaining for municipal employees has been established.

the law.[33] A procedure that offers public employees a seemingly fair alternative to the strike, however, may change the community's sense of the propriety of the strike and may in the long run influence the attitude of public employees. They may in time reach that desirable state of accepting an award that they find less than totally fair. This is the goal of compulsory arbitration, and is what differentiates it from nonfinality procedures. No moral imperative, above and beyond the preexisting moral imperative of not breaking the no-strike law, is generated by nonfinality procedures such as fact-finding with recommendations. They are advisory only. An aim of arbitration binding on both parties is to generate just such an imperative. Again, however, total success cannot be expected.

The second factor limiting the effectiveness of arbitration is that it deters collective bargaining. The point is simple enough. Either the public employer or the union will reckon that an arbitration award will be more advantageous than a negotiated settlement. That party will then employ tactics to ensure arbitration by bargaining without a sincere desire to reach agreement.[34]

It is almost impossible wholly to solve this problem; but the route to partial and perhaps satisfactory resolution is to fashion a procedure sufficiently diverse and uncertain as to make a negotiated settlement more attractive to the parties than arbitration.

The composition of an arbitration panel can importantly influence its award. Honest men acting disinterestedly often see things differently. The behaviorists are surely right in thinking that results are influenced by the perspectives of decision makers. Thus, to the extent that the composition of an arbitration panel is unknown beforehand and is outside the control of the parties, some uncertainty will exist. On the other hand, the parties are more likely to have confidence in an award rendered by arbitra-

33. "There is a readily discernible, sharply upward trend in the number of strikes in Government employment over the last decade and in the number of employees involved. From a total of only 15 strikes involving 1,700 workers in 1958, the numbers have grown to 254 strikes of 202,000 employees in 1968. . . . Preliminary figures for 1969 and estimates for the current year indicate the trend continues unabated." Twentieth Century Fund, Task Force on Labor Disputes in Public Employment, *Pickets at City Hall* (1970), p. 31. For details, see Appendix B, below.

34. The problem is discussed in more detail in Wellington, *Labor and the Legal Process,* pp. 288–91.

tors they have chosen. This tension can be eased by allowing each party to select one member of a three-man panel.

Another device to reduce the chilling effect is "one-or-the-other" arbitration, in which the arbitrator's choice would be limited to either the employer's final position or the union's final position—all of one or all of the other.[35] This creates some uncertainty but very high stakes, and the fact that the stakes are so high is counted on by its advocates to make "one-or-the-other" arbitration work. The predictions made are as follows: Employer and union, realizing that the arbitrator's power is limited to accepting the entire proposed contract of one or the other party, will each bargain in good faith and in great earnestness to reach an agreement. If this process fails to produce agreement, it will, nevertheless, narrow very substantially the area of disagreement as each party strains for a favorable decision from the arbitrators by attempting to make its position appear the more reasonable of the two.[36]

One-or-the-other arbitration has, however, substantive difficulties suggesting that it may work better in some disputes than in others.[37] If the parties assume positions out of ideological commitment rather than practical needs, the original disagreement may not be narrowed in the bargaining process by the all-or-nothing nature of possible arbitration.[38] The arbitrators, moreover, occasionally may not know what the effects of certain proposals would be. There is sometimes the danger of the seemingly more

35. See C. M. Stevens, "Is Compulsory Arbitration Compatible with Bargaining?" 5 *Industrial Relations* 38 (February 1966). The President has proposed a form of one-or-the-other arbitration in national transportation disputes. See 73 *Lab. Rel. Rep.* 197 (March 9, 1970).

36. With the agreement of the parties, one-or-the-other arbitration was used in a teacher–board of education dispute in Connecticut. The parties came to advisory arbitration after serious good faith bargaining had substantially narrowed the differences between them. The one-or-the-other suggestion, after it was explained to the parties and agreed to by them, led to several hours of bargaining that almost resulted in a contract.

37. Some insight into people's attitudes toward arbitration may be gleaned from their reactions to one-or-the-other arbitration. Perhaps it is because so many see arbitration as "adding up the claims on both sides of a dispute and dividing the sum by two" (*Local Union No. 28, International Brotherhood of Electrical Workers v. Maryland Chapter, National Electric Contractors Association,* 194 F. Supp. 494, 497 [D. Md., 1961]) that their first reaction to the one-or-the-other variety is to call it a game of Russian roulette.

38. This is more of a problem in the public sector than it is in the private. See pp. 21–24, above.

reasonable proposal being disruptive or otherwise impracticable. This may be an aggravated difficulty in the public sector where the complexity of municipal fiscal affairs or the heated political atmosphere surrounding particular nonmonetary issues obscures the stakes in the dispute.

BINDING ARBITRATION: LEGAL CONSIDERATIONS

The major legal threat—and puny it is—to compulsory and binding arbitration is the doctrine of illegal delegation. The constitution of each state gives legislative power to the legislature. The question is, to what extent can the legislature delegate that power? Of course it can delegate power over the wages and conditions of employment of municipal employees to municipal legislatures. If collective bargaining is legal in a state, the further delegation required by collective bargaining is legal. But the legislative body may exercise some continuing control. In Connecticut, for example, bargaining is between the executive and the employee representative, but the legislative body (the city council or the board of aldermen) must approve or disapprove in toto any contract negotiated by these parties with budgetary consequences.[39] Binding arbitration, however, if it means anything, means that it binds the legislative body as well as the executive and the employee representative; and this, it might be thought, could pose difficulties.

As it has evolved, the delegation doctrine, at least in most jurisdictions, is satisfied if there is a rational reason for the delegation, and if power is given to a state official who is directed to exercise it according to decisional standards supplied by the legislature.[40] This is probably too loose a formulation to satisfy the requirements for a legal delegation in any particular jurisdiction, but it should make clear that a legislature can, if it is careful, draft a binding arbitration statute and be reasonably confident that the statute will be held constitutional.

The most illuminating case addressing the constitutionality of

39. Conn. Gen. Stat. Ann., § 7-474 (Supp. 1970).

40. See, for example, *City of Warwick* v. *Warwick Regular Firemen's Association*, 256 A.2d 206 (R.I. 1969); "Collective Bargaining for Public Employees and the Prevention of Strikes in the Public Sector," 68 *Mich. L. Rev.* 260, 279–88 (1969).

binding arbitration involves a Rhode Island statute giving the right of collective bargaining to firefighters, and providing: "In the event that the bargaining agent and the corporate authorities are unable, within 30 days . . . to reach an agreement . . . all unresolved issues shall be submitted to arbitration."[41] Each party is given the responsibility of selecting an arbitrator; the two arbitrators selected are themselves to choose a third, who serves as chairman of the panel.[42]

This method of selecting the arbitration panel raises more legal difficulties than would other approaches. It makes it harder for a court to find that the arbitrators are state officials than would, for example, a statute that empowered the governor to appoint a standing panel of fifteen or twenty men from which a three-man arbitration board was chosen by the parties for a particular case. The Rhode Island Supreme Court, however, moved surely to its holding that the arbitrators were state officials and that the three-man panel was a state agency. Said the court:

> We find that the legislature delegated to each of the arbitrators a portion of the sovereign and legislative power of the government, particularly the power to fix the salaries of public employees, clearly a legislative function. It is clear that each arbitrator is free to perform this duty without control or supervision from any superior. It is also to be observed that the provisions . . . of the act establish a fixed term and specific duties for the incumbent. It is our conclusion then that an arbitrator appointed under the pertinent provisions of the statute is a public officer and that collectively the three constitute a public board or agency.[43]

The court also had no trouble, under the Rhode Island statute, with the question of decisional standards. "In the instant case," the court said, "the legislature prescribed standards for the exercise of the delegated power that clearly are reasonably open to the conclusion that the exercise of power by the arbitrators would be sufficiently confined to meet the constitutional requirements." The statute, as the court tells us,

> sets out specifically a number of comprehensive limitations on the actions of a board of arbitration when exercising the power delegated. They require that certain factors "be given weight by the arbitrators in arriving at a decision. . . ." These factors include specifically a compari-

41. R.I. Gen. Laws, § 28-9.1–7 (1961).
42. R.I. Gen. Laws, § 28-9.1–8 (Supp. 1970).
43. *City of Warwick* v. *Warwick Regular Firemen's Association,* 256 A.2d 206 (R.I., 1969), at 210–11.

son of wage rates or hourly conditions of employment of the fire department in question with prevailing wage rates or hourly conditions of employment of skilled employees of the building trades and industry in the local operating area. They require also that consideration and weight be given to the wage rates or hourly conditions of employment of the fire department in question in comparison to similar wage rates or hourly conditions of employment of other cities or towns of comparable size. They require that weight be given to the interest and welfare of the public and specifically spell out that weight be given to the hazards of the employment and physical and educational qualifications of the employee, and the job training and skills. In our opinion, these standards clearly are sufficient to meet the constitutional requirement that the delegated power be confined by reasonable norms or standards.[44]

Other states are experimenting with compulsory and binding arbitration in portions of the public sector, but experience remains limited. Michigan has a Police and Firemen's Arbitration Act, which became effective on October 1, 1969, and is due to expire June 30, 1972.[45] Decisional standards to be used, "as applicable," are spelled out in some detail in the Michigan law.[46] In

44. *Ibid.*, p. 211.
45. Mich. Comp. Laws Ann., §§ 423.231–.247 (Supp. 1970).
46. They are found in § 423.239, and include:
    (a) The lawful authority of the employer.
    (b) Stipulation of the parties.
    (c) The interests and welfare of the public and the financial ability of the unit of government to meet those costs.
    (d) Comparison of the wages, hours and conditions of employment of the employees involved in the arbitration proceeding with the wages, hours and conditions of employment of other employees performing similar services and with other employees generally:
        (i) In public employment in comparable communities.
        (ii) In private employment in comparable communities.
    (e) The average consumer prices for goods and services, commonly known as the cost of living.
    (f) The overall compensation presently received by the employees, including direct wage compensation, vacations, holidays and other excused time, insurance and pensions, medical and hospitalization benefits, the continuity and stability of employment, and all other benefits received.
    (g) Changes in any of the foregoing circumstances during the pendency of the arbitration proceedings.
    (h) Such other factors, not confined to the foregoing, which are normally or traditionally taken into consideration in the determination of wages, hours and conditions of employment through voluntary collective bargaining, mediation, fact-finding, arbitration or otherwise between the parties, in the public service or in private employment.

contrast, the Pennsylvania Police and Firemen Arbitration Act contains no standards, other than the general policy of the statute, to guide the arbitrators.[47] While this does not violate the delegation doctrine as it has evolved in Pennsylvania,[48] it probably would subject a similarly drafted statute to constitutional attack in a number of jurisdictions.[49]

LEGISLATIVE FINALITY

A very different approach to the impasse problem is suggested in the Taylor Committee Report, which led to the enactment of New York's Public Employees' Fair Employment Law. The Taylor Committee suggested "that in the event of the rejection of a fact-finding recommendation, the legislative body or committee hold a form of 'show cause hearing' at which the parties review their positions with respect to the recommendations of the fact-finding board. The appropriate budgetary allotment or other regulations are then to be enacted by the legislative body."[50]

The statute as initially enacted did not adopt this proposal, but a 1969 amendment provides that:

> In the event that either the public employer or the employee organization does not accept in whole or in part the recommendations of the fact-finding board, (i) the chief executive officer of the government involved shall, within ten days after receipt of the findings of fact and recommendations of the fact-finding board, submit to the legislative body of the government involved a copy of the findings of fact and recommendations of the fact-finding board, together with his recommendations for settling the dispute; (ii) the employee organization may submit to such legislative body its recommendations for settling the dispute; (iii) the legislative body or a duly authorized committee thereof shall forthwith conduct a hearing at which the parties shall be required to explain their positions with respect to the report of the fact-finding board; and (iv) thereafter, the legislative body shall take such action as it deems to be in the public interest, including the interest of the public employees involved.[51]

47. Pa. Stat. Ann., Tit. 43, §§ 217.1–.10 (Supp. 1970).

48. *Harney* v. *Russo*, 435 Pa. 183, 255 A.2d 560 (1969).

49. See generally K. Davis, *Administrative Law Treatise* (West Publishing Co., 1958), § 2.15.

50. Governor's Committee on Public Employee Relations, *Final Report* (State of New York, 1966), p. 39.

51. N.Y. Civ. Serv. Law, § 209, Para. 3(e) (McKinney Supp. 1970).

One difficulty with this legislative finality approach is that in some situations the employer ("chief executive officer of the government involved") and "the legislative body of the government involved" may in fact be the same—a school board with independent fiscal authority, for example. In other situations it may be that "the legislative body of the government involved" has already acted, indeed has precipitated the crisis by turning down a collective agreement. This could certainly happen in Connecticut if the legislative finality approach was appended to that state's municipal bargaining law.

Another troublesome question is whether it is desirable for the legislature to deal in detail with labor relations. This varies, to be sure, from legislative body to legislative body and also with the nature of a particular labor dispute. But the long-run fear must be that public employee unions will bypass the executive, where the executive is the public employer, whenever they think they can do better with the legislature. This is a serious problem today in many municipalities that are developing collective bargaining relationships with their employees. The legislative finality proposal, if widely adopted, could exacerbate this unhappy state of affairs.

CHOICE OF PROCEDURES

None of the difficulties with legislative finality, however, requires its total rejection. For if it were part of a choice-of-procedures statute—one that permitted a choice among a number of post-impasse procedures—it could be employed selectively. It would not be used where the legislature had already spoken. And, because it would be used only from time to time, it would not aggravate the bypass problem, at least not very much.

The choice-of-procedures approach—a fairly old idea in the area of emergency disputes in the private sector[52]—has two major advantages. First, it tailors the post-impasse procedure to the particular dispute. Because one-or-the-other arbitration, for example, is

52. See, for example, W. Wirtz, "The 'Choice-of-Procedures' Approach to National Emergency Disputes," in I. Bernstein, H. Enarson, R. Fleming (eds.), *Emergency Disputes and National Policy* (Harper, 1955), p. 149; G. Shultz, "The Massachusetts Choice-of-Procedures Approach to Emergency Disputes," 10 *Ind. & Lab. Rel. Rev.* 359 (1957); A. Cox, *Law and the National Labor Policy* (University of California, Institute of Industrial Relations, 1960), pp. 55–58.

suited only to some situations, the technique of selective application would seem desirable.

The second major advantage of a choice of procedures is that it builds uncertainty into the post-impasse stage and thereby makes it difficult for the parties to estimate the consequences of failing to agree. Because neither party is likely to find every procedure favorable to achieving its demands, the fear that the least desirable may be chosen will itself generate settlement pressures.[53]

Under such an approach, the agency charged with enforcing the state public employee law would be empowered, after investigation, to determine the procedure best suited to the particular dispute, be it fact-finding with recommendations, regular arbitration, the one-or-the-other variety, or legislative finality. This breadth of choice should be sufficient both to create uncertainty and to permit choice of an appropriate procedure.

A choice-of-procedures approach, like every other approach consistent with an open society, is no panacea. It will not stop all strikes but it has the best chance of reducing their incidence. And that is all we have any right to expect.

Penalties for Striking

In a system of labor relations that bans the strike, the proper role of sanctions is no less vexing a problem than the proper design for post-impasse procedures. Only the outer boundaries of the problem are reasonably clear. The declaration that the strike is illegal must be more than hortatory, and the sanctions for breach of the primary rule must not be so harsh as to engender a feeling of revulsion in the community. Within these boundaries the aim of sanctions is to deter strikes effectively and to do justice. At best, this is a complicated business. Not only is there the response of the general community; there is also the response of the public employees involved. In some situations, for example, the incarceration of a union leader for contempt will turn that leader into a martyr and stiffen support for the strike. Yet it is also true that fairness or justice requires that like situations be treated

53. Wirtz, pp. 158–59.

alike. And it may be difficult to show forbearance toward one union leader and incarcerate another.

Harsh penalties automatically invoked, moreover, run the risk of converting an economic strike into a strike for amnesty that will be difficult to settle without openly abandoning the law. The harsher the penalties, the less the strikers will feel they have to lose, and the effect may be to extend rather than end the strike. These considerations suggest gradually escalating sanctions that seek to make the cost of continuing the strike at any point in time greater than the cost of ending it.

Other problems exist as well. To what extent should sanctions be directed against the organization, its leaders, or its members? The answer to this question depends in part upon the prevalence of wildcat strikes, and may also be influenced by what has come to be known as the ratification problem; that is, the increasing frequency with which union members turn down negotiated settlements.[54] Both phenomena are manifestations of rank-and-file militancy that override union leadership, and, where either exists, the threat of sanctions against the membership may be necessary if strikes are to be reduced. This threat, indeed, may be essential to any attempt by the leadership to assert control.

Different sanctions, of course, are appropriate to different situations. This argues for flexibility, but with some guidelines.

Many states use the courts to develop sanctions. In the *Holland* case, the Michigan Supreme Court suggested that a trial court "inquire into whether the public employer has refused to bargain in good faith, whether an injunction should be issued at all, and if so, on what terms and for what period in light of the whole record to be adduced."[55] Apart from the issue of good faith, it is far from clear what the Michigan court would have a trial court examine. It may be that the process of "litigating elucidation" is a good way to develop differentiated sanctions for different situations, but it requires considerable wisdom on the part of judges. For if like

54. One classic example is the airline strike of 1966. President Johnson announced on television a settlement between five major carriers and the International Association of Machinists only to have the union membership repudiate it within two days. See *New York Times,* Aug. 1, 1966, p. 1. Another example is the railroad-shopcraft dispute of 1970; see, for example, 73 *Lab Rel. Rep.* 297 (April 13, 1970).

55. *Holland School District* v. *Holland Education Association,* 380 Mich. 314, 327, 157 N.W. 2d 206, 211 (1968).

cases are not treated alike, the system is unfair and probably unworkable. There is no reason to think that judge-created sanctions will be more effective than those prescribed by the legislature—or even as effective. The imprimatur of the political process may be necessary to the creation of a moral imperative against striking, or to the dissipation of the belief that stern sanctions for striking are inconsistent with our notions about fundamental freedoms.

One important differentiating factor is the procedures that have been employed prior to the strike. Those procedures that seek to substitute for the strike a fair method of dispute resolution must themselves be protected. For example, a strike in the teeth of a binding arbitration award should be met with the maximum of sternness consistent with the community's sense of fairness. Yet the Michigan Police and Firemen's Arbitration Act seems to undercut its policy of limited, binding arbitration. The statute provides that, "no person shall be sentenced to a term of imprisonment for any violation of the provisions of this act or an order of the arbitration panel." The statute does provide, however, that if a party "willfully disobeys a lawful order of enforcement [of an award by a court] or willfully encourages or offers resistance to such order . . . the punishment for each day that such contempt persists may be a fine fixed in the discretion of the court in an amount not to exceed $250.00 per day."[56]

There is considerable diversity as to sanctions among other states with public employee bargaining statutes. Connecticut's Municipal Employee Relations Act is silent except to provide that "nothing [in this act] shall constitute a grant of the right to strike to employees of any municipal employer and such strikes are prohibited."[57] Connecticut has not been free of strikes, and the sanction used has been the injunction.[58]

Contrast section 210 of the New York law, which imposes sanctions on employees who engage in a strike: "probation for a term of one year" and deduction from compensation of "an amount equal to twice his daily rate of pay for each day or part thereof"

56. Mich. Comp. Laws. Ann., §§ 423.246 and 423.241 (Supp. 1970).

57. Conn. Gen. Stat. Ann., § 7-475 (Supp. 1970).

58. See, for example, "Injunction against Strike by Employees of New Haven Department of Public Works," reported in *Government Employee Relations Report*, No. 283 (Feb. 10, 1969), p. B-9.

that an employee is on strike. It also penalizes the employee organization through the loss of membership dues deduction for a period to be determined by the Public Employment Relations Board. Moreover, section 211 mandates "the chief legal officer of the government involved" to apply for an injunction. Section 210 has elaborate procedural safeguards and builds flexibility into the sanction aimed at the union. As it applies to individual employees, however, section 210 seems to be rather inflexible and therefore in some situations will be overly harsh.[59]

Within the boundaries that describe the role of sanctions in the no-strike model—more than hortatory but within the community's sense of fairness—each state must experiment and find its own way. Time will help the policymaker reach evaluative judgments; but it is doubtful that a clear picture of a proper structure will ever emerge. Nor should there be any expectation that wise sanctions will wholly eliminate strikes. Neither sanctions nor impasse procedures, alone or in combination, can do more than ease the situation. In some cities and states this will be enough. Society can tolerate some flouting of the no-strike norm without its generating disrespect for law; and the political process can tolerate some without becoming too distorted. In other localities the prohibition on strikes may not work, no matter what. Where this is the case, the task for policymakers will be to accept the strike and reduce its effects. There are more ways to do this than may be generally thought.

59. N.Y. Civ. Serv. Law, §§ 210 and 211 (McKinney Supp. 1970).

CHAPTER TWELVE

The Legal Strike Model

The essentiality of governmental services has been urged by some as the touchstone with which to judge the permissibility of public employee strikes.[1] Unfortunately, however, commentators often have not recognized that, when so used, this concept encompasses three distinct problems: first, the fact that disruption of some services will create an immediate danger to public health and safety; second, the inelasticity of demand for most governmental services; and, finally, the vulnerability of the typical large city political structure to the strike weapon. A statutory scheme that permits strikes must take each of these aspects of the essentiality problem into account.

The Emergency Dispute Problem

Assume for analytic purposes that the emergency dispute problem is the only one the municipality need consider. Clearly, where a strike creates an immediate danger to public health and safety, the strike weapon should be outlawed and resort to the prescribed post-impasse procedures made mandatory. Where the length of the strike determines the magnitude of the danger, however, special

1. See, for example, T. St. Antoine, "The Consent of the Governed: Public Employee Unions and the Law," 15 *Law Quadrangle Notes* 9–13 (Fall 1970).

procedures for invoking post-impasse procedures are necessary. For the strike, by hypothesis, is tolerable for a time. One approach would be to empower a public official, the governor or mayor, to invoke the procedures when he determines that a health or welfare danger exists. This factual determination should be final and not subject to judicial review. While such review exists under Title II of the Taft-Hartley Act,[2] its extension to the public sector seems unwise. To require that a court review a purely prudential decision entails that the court do little more than rubber-stamp what has been done. This is not a good way to use courts.

A difficulty with giving the executive authority to determine when a strike must stop is that he is apt to be a party to the dispute. If it is thought that the appearance of unfairness will significantly lessen the law's acceptability, it may be preferable to entrust the power to determine whether an emergency exists to an independent, specialized agency, such as the one empowered to administer the public employee bargaining law. That agency would act upon the petition of the public employer. Its procedures should ensure a speedy decision, which, again, should be final. However, the employer should be free, after a period of time, to renew a rejected petition on grounds of changed conditions.

In the private sector, the question of when a strike constitutes a genuine emergency has, however, never been resolved with finality. The reason is not that an emergency cannot be defined in a way that will satisfy informed opinion,[3] but rather that the public inevitably finds such a definition too narrow. Indeed, many of the cases of ad hoc intervention by the President, or of resort to the "cooling off" provisions of Taft-Hartley, have not involved disputes that were, strictly speaking, emergencies. The political pressures surrounding strikes that are severely inconvenient but not dangerous are such that strict obedience to the criterion of actual emergency would involve too great a political risk for a President to incur.[4]

2. 29 U.S.C. § 178 (1964); *United Steelworkers of America* v. *United States*, 361 U.S. 39 (1959).

3. G. Hildebrand, "An Economic Definition of an Emergency Dispute," in I. Bernstein et al., *Emergency Disputes and National Policy* (Harper, 1955), p. 3.

4. H. Wellington, *Labor and the Legal Process* (Yale University Press, 1968), pp. 270–74.

The feasibility of a nonemergency strike model in the public sector is, therefore, doubtful from the start, for it requires that the law distinguish between true emergency and inconvenience. That is the very distinction that has proved unacceptable in the private sector. Most strikes in the public sector—all those worth staging[5] —inconvenience a substantial part of the community. If the total ban on strikes by public employees is to be relaxed, political adherence to a distinction between true emergencies and real inconvenience will be needed.

Paradoxically, this may make the use of a strict definition of an emergency politically more acceptable in the public sector than in the private. Contrary to the myth, it is often in the interest of a striking union in the private sector to involve the government in the search for a settlement. Long strikes frequently work to the advantage of the employer, and a union that can avoid the long strike by invoking government pressures for a settlement may have strengthened its hand at the bargaining table.[6] One reason for the unacceptability of the strict definition of an emergency in the private sector, therefore, may be the interest of labor in seeing the distinction between emergency and inconvenience blurred.

Public employee unions, however, may view the problem differently. Their choice is not between accepting a rational distinction or gaining helpful government intervention. Rather, they must choose between accepting the distinction between strikes that create an emergency and those that inconvenience or a complete statutory ban on strikes. For this reason, such a distinction may be more acceptable politically in the public sector than it has proved to be in the private.

On the other hand, the fact of inconvenience remains and the distinction must be accepted by what may be a reluctant public. This probably means that where discretion to determine whether an emergency exists is delegated, it should go to the independent,

5. G. Taylor, "Public Employment: Strikes or Precedures?" 20 *Industrial and Labor Relations Review* 617 (1967).

6. "Government intervention and its anticipation are very likely to increase the probability of the short strike, and to make the short strike pay off, by frustrating normal negotiation and removing the option of the long strike." E. Livernash, "The Relation of Power to the Structure and Process of Collective Bargaining," 6 *Journal of Law and Economics* 10, 15 (1963).

administrative tribunal rather than to an elected public official who will be politically unable to apply the distinction.

A structure that permits strikes to continue only until they create emergency conditions may, however, chill collective bargaining, because the parties will be able to predict the length of the strike and calculate accordingly. The party that stands to gain by waiting out the strike will do so. Much of this effect can be mitigated by using a choice of procedures as a post-impasse structure and by taking whatever steps are available in a particular dispute to create uncertainty as to the length of time the strike will be permitted.[7]

The definition of strike-created emergency conditions should not be overly difficult to write, though local conditions will produce the usual variations. There must be an immediate danger of serious injury to public health and safety. Police and fire services, it would seem, may not be fully disrupted for any amount of time without such a danger being created. Here the damage occurs so quickly and in such unforeseen ways that no hiatus can be safely permitted.[8] Other kinds of strikes are not so clear-cut. The disruption of utility services, for instance, may not create an emergency for some time, depending on the degree of disruption, the nature of the service, the time of year, the availability of substitutes at a subsistence level, the extent of automation, and other factors.

A strike in health services is most critical where the operation of hospitals is concerned. But even with hospitals, such variables as the ability to maintain partial operations, the location of non-struck hospitals, and the time of year may keep the impact of the strike below the emergency level.

Sanitation disputes similarly do not inevitably endanger public health and safety. The problem is most acute in large urban areas, but a suburb with an accessible dump may run little danger. Even transportation strikes may be tolerated for a period, sometimes until settlement, depending on the availability of substitutes and the extent to which the damage is mainly economic. Strikes by welfare employees probably do not constitute an emergency immediately. The disruption of services surrounding public housing

7. See Chap. 11, pp. 185–86, above.

8. The 1969 police and firefighters' strike in Montreal suggests that a real danger to health and safety can occur within hours of the start of a walkout.

will create emergencies most often in cold weather and in circumstances in which the tenants are unable to make minimal provision for themselves. And in education, most experience has shown that the risk is to political careers rather than to the health and safety of the public. Lost school days can be recaptured, often at times of the year that might make teachers think twice before striking. Strikes by support personnel must be judged by the extent to which they disrupt related functions. Other governmental services do not by any standard seem to threaten the health and safety of the public or even produce significant inconvenience.

Two things, then, are clear. First, the size of a municipality and the degree to which it is subject to strike-created emergencies are related. The extent of division of labor and the distance to alternative services combine to make large cities highly vulnerable. The problem of public employees is truly part of the "urban crisis." Second, strikes by most public employees that fall short of emergencies are nevertheless severely inconvenient to a significant segment of the community. If there are to be strikes, that is the minimum price that must be paid.

To sum up: the emergency dispute problem does not compel a complete ban on strikes. Many public employee strikes are not a danger to health and safety, at least not immediately.[9] And while nonemergency strikes cause inconvenience, that may not be reason enough to ban strikes.

The Inelastic Demand Problem

The second sense in which essentiality may be used as the touchstone upon which the strike question is resolved relates to the inelasticity of demand for most governmental services. Because there are few close substitutes for such services and virtually no fear of entry by a nonunion rival, the demand for many governmental services is relatively insensitive to price. And because the demand for labor is derived from the demand for the product, public employee unions face a relatively insignificant trade-off between benefits received and unemployment incurred in pursuing their demands.

9. See J. Burton, Jr., and C. Krider, "The Role and Consequences of Strikes by Public Employees," 79 *Yale Law Journal* 418, 432 ff. (January 1970).

It must be conceded that government can do little about the lack of close substitutes for its services. Indeed, it is often the very lack of substitutes that led government to undertake these functions in the first place. But the inelasticity of demand for governmental services does not necessarily mean excessive wages for governmental employees, any more than the inelasticity of demand for some agricultural products means excessive income for farmers. It is the lack of competition—monopoly—that permits producers to take advantage of an inelastic demand schedule. And where unions are concerned, it is principally the strike and the strike threat that enable them to exploit such an advantageous market position. If measures are employed that reduce the effectiveness of the strike weapon, at least part of the difficulty created by the inelasticity of demand for governmental services will be solved. That problem is considered next.

The Problem of the City's Vulnerability

The final sense in which essentiality is used goes to the effectiveness of the public employee strike. Such strikes generally inconvenience people and these people are also voters. Other things being equal, they will vote in a way that eliminates the inconvenience; that is, that avoids or brings about an end to the strike. And all too often, other things will be equal.[10] Because the cost of a settlement may frequently be passed on to larger political units or hidden in the bowels of an incomprehensible municipal budget, voters will tend to choose political leaders who avoid inconveniencing strikes over those who work to minimize the costs of settlements at the price of a strike. Costs that are not imposed on voters are hardly likely to deter them from pressuring for a

10. This is not to suggest that large numbers of politicians will have their careers terminated as a result of large numbers of strikes, for they are far too shrewd not to appreciate the risk. These facts of life are already more apparent to the politicians than to industrial relations commentators, which is perhaps to be expected. Mayor Lindsay's early and generous settlement in an election year with the United Federation of Teachers showed his lack of confidence in the repeated assertions by labor "experts" that strikes in the public sector do not differ from those in the private. That insight, and his great luck in having his most formidable opponents eliminated in the Democratic primary, may have been the most important factors in his election victory.

settlement, no matter what its size. And costs effectively hidden by the genius of municipal accountants, as well as understated by the parties, will not induce voters to urge firmness by their elected officials in the face of an inconveniencing strike. The net effect is that the typical municipal political structure is altogether too vulnerable to strikes by public employees, and other groups in the political process are thereby disadvantaged. This is true whether the strike is over monetary or nonmonetary issues, although in the latter case organized groups whose interests are threatened by union demands may create countervailing pressures of varying impact.

The suggestions below aim to reduce the vulnerability of the public employer. They are neither mutually exclusive nor always complementary. Depending on local variables, they may be employed individually or together.

CONTINGENCY PLANNING

The first things government should consider are various ways in which the effect of strikes by public employees can be mitigated. To this end, a municipality with a potential for public employee labor trouble should engage in careful contingency planning. There are, of course, limits to what can be accomplished through planning, particularly where the unions involved regard any attempt to find substitutes for struck services as a form of strikebreaking and use all of their considerable powers to stop it.[11] Nevertheless, some things can be done. Prepared emergency traffic patterns and parking facilities can offset some of the consequences of a transit strike. Contingency plans as to the use of neighboring hospitals may avoid disasters in a hospital strike. Automating the most critical functions before a dispute occurs can reduce the impact of a strike enormously. Many utility strikes today are hardly noticed by the public because automation permits continued service. And prepared written directions to businesses and individuals indicating how they may help themselves and others can limit the impact of many kinds of strikes. Again, the helpful-

11. The reaction of the New York City sanitation workers to Mayor Lindsay's threat of using the National Guard to pick up the garbage was both volatile and effective. It stirred the emotions of those who view "strikebreaking" with contempt and caused Governor Nelson Rockefeller to refuse to abide by the mayor's wishes.

ness of such measures can be easily overstated, but there may be a great temptation to procrastinate, either because of lethargy or a desire not to appear provocative.

PARTIAL OPERATIONS

Another approach deserves serious consideration. It seems evident that emergencies, and the most severe inconveniences caused by strikes, can be avoided by partial operation of the struck facility. Partial operation, moreover, can be tailored so as to leave substantial pressure on government to settle. Policemen can keep order without giving out parking tickets, directing traffic, arresting for minor offenses, doing paper work, or testifying for the prosecution in criminal cases. Firemen can prevent conflagrations without doing the normal housekeeping details. Welfare checks can be processed, and all other welfare services cease. Garbage can be collected, but less often. Subway service can be reduced by half.

The goal of any partial operation scheme is, first, to ensure performance of those functions essential to health and safety and the avoidance of severe inconveniences; and, second, to maintain sufficient pressure on government to settle. From the union's point of view the advantage is a legal, albeit partial, strike and some continuing income for its members.

Partial operation schemes will, of course, work best as law if agreed to by the parties. In the private sector, agreement on such schemes has been so infrequent or nonexistent as to discourage, until recently, much inquiry along this route. But private sector unions have the right to strike and often are helped by government intervention. In the public sector, the right to strike has been withheld and may be an acceptable quid for the quo of continuing specified operations. Such operations, moreover, may be spread among the affected workers so they all receive some compensation during the strike period.

Consideration of partial operations in the private sector has perennially raised the issue as to which of several plants or companies should continue to operate under the arrangement.[12] The

12. Partial operations in the private sector usually permit one or more firms and one group of workers to profit while the rest suffer the effects of a strike. Thus, it is the internal divisions within the employer group and unions that prevent agreement.

inability to find a way to spread the benefits of partial operation has been one of the reefs on which such schemes have been wrecked. In the public sector, the lack of competing employers and the relative ease with which almost all the employees can share[13] may facilitate the working out of such arrangements, which can then be enacted into legislation.

CHANGING THE POLITICAL PROCESS

In addition to taking steps that lessen the impact of strikes by public employees, government should consider certain measures that tend to decrease public willingness to call for settlements without sufficient regard for the costs involved. Such measures, if institutionalized, might be accompanied by a relaxation on the ban against strikes in nonemergency situations.

One reason for vulnerability is that the cost of settlement is hard to find in a municipal budget. Any measure that sharpens the public's awareness of the cost of a settlement, therefore, will tend to decrease the political pressure for a precipitous settlement.

A tactic more useful in small and middle-sized communities than in giant urban centers is to publish the salaries of the individual public employees involved by name. Where these salaries seem higher than those received for comparable work in the private sector, public sympathy for the strikers will not be very great, and political leaders may be less fearful of a backlash at the polls because they resist union demands at the price of a strike. In Waterbury, Connecticut, a taxpayers' revolt over teachers' salaries was caused by just such a tactic.[14]

Another device might be to specify in tax bills the allocation of taxes among various functions of government or the amount attributable to collective agreements. Taxpayer groups and the like may thus be aided in leading opposition against union demands.

Another source of vulnerability is the municipalities' ability to pass costs on to larger political units. Voters who do not pay the

13. If the subways operate at 50 percent capacity, for instance, it ought to be possible to find ways to see that all employees work around 50 percent of their normal time.

14. D. Lewis and F. Lynch, "Budgets and Public Bargaining" (unpublished MS, Yale Law School, 1969).

costs of a settlement will not encourage their elected officials to resist union demands. There is one measure that serves both to put the costs of the settlement on those who have the greatest incentive to call for settlement and to increase the visibility of those costs. One not uncommon and suggestive feature of the municipal scene is the fiscally independent school district.[15] Such districts have independent power to finance their budgets by raising taxes directly without the approval of a reviewing body. It may be possible to fashion analogues of such districts for bargaining units of public employees by creating coextensive independent tax districts. Such "bargaining-tax" districts (which, geographically, may be as large as the governmental entity) might finance the performance of the whole function involved, as the fiscally independent school districts do, or merely raise the amount necessary to finance the monetary costs of a collective agreement.

The advantage of tax districts coextensive with bargaining units is evident. Those who clamor for a settlement will see the cost in the plainest possible way. In addition, the ability of a municipality to pass these costs on will be limited since the money will be raised automatically from the specific tax district. A similar device is the imposition of user costs on those who benefit from municipal services.

The subsidization by the state or federal government of municipal functions from which funds have been derived for collective bargaining purposes may seem to be no more than an indirect means of paying the costs of collective bargaining. It seems doubtful, however, that state or federal governments will regulate their subsidies so carefully that municipalities with strong public employee unions will get proportionately more money for other functions than municipalities without such unions. If that is the case, the ability of some municipalities to pass on the costs of settlements will be lessened. Nor will unrestricted money, passed to cities through revenue sharing schemes, lessen public resistance to generous settlements when they must be financed solely out of "bargaining-tax" districts.

Other structural changes in the organization of municipal governments may permit nonemergency strikes but penalize their use

15. See M. Lieberman and M. Moskow, *Collective Negotiations for Teachers; An Approach to School Administration* (Rand McNally, 1966), pp. 277 ff.

in some way. Settlements reached after a strike might be subject to approval by a referendum among registered voters. The referendum might ask the voters to approve the estimated tax consequences of the settlement. If conducted within the framework of tax districts coextensive with bargaining units, the referendum would not only ratify the settlement but also levy the necessary taxes.[16]

Where analogous structures actually exist, effective pressure has been exerted on the size of financial settlements. In Portland, Oregon, the local education tax cannot increase more than 6 percent per year without a local vote or a special levy. As a result, the settlements reached appear to call for considerably less money than would have been the case had the school board and union been free to bargain without having to persuade the voters.[17] And in San Francisco the only substantial check on the ability of public employee unions to achieve their demands through political pressure has been the willingness of the city's Chamber of Commerce to threaten to use local procedures permitting wage rates to be submitted to a referendum. Indeed, the principal negotiations in San Francisco are often between the unions and the chamber.

The referendum device increases the visibility of a settlement's cost and places it on those voters with the most power to resist. Furthermore, union leaders are encouraged to make their deal with elected officials rather than risk the unknowns of a referendum. Such settlements are apt to be smaller than those that would follow strikes under present structures. The officials, moreover, have an incentive to settle and thereby claim credit for avoiding a strike, but are able, if no settlement is reached, to escape the dilemma of choosing between the wrath of those inconvenienced by a strike and those enraged by increased taxes. The

16. This device may in some circumstances constitute overkill. See generally, C. Rehmus, "Constraints on Local Governments in Public Employee Bargaining," 67 *Mich. L. Rev.* 919 (1969). The example of Youngstown, Ohio, where taxpayers refused to authorize sufficient funds to keep the schools open for a full school year, suggests that considerable resistance to tax increases can be expected where specific items are put to a referendum. *Government Employee Relations Report,* No. 273 (Dec. 2, 1968), p. B-4. On the other hand, such a mechanism may be wholly inadequate when a union represents a small number of employees, because their total wage bill may never be enough to affect individual voters adversely.

17. Lewis and Lynch, "Budgets and Public Bargaining," pp. 34 ff.

officials in such structures, once an impasse is reached and a strike called, are able to assume a more neutral stance because they lack the power to make a final settlement. Thus, in Portland and San Francisco, local officials sometimes have been more concerned with helping the unions estimate what the voters will accept than with acting as true adversaries. This has been so even though the referendum device in neither case requires that a strike precede it.

All of these suggestions indicate the direction in which collective bargaining structures in public employment must go if nonemergency strikes are to be permitted. Arrangements that lessen the impact of such strikes should be created and the costs of settlement made more visible. Those who can decide to settle a dispute must know the costs of that settlement and must bear them. Where possible, incentives to settle without a strike should be created, enabling public officials to be relieved of the dilemma in which strikes now put them. These suggestions are just that, and they are not exhaustive. Local conditions will determine the appropriateness of any particular device and of permitting nonemergency strikes at all. And such conditions will undoubtedly suggest other devices. Experimentation is necessary, for it is clear that the strike ban, wise as it is in theory, will not work in all places at all times.[18]

18. The U.S. Bureau of Labor Statistics' study, *Work Stoppages in Government, 1958–68* (1970), shows substantial differences among the Midwest, Northeast, South, and West in the number of strikes by government employees during the decade. The study is reproduced in *GERR*, No. 350 (May 25, 1970), p. D-1. See particularly pp. D-8, D-9, and D-15.

Postscript

During the 1970–71 negotiations between New York City and its uniformed employees, Mr. Michael J. Maye, the president of the Uniformed Firefighters Association, was quoted to good effect in the *New York Times:* " 'They say there's no money for us,' Mr. Maye almost shouts. 'Well, fire protection has gone from 4 percent to 3 percent of the budget. There's a drain all right, and who's getting it? We know. Welfare has gone from 10 percent to 22 percent—there's plenty of money for that.' "[1]

Mr. Maye knows better than most that the principal issue in public employee unionism is the distribution of political power among those groups pressing claims on government. And, one may assume, he has no doubt that the unions' share of political power should be increased. Indeed, it would seem that every responsible union leader must be committed to the proposition that what's good for public employees is good for the cities, counties, and states of the nation.

Our rejection of that proposition has served as the major normative premise of this book. We believe that in the cities, counties, and states there are other claimants with needs at least as pressing as those of the public employees. Such claimants can never have the power the unions will win if we mindlessly import into the public sector all the collective bargaining practices developed in the private sector. Make no mistake about it, government is *not* "just another industry."

1. *New York Times,* Dec. 20, 1970, Sec. 1, p. 51.

APPENDIX A

State Public Employee Labor Provisions

Table A-1 presents a survey of public labor law in each of the fifty states. Statutes of limited application, such as those applying only to a single agency or authority, have not been included. Table A-2 presents a more detailed statutory analysis, but includes only selected state statutes.

The major source of information in the compilation of these listings has been the tables published in Advisory Commission on Intergovernmental Relations, *Labor-Management Policies for State and Local Government* (1969), pp. 13–18, 20–22. The tables have been updated through September 1970 by comparing the provisions listed with the statutes compiled in relevant issues of *Government Employee Relations Report* and Volumes 4 and 4A of the *Labor Relations Reporter*. Both are published by the Bureau of National Affairs.

TABLE A-1. *Categories of Public Employees under State Legal and Administrative Labor Relations Authorizations, by Selected Labor Provisions, September 1970*[a]

State	*Right to organize*	*Right to present proposals*	*Right to meet and confer*[b]	*Right to bargain collectively*[b]	*Detailed recognition procedures*	*Union security*[c]	*Dispute settlement provisions*	*Strike prohibition*
Alabama	Fire (L)	Fire (L)	. . .	Water works board (A)	. . .	. . .	Fire (L) All (A)	. . .
Alaska	Teachers (L)	. . .	. . .	All (L) **Teachers** (L)	Teachers (L)	. . .	Teachers (L)	. . .
Arizona	All (L)	. . .	. . .	. . .	. . .	. . .	. . .	. . .
Arkansas	All (L)	. . .	. . .	State (A)	. . .	. . .	. . .	State (A)
California	All (L) Fire (L) Teachers (L)	Fire (L)	**All, except teachers** (L) **Teachers** (L)	Hospital district (A)	Teachers (L)	Right to refrain, all (L) Teachers (L)	All, except teachers (L) Teachers (L)	Fire (L) City (C) Public utility (C)
Colorado	. . .	. . .	. . .	. . .	. . .	. . .	. . .	. . .
Connecticut	Local (L) Teachers (L)	. . .	. . .	**Local** (L) **Teachers** (L)	Local (L) Teachers (L)	Right to refrain, teachers (L)	Local (L) Teachers (L)	Local (L) Teachers (L) All (C)
Delaware	All, except teachers (L)[d] Teachers (L)	. . .	. . .	Municipal (L) **State and county** (L) **Teachers** (L)	All, except teachers (L)[d]	Right to refrain, teachers (L)	All, except teachers (L)[d]	All, except teachers (L) Public transit
Florida	All (L) Fire (L)	All (L)	Teachers (L)	**Fire** (L)	. . .	Right to refrain, all (L)	Fire (L) Teachers (L)	All (L)
Georgia	. . .	. . .	. . .	School boards (A)	. . .	. . .	. . .	State (L) Teachers (A)

Hawaii	All (L)	. . .	. . .	**All** (L)	All (L)	Agency shop, all (L)	All (L)	. . .
Idaho	Fire (L) All (A)	. . .	. . .	City (A) **Fire** (L)	. . .	. . .	Fire (L)	. . .
Illinois	Fire (L) State (L) Teachers (C)	. . .	. . .	Transit authority (L) State (L) Board of education (C)	. . .	. . .	Fire (L) Transit authority (L)	All (C)
Indiana	Teachers (L) All (A)	. . .	All (A)	. . .	. . .	. . .	Public utility (L)	All (C)
Iowa	All (C) State (A)	All (L)	. . .	All (C)	. . .	. . .	Fire (L)	All (C) State (A)
Kansas	All (L) Teachers (L)	. . .	. . .	**Teachers** (L)	Teachers (L)	Right to refrain, teachers (L)	Public utility (L)	. . .
Kentucky	State (L) All (A) Teachers (A)	. . .	City (A) Teachers (A) State (L, A)	. . .	. . .	. . .	. . .	State (L) All (C)
Louisiana	Public transportation (L) Fire and police (A)	. . .	. . .	**Public transportation** (L)	. . .	. . .	Public transportation (L)	. . .
Maine	Local (L) All (A)	Local (L) All (A)	. . .	**Fire** (L) **Local** (L)	Fire (L) Local (L)	. . .	Fire (L) Local (L)	Fire (L) Local (L)
Maryland	Teachers (L)	. . .	. . .	**Teachers** (L)	Teachers (L)	Right to refrain, teachers (L)	Teachers (L)	Teachers (L)
Massachusetts	Local (L) State, except police (L)	. . .	. . .	**Local** (L) **State, except police** (L)	Local (L) State, except police (L)	Right to refrain, state (L), local (L)	Local (L) State, except police (L)	Local (L) State (L)

TABLE A-1 *Continued*

State	*Right to organize*	*Right to present proposals*	*Right to meet and confer*[b]	*Right to bargain collectively*[b]	*Detailed recognition procedures*	*Union security*[c]	*Dispute settlement provisions*	*Strike prohibition*
Michigan	All (L)	...	...	**All** (L)	All (L)	Agency shop, local (C)	All (L) Police and fire (L)	All (L)
Minnesota	All, except teachers (L) Teachers (L)	...	**All, except teachers** (L) **Teachers** (L)[e]	**Nonprofit hospital** (L)	All, except teachers (L) Teachers (L)	Right to refrain, all except teachers (L)	All, except teachers (L) Teachers (L)	All (L)
Mississippi	...	...	...	...	...	...	...	...
Missouri	All, except police and teachers (L) Teachers (A)	Teachers (A)	Teachers (A) **All, except police and teachers** (L)	...	...	Right to refrain, all except police and teachers (L) No agency shop, state (C)	All (L) Fire (L)	All (L)
Montana	Nurses (L) County (A)	...	...	County (A) **Nurses** (L)	Nurses (L)	...	...	...
Nebraska	Fire (L) Teachers (L) Local (L) All (L)	...	Teachers (L)	All (L) Local (L)	All (L) Teachers (L)	Right to refrain, all (L) Teachers (L)	All (L), Fire (L) Teachers (L) Public utility (L) Local (L)	All (L)

Nevada	Local (L)	...	...	**Local** (L)	Local (L)	Right to refrain, local (L)	Local (L)	All (L)
New Hampshire	City (L) State (L)	...	...	City (L) **State** (L)	State (L)	Agency shop, local (C) Right to refrain, state (L)	...	All (C) State (L)
New Jersey	All (L)	...	...	**All** (L)	...	Right to refrain, all (L)	Public utility (L) All (L)	Public utility (L) All (C)
New Mexico	Mass transportation (L) All (A)	...	All (A)	Mass transportation (L) City (C)	...	...	...	All (A) Teachers (L) Mass transportation (L)
New York	All (L)	...	...	**All** (L)	All (L)	Right to refrain, all (L)	All (L)	All (L)
North Carolina	All (C)	...	...	...	...	...	...	...
North Dakota	All (L) Teachers (L)	...	...	All (A) **Teachers** (L)	Teachers (L)	Right to refrain, teachers (L)	All (L) Teachers (L)	City (C) Teachers (L)
Ohio	...	...	...	...	...	No agency shop, city (C)		All (L)
Oklahoma	State (A)	...	...	...	...	...	...	State (A, C)

TABLE A-1 *Continued*

State	*Right to organize*	*Right to present proposals*	*Right to meet and confer*[b]	*Right to bargain collectively*[b]	*Detailed recognition procedures*	*Union security*[c]	*Dispute settlement provisions*	*Strike prohibition*
Oregon	State and local (L)[d] Teachers (L) Nurses (L)	. . .	**Teachers** (L)	Local (L) **State** (L) **Nurses** (L)	Teachers (L) Nurses (L)	Right to refrain, state (L)	State and local (L)[d] Teachers (L) Nurses (L)	Nurses (L) State and local (L)[d]
Pennsyl-vania	All (L)	. . .	. . .	**Fire, police** (L) **All** (L)	All (L)	Right to refrain, all (L)	Fire, police (L) All (L) Public utility (L)	. . .
Rhode Island	Local (L) Fire (L) Police (L) State (L) Teachers (L)	. . .	. . .	**Local** (L) **Fire** (L) **Police** (L) **State** (L) **Teachers** (L)	Local (L) Teachers (L)	Right to refrain, state (L)	Fire (L) Police (L) Local (L) Teachers (L)	All (L) Local (L) Fire (L) Police (L) State (L)
South Carolina		. . .	. . .	. . .	. . .	. . .	. . .	All (A)
South Dakota	All (L)	. . .	**All** (L)	. . .	All (L)	Right to refrain, all (L)	. . .	All (L)
Tennessee	. . .	. . .	. . .	. . .	. . .	. . .	. . .	All (C)
Texas	All (L)	All (A)	. . .	. . .	. . .	. . .	. . .	All (L)
Utah	All (L)	. . .	. . .	Local (A) State (A)	. . .	Right to refrain, all (L)	. . .	All (A)

Vermont	State (L) City, except professionals (L) Teachers (L)	. . .	. . .	**State** (L) **City, except professionals** (L) **Teachers** (L)	State (L) Teachers (L)	Right to refrain, state (L); city, except professionals (L) Teachers (L)	State (L) City, except professionals (L) Teachers (L)	State (L) Fire (L)
Virginia	All (L)	All (L)	. . .	City (A)	. . .	. . .	. . .	All (L) Hospital (L)
Washington	Local (L) Teachers (L)	. . .	. . .	Public utility (L) **Local** (L) **Teachers** (L)	Local (L) Teachers (L)	. . .	Local (L) Teachers (L)	Local (L) Hospital (L)
West Virginia	All (A)	All (A)	. . .	. . .	. . .	. . .	. . .	All (A)
Wisconsin	Local, except police (L) State (L)	. . .	. . .	**Local, except police** (L) **State** (L)	Local, except police (L) State (L)	Right to refrain, local, except police (L), state (L)	Local, except police (L) State (L) Public utility (L)	Local, except police (L) State (L) All (L)
Wyoming	Fire (L)	. . .	. . .	**Fire** (L)	. . .	. . .	Fire (L)	. . .

Sources: Advisory Commission on Intergovernmental Relations, *Labor-Management Policies for State and Local Government* (ACIR, 1969), pp. 13–18, updated from Bureau of National Affairs, *Government Employee Relations Report*, relevant issues, and BNA, *Labor Relations Reporter*, "State Laws," Vols. 4 and 4A, with supplements (BNA, as of September 1970). The data drawn from these sources have been amended and adapted by the authors at various points when their interpretations of the regulations differed from those presented in the sources.

a. Each listing in any given cell of this table indicates a separate law (L), attorney general's opinion (A), or court decision (C), and a specific category of public employee. For example, "All (L)" indicates that all public employees are covered by one statute, whereas "State (L), Local (L)" indicates that all public employees are also covered, but by two separate statutes. "State" denotes state employees; "local" denotes employees of state political subdivisions; "all" denotes both. Other entries, such as "fire" and "teachers," indicate the various categories that such terms imply.

b. **Bold type** denotes **mandatory** provisions; ordinary type denotes permissive provisions.

c. Union security refers to the protection of union status by provisions in union agreements establishing agency shop or other types of shop or membership requirements. In an agency shop, employees are not required to join the union but are required to pay an amount equal to the initiation fee and regular dues. Right to refrain indicates that employees have the right to refrain from joining a union of public employees.

d. Municipal employees are not included unless the municipality has elected to be covered by the statute.

e. On monetary issues, teachers meet and confer "in an effort to reach agreement." On other issues, they meet and confer only to exchange views.

TABLE A-2. *Provisions of Selected State Public Labor Relations Statutes, September 1970*

Provision	*Alaska (1959, 1968)*	*California (1961, 1968, 1970)*	*Connecticut (1965, 1967, 1969)*	*Delaware (1970)*	*Hawaii (1970)*	*Maine (1969, 1970)*	*Massachusetts (1962, 1965, 1969)*	*Michigan (1947, 1965)*	*Minnesota (1965)*	*Missouri (1967, 1969)*	*Nebraska (1969)*	*Nevada (1969)*	*New Hampshire (1969)*	*New Jersey (1968)*	*New York (1967, 1969, 1970)*	*Oregon (1965, 1969)*	*Pennsylvania (1970)*	*Rhode Island (1967)*	*South Dakota (1970)*	*Vermont (1969)*	*Washington (1961, 1967)*	*Wisconsin (1966)*
Coverage																						
State public employees	×	×	–	×	×	–	×	×	×	×	–	–	×	×	×	×	×	–	×	×	×	×
Local public employees	×	×	×	×	×	×	×	×	×	×	×	×	–	×	×	×	×	×	×	–	×	–
Public school teachers	×	–	–	–	×	×	×	×	–	–	–	×	–	×	×	–	×	–	×	–	–	–
Local police	×	×	×	×	×	×	×	×	×	–	×	×	–	×	×	×	–	–	×	–	×	–
Firemen	×	×	×	×	×	×	×	×	×	×	×	×	–	×	×	×	–	–	×	–	×	–
Collective negotiations																						
Mandatory	–	–	×	×[a]	×	×	×	×	–	–	–	×	×	×	×	×[a]	×	×	–	×	×	×
Permitted but not mandatory	×	–	–	×[b]	–	–	–	–	–	–	×	–	–	–	–	×[b]	–	–	–	–	–	–
Employer-employee meetings and conferences required	–	×	–	–	–	–	–	–	×	×	–	–	–	–	–	–	–	–	×	–	–	–
Binding written agreement required	–	–	×	×	×	×	×	×	–	–	–	–	×	×	×	–	×	×	–	×	×	×
Scope of negotiations restricted	–	×[c]	–	–	–	×[d,e]	–	×[d]	–	–	–	–	×	–	–	–	×	–	–	–	×[d]	×

Representation																						
Exclusive procedures	–	–	×	×	×	×	×	×	–	×	×	×	×	×	×	×	×	×	–	×	×	×
Formal procedures	–	–	–	–	–	–	–	–	×	–	–	–	–	–	×	–	–	–	×	–	–	–
Informal procedures	–	–	–	–	–	–	–	–	×	–	–	–	–	–	–	–	–	–	×	–	–	–
Parties permitted to establish their own procedures	–	×	–	–	–	–	–	–	–	–	–	–	–	–	–	×	–	–	–	–	–	–
No provision regarding procedures	×	–	–	–	–	–	–	–	–	–	–	–	–	–	–	–	–	–	–	–	–	–
Dues checkoff authorized	–	–	×	×	×	–	–	–	–	–	–	–	×	–	×	–	×	–	–	–	×	×
Settlement of disputes																						
Mediation	×	×	×	×	×	×	×	×	×	–	×	×	×	×	×	×	×	×	–	×	×	×
Fact-finding	–	–	×	–	×	×	×	–	×	–	×	×	×	×	×	×	×	–	–	×	–	×
Arbitration	–	–	×	×	×	×	×	–	–	–	–	–	×	×	×	×	×	×	–	×	–	×
Parties permitted to establish their own procedures	–	–	–	–	×	–	–	–	–	–	–	–	×	–	×	–	–	–	×	–	–	–
No provision	–	–	–	–	–	–	–	–	–	×	–	–	–	–	–	–	–	–	–	–	–	–
Unfair practices																						
Detailed specifications for both employees and employers	–	–	×	–	×	×	×	–	–	–	–	–	–	–	×	–	×	×	–	×	×	×
Simple noninterference clause	–	×	–	×	–	–	–	×	×	×	–	×	×	×	–	×	–	–	×	–	–	–
No provision	×	–	–	–	–	–	–	–	–	–	×	–	–	–	–	–	–	–	–	–	–	–
Administrative machinery																						
Existing state agency	×	–	×	×	–	–	×	×	×	×	×	–	–	–	–	–	×	×	×	–	×	×
New independent state agency	–	–	–	–	×	×	–	–	–	–	–	×	×	×	×	×	–	–	–	×	–	–
Local agency employer	–	×[f]	–	–	–	–	–	–	–	–	–	–	–	–	–	–	–	–	–	–	–	–

Sources: Advisory Commission on Intergovernmental Relations, *Labor-Management Policies for State and Local Government* (ACIR, 1969), pp. 20–22, updated from Bureau of National Affairs, *Government Employee Relations Report*, relevant issues, and BNA, *Labor Relations Reporter*, "State Laws," Vols. 4 and 4A, with supplements (BNA, as of September 1970). The data drawn from these sources have been amended and adapted by the authors at various points when their interpretations of the regulations differed from those presented in the sources.

a. State employees.
b. Local employees.
c. Excludes mission of the agency only from scope of discussions.
d. Matters delegated to the civil service commission are not negotiable.
e. Educational policies do not have to be negotiated with teachers.
f. Employing agency for state employees.

APPENDIX B

Statistics on Public Work Stoppages

TABLE B-1. *Work Stoppages by State and Local Government Employees, 1958–69*

Year	State and local governments: Number of stoppages	State and local governments: Number of workers involved	State and local governments: Man-days of idleness during year	Local government only: Number of stoppages	Local government only: Number of workers involved	Local government only: Man-days of idleness during year
1958	15	1,720	7,510	14	1,690	7,450
1959	26	2,240	11,500	22	1,830	9,850
1960	36	28,600	58,400	33	27,600	57,200
1961	28	6,610	15,300	28	6,610	15,300
1962	23	26,910	45,300	21	25,300	43,100
1963	29	4,840	15,400	27	4,560	13,300
1964	41	22,700	70,800	37	22,500	67,700
1965	42	11,900	146,000	42	11,900	145,000
1966	142	105,000	455,000	133	102,000	449,000
1967	181	132,000	1,250,000	169	127,000	1,230,000
1968	251	200,120	2,535,600	235	190,900	2,492,800
1969	409	159,400	744,600	372	139,000	592,200

Source: U.S. Bureau of Labor Statistics, *Work Stoppages in Government, 1958–68*, Report 348 (1970), Table 1, supplemented with unpublished data for 1969 from the Bureau of Labor Statistics.

TABLE B-2. *Number of Workers Involved in Work Stoppages as a Fraction of Total Employment, 1958–69*

In percent

Year	All stoppages	Government stoppages: Total	State	Local
1958	3.9	0.022	0.002	0.04
1959	3.3	0.028	0.030	0.04
1960	2.4	0.340	0.060	0.60
1961	2.6	0.077	—	0.14
1962	2.2	0.350	0.100	0.50
1963	1.1	0.052	0.020	0.09
1964	2.7	0.240	0.020	0.40
1965	2.5	0.120	—	0.20
1966	3.0	0.970	0.100	1.70
1967	4.3	1.140	0.200	1.90
1968	3.8	1.650	0.400	2.70
1969	3.5	n.a.	n.a.	n.a.

Source: U.S. Bureau of Labor Statistics, *Work Stoppages in Government, 1958–68*, Table 2, supplemented with unpublished data for 1969 from the Bureau of Labor Statistics.

n.a. Not available.

TABLE B-3. *Number of Workers Involved in Work Stoppages, Yearly Averages, 1958–69*

Year	All stoppages	Government stoppages: Total	State	Local
1958	558	115	30	121
1959	507	86	102	83
1960	396	794	323	836
1961	431	236	—	236
1962	340	1,105	830	1,205
1963	280	167	140	169
1964	449	554	70	608
1965	391	283	—	283
1966	445	739	343	767
1967	625	729	389	751
1968	525	791	581	812
1969	435	389	554	374

Source: U.S. Bureau of Labor Statistics, *Work Stoppages in Government, 1958–68*, Table 3, supplemented with unpublished data for 1969 from the Bureau of Labor Statistics.

TABLE B-4. *Idleness Caused by Work Stoppages, 1958–69*
In man-days per idle worker

Year	*All stoppages*	*Government stoppages*		
		Total	*State*	*Local*
1958	11.6	4.4	2.0	4.4
1959	36.7	5.1	4.0	5.4
1960	14.5	2.0	1.2	2.1
1961	11.2	2.3	—	2.3
1962	15.0	2.5[a]	1.4	1.7
1963	17.1	3.2	7.7	2.9
1964	14.0	3.1	11.3	3.0
1965	15.1	12.3	—	12.2
1966	12.9	4.3	1.9	4.4
1967	14.7	9.5	3.5	9.7
1968	18.5	12.6[b]	4.6	13.1
1969	17.3	4.7[c]	7.4	4.3

Source: U.S. Bureau of Labor Statistics, *Work Stoppages in Government, 1958–68,* Table 4, supplemented with unpublished data for 1969 from the Bureau of Labor Statistics.

a. Includes five stoppages of federal employees resulting in an average of 8.1 man-days of idleness per worker involved.

b. Includes three stoppages of federal employees resulting in an average of 5.7 man-days of idleness per worker involved.

c. Includes two stoppages of federal employees resulting in an average of 1.8 man-days of idleness per worker involved.

TABLE B-5. *Public Work Stoppages by Major Issue, 1958–69*

Year	Number of stoppages	Number of workers involved	Man-days of idleness during year	Number of stoppages	Number of workers involved	Man-days of idleness during year
	General wage changes and supplementary benefits			*Union organization and security*		
1958	8	1,130	4,760	2	340	1,990
1959	7	950	2,640	9	820	4,580
1960	19	16,600	40,800	8	6,220	9,610
1961	22	5,970	13,600	1	20	20
1962	10	25,500	40,300	5	380	840
1963	15	1,700	8,350	5	2,750	6,060
1964	26	9,620	37,300	8	2,550	7,680
1965	25	9,830	128,000	12	850	11,500
1966	78	58,200	355,000	36	11,600	45,600
1967	28	118,000	1,040,000	29	6,670	99,300
1968	146	110,300	759,200	60	33,600	90,100
1969	285	121,600	529,100	63	14,400	145,000
	Job security[a]			*Administration matters*[a,b]		
1958	—	—	—	—	—	—
1959	—	—	—	—	—	—
1960	—	—	—	—	—	—
1961	—	—	—	—	—	—
1962	2	30	200	8	2,380	6,100
1963	2	90	170	5	170	340
1964	—	—	—	7	10,600	25,900
1965	1	80	80	1	10	50
1966	2	170	1,680	21	33,300	46,500
1967	2	730	1,430	19	2,670	5,630
1968	2	90	200	33	52,200	1,684,200
1969	7	1,400	3,300	38	19,200	33,500
	Interunion or intra-union matters			*Other working conditions*		
1958	—	—	60	5	250	700
1959	2	40	180	8	430	4,060
1960	1	10	10	8	5,770	8,010
1961	1	10	20	4	610	1,640
1962	3	2,870	31,700	—	—	—
1963	1	30	120	1	100	400
1964	—	—	—	—	—	—
1965	2	980	6,160	—	—	—
1966	5	1,760	5,840	—	—	—
1967	1	90	360	2	4,030	99,900
1968	5	2,700	4,900	5	1,700	6,200
1969	3	700	7,500	13	2,300	26,700

Source: U.S. Bureau of Labor Statistics, *Work Stoppages in Government, 1958–68*, Table 6, supplemented with unpublished data for 1969 from the Bureau of Labor Statistics.

a. Job security and administration matters were included in "other working conditions," 1958–61.

b. Administration matters include physical surroundings, safety, supervision, shift work, work assignments, speed-up, work rules, overtime, discipline, and discharge, and other matters such as the size of the state budget, caseloads for welfare workers, and so forth.

TABLE B-6. *Public Work Stoppages by Type of Work, 1958–69*

Year	Number of stoppages	Number of workers involved	Man-days of idleness during year	Number of stoppages	Number of workers involved	Man-days of idleness during year	Number of stoppages	Number of workers involved	Man-days of idleness during year
	Administration and protection services			*Sanitation services*			*Public schools and libraries*		
1958	3	620	2,230	7	950	4,890	—	—	—
1959	3	130	1,560	7	390	1,020	5	410	1,400
1960	2	130	760	12	8,180	21,400	5	10,200	17,000
1961	2	40	1,000	12	1,390	3,550	2	90	180
1962	—	—	—	5	850	4,100	6	23,900	37,700
1963	2	120	240	8	1,760	7,720	7	2,540	5,080
1964	1	30	30	5	700	1,550	18	17,100	40,600
1965	3	6,620	114,000	16	1,750	8,030	9	1,930	13,800
1966	19	9,360	50,300	36	7,500	24,700	54	44,800	78,300
1967	24	22,200	197,000	23	3,100	17,300	89	96,200	983,000
1968	28	10,600	44,300	63	27,500	200,100	112	148,000	2,193,800
1969	56	8,290	38,300	51	14,300	75,500	230	117,000	481,000
	Publicly owned transportation			*Publicly owned utilities*			*Streets and highways*		
1958	—	—	—	2	40	230	1	10	40
1959	—	—	—	—	—	—	6	660	5,310
1960	2	8,340	16,100	1	10	10	11	920	2,310
1961	2	4,520	4,520	5	350	4,690	3	150	1,170

1962	4	1,700	2,340	8	3,510	33,200	4	140	390
1963	—	—	—	3	90	580	6	260	1,580
1964	4	3,840	18,300	3	380	850	9	560	4,250
1965	1	180	4,620	3	80	230	6	650	3,700
1966	2	34,900	275,000	6	130	1,510	2	60	210
1967	6	1,530	5,360	5	670	4,780	5	1,330	3,030
1968	1	10	30	10	3,200	17,100	5	100	1,000
1969	8	700	3,370	10	2,480	21,300	19	6,310	65,400
	Museums, art galleries, and botanical and zoological gardens			*Hospitals and other health services*[a]			*Miscellaneous services*		
1958	—	—	—	—	—	—	2	100	130
1959	3	610	1,990	—	—	—	2	40	180
1960	1	200	200	—	—	—	2	610	610
1961	1	60	60	—	—	—	1	10	150
1962	—	—	—	—	—	—	1	1,070	1,430
1963	—	—	—	1	10	30	2	80	210
1964	—	—	—	—	—	—	1	140	5,290
1965	1	250	500	1	160	1,120	2	250	250
1966	—	—	—	17	7,760	23,400	6	520	1,420
1967	—	—	—	19	1,200	26,800	10	5,470	8,860
1968	2	100	1,100	21	11,000	83,500	12	1,400	4,200
1969	—	—	—	24	9,590	56,900	13	1,320	3,920

Source: U.S. Bureau of Labor Statistics, *Work Stoppages in Government, 1958–68,* Table 8, supplemented with unpublished data for 1969 from the Bureau of Labor Statistics.

a. "Hospitals and other health services" were included in "miscellaneous services" in 1958–62.

Index of Cases Cited

General Index